NATIONAL IMAGINARIES, AMERICAN IDENTITIES

NATIONAL IMAGINARIES, AMERICAN IDENTITIES

THE CULTURAL WORK OF AMERICAN ICONOGRAPHY

*Edited by Larry J. Reynolds
and Gordon Hutner*

PRINCETON UNIVERSITY PRESS   PRINCETON AND OXFORD

Copyright © 2000 by Princeton University Press
Published by Princeton University Press, 41 William Street,
Princeton, New Jersey 08540
In the United Kingdom: Princeton University Press,
3 Market Place, Woodstock, Oxfordshire OX20 1SY
All Rights Reserved.

Library of Congress Cataloging-in-Publication Data
National imaginaries, American identities:
the cultural work of American iconography / edited by
Larry J. Reynolds and Gordon Hutner.
p. cm.
Includes bibliographical references.
ISBN 0-691-00994-5 (alk. paper)—ISBN 0-691-00995-3 (pbk. : alk. paper))

1. United States—Civilization. 2. Symbolism—Social aspects—United
States—History. 3. National characteristics, American. 4. Group identity—United
States—History. 5. Arts and society—United States—History. I. Reynolds,
Larry J. (Larry John), 1942– II. Hutner, Gordon
E169.1 .N3744 2001
973–dc21   00-034666

This book has been composed in Janson

The paper used in this publication meets the minimum requirements
of ANSI/NISO Z39.48-1992 (R1997) (*Permanence of Paper*)

www.pup.princeton.edu

Printed in the United States of America

1   3   5   7   9   10   8   6   4   2

1   3   5   7   9   10   8   6   4   2

To the twins

CHARLOTTE AND LOGAN REYNOLDS,

DAN AND JAKE HUTNER

Contents

Illustrations

Acknowledgments

THIS BOOK began as a lecture series sponsored by the Interdisciplinary Group for Historical Literary Study (IGHLS) at Texas A&M University. The fellows of that group, working in cooperation with the editors of this volume, originated the project and supported it in many ways. We wish to thank them and also the Texas A&M College of Liberal Arts and the Center for Humanities Research, which provided financial support for this volume. We would also like to thank Oxford University Press for its support for *American Literary History*, the journal in which the first version of these essays originally appeared. We note with sadness that Jenny Franchot did not live to see the final product.

Larry Reynolds wishes to thank Dennis Berthold, Sean Chadwell, Jeffrey Cox, Susan Egenolf, Marian Eide, Chac-Pyong Song, David McWhirter, and the anonymous reader for Princeton University Press for their useful suggestions for the introduction. Gordon Hutner wishes to thank Dale Bauer, Stephen Karian, Jami Moss, and Deborah Siegel for their help at various stages.

Contributors

VOLUME EDITORS

Gordon Hutner
Professor of English at the University of Kentucky, he is the editor of *American Literary History*.

Larry J. Reynolds
Professor of English and Thomas Franklin Mayo Professor of Liberal Arts at Texas A&M University, he is the author of *European Revolutions and the American Literary Renaissance* and coeditor of *"These Sad but Glorious Days": Dispatches from Europe, 1846–1850* and *New Historical Literary Study*.

ESSAY AUTHORS

Dennis Berthold
Professor of English at Texas A&M University, he has published essays on Charles Brockden Brown, Nathaniel Hawthorne, James Russell Lowell, Constance Fenimore Woolson, and Mark Twain. His essay on Herman Melville and the Astor Place riots appeared in the September 1999 issue of *American Literature*, and his annotations to Melville's Burgundy Club sketches and poems will appear in the forthcoming Northwestern-Newberry edition of *Billy Budd and Other Late Manuscripts*. He is currently completing a book on Melville and Italy.

Jenny Franchot
Late of the University of California at Berkeley, she was an associate professor there and author of *Roads to Rome: The Antebellum Protestant Encounter with Catholicism* (University of California Press, 1994).

Eric Lott
He teaches American Studies at the University of Virginia. He is the author of *Love and Theft: Blackface Minstrelsy and the American Working Class* (Oxford University Press, 1993) and the forthcoming *Darkness U.S.A.: The Cultural Contradictions of American Racism*.

José E. Limón
Professor of English, anthropology, and Mexican-American Studies at the University of Texas at Austin, his most recent book is *American Encounters:*

Greater Mexico, the United States and the Erotics of Culture (Beacon Press, 1998). He has also published *Dancing with the Devil: Society and Cultural Poetics in Mexican-American South Texas* (University of Wisconsin Press, 1994).

Shirley Samuels

She is H. Fletcher Brown Chair of the Humanities at the University of Delaware. She has published *Romances of the Republic: Women, the Family, and Violence in the Literature of the Early American Nation* (Oxford University Press, 1996) and has also edited *The Culture of Sentiment: Race, Gender, and Sentimentality in Nineteenth-Century America* (Oxford University Press, 1992). This essay is part of a new project on the iconography of political cartoons, sensation fiction, and historical novels about the Civil War.

Bryan C. Taylor

Associate Professor in the Department of Communication at the University of Colorado, Boulder, he is currently working on a book about images of the Cold War in communication research.

Cecelia Tichi

She teaches American literature at Vanderbilt University, where she directs the American and Southern Studies Program. She is at work on a book on bodily identity and the American environment.

Alan Trachtenberg

He is the Neil Gray, Jr. Professor of English and American Studies at Yale University.

Maurice Wallace

Assistant Professor of English and African and African American Studies at Duke University, his book *Constructing the Black Masculine: Identity and Ideality in African American Men's Literature and Culture* is forthcoming from Duke University Press. He is also at work on a book-length study of the criminological and penal preoccupations in the life and works of James Baldwin, entitled *Hostile Witness: Crime and Criminality in the Works of James Baldwin.*

NATIONAL IMAGINARIES, AMERICAN IDENTITIES

American Cultural Iconography

LARRY J. REYNOLDS

THE FOLLOWING essays exemplify some of the best new work in the emerging critical practice that we call American cultural iconography. During the past three decades, this practice has become increasingly visible and even prominent in American studies through a growing body of criticism identifiable by its use of visual and verbal images to explore American cultural formations—from Indians, women, and the West to the Black Panthers, Whiteness, and the American fetus. While once confined to art history and used for descriptive purposes, iconography has established itself as a penetrating means of cultural criticism in numerous areas of study, including photography, cultural studies, film and media studies, race and gender studies, postcolonial studies, and border studies, as the essays in this volume reveal. Because of its diffusion, cultural iconography has remained until now largely unself-conscious and noncoherent. This collection not only identifies this new critical practice but also shows its scope and interpretive power.

The emergence of American cultural iconography has been stimulated by three related contemporary developments in humanities research. The most obvious of these is interdisciplinarity, which has flourished in the 1980s and 1990s, especially in American studies, where a growing number of scholars have turned to a wider and wider range of historical and visual materials in their work. Literary scholars, especially, have crossed disciplinary boundaries to study paintings, sculptures, monuments, photographs, tourist sites, advertisements, posters, magazine illustrations, political cartoons, and movie stills to support a range of investigations into American cultural history. This growing attention to visual texts owes much to the example of British cultural studies, which is also responsible for a second related development, the increasing interest in popular culture and its visual mediations. During the past thirty years, "Literature" and "Art" have lost much of the privileged ontological status they once enjoyed in the academy, as the Arnoldian concept of culture has been replaced by a more inclusive, holistic concept, now understood as the entire range of practices, representations, languages, and customs of a particular society (see Hall, "Gramsci's Relevance").[1] A third, related development, perhaps more indigenous in origin, has been the explosion of images under late American capitalism and the concomitant "pictoral turn," as W.J.T. Mitchell calls it, in humanities studies (*Picture Theory* 11).[2] Though much of this "turn" has involved theoretical explorations of visuality, images, and image/text relations (now called "visual culture studies"),[3] it has also involved empirical study of particular sets of representational images, ultimately, the domain of iconography.

The American cultural iconography found in these essays spans the eighteenth century to the present and treats iconic materials ranging from portraits, photographs, and political cartoons to landscape art, religious icons, and film. Although no argument for U.S. exceptionalism will be made here, the essays do frequently remind us that the fervid and violent iconoclasm of seventeenth-century Puritanism endowed images and image making with lasting, and contested, significance in North America. Puritan iconoclasts, as Ann Kibbey has shown, believed deeply in the power of visual images, which they regarded with attraction and fear, at times collapsing the distinction between offending images and actual human beings (Kibbey 45).[4] Even when the functions of sacred images were appropriated for political and social purposes within American Protestant culture of the eighteenth century and later, this intense ambivalence persisted.[5] Moreover, the constitutive roles of race and sexuality in American identity formation also endowed the image and the visual field (where race and sexuality are most obviously determined) with profound cultural significance. A number of the essays collected here respond to these concerns by exploring the interplay of images and narratives in American identity formation; these we have grouped under the heading "Between Image and Narrative: Figuring American Collectivity." Another set of essays treats the related issue of the politics of representation, and these we have assembled under the heading "Representational Frameworks and Their Others: The Politics of Racialized Gender and Sexuality." These groupings are meant to be suggestive, not restrictive, of course, and the reader will find that the essays speak to each other between, as well as within, these broad thematic divisions.

1

In shaping empirical work in a number of areas of study, American cultural iconography has drawn upon an array of overlapping theoretical perspectives, four of which stand out as particularly influential: semiotics, marxism, psychoanalysis, and Foucauldian poststructuralism. This introduction offers a sketch of this background, tracing its cumulative effects upon American cultural iconography, especially as exemplified by the nine essays in this volume. The genealogy that emerges shows not a simple line of descent but rather a complicated evolution in which the formalist and structuralist work of the first half of the twentieth century becomes increasingly invested in cultural critique owing to developments in literary and cultural theory.

By far the most persistent theoretical influence upon contemporary cultural iconography has been semiotics. The nineteenth-century American philosopher Charles Sanders Peirce coined that term to denote the study of signs—such as words, images, gestures, and clothing—which all convey meaning through a system of cultural codes and conventions. Peirce distinguished the icon from the index and the symbol by defining the icon as a sign related to its referent by means of resemblance or analogy (such as a picture of a wolf), whereas the index is related by causal or physical means (such as a pawprint) and the symbol by means of a convention other than resemblance (such as the word "wolf") (see Pierce 156–73). Semiotics, especially as developed by the Swiss linguist Ferdinand de Saussure, has informed twentieth-century literary studies, anthropology, psychoanalytic theory, film theory, art history, and the history of photography in so basic a way that, in a sense, cultural iconography is a method that has arisen to meet an inevitable change in humanistic inquiry.

The influence of semiotics upon American cultural iconography has been especially effective in the study of photographs, for to the uninformed eye, these images appear the most iconic and natural of all visual signs. Even Peirce did not fully appreciate their multiple levels of signification, although he did observe that they are both iconic (resembling the objects they represent) and indexical (linked to the real through traces of light). As modern semioticians have revealed, they also convey meaning through codes and conventions only slightly less determined than those of paintings. Their iconicity, in other words, is constructed as well as "natural." As Joel Snyder has shown, the camera was designed to help in the creation of "realistic" paintings, and early Renaissance art "provided the standard for the kind of image the camera was designed to produce" (511).

The most instructive theoretical meditations on photography have been those of the twentieth-century French semiotician Roland Barthes, who posited that the photograph paradoxically fuses two messages, "one without a code (the photographic analogue), the other with a code (the 'art', or the treatment, or the 'writing', or the rhetoric, of the photograph)" ("The Photographic Message" 19).[6] Snyder has offered some qualifications to the claim of analogy for the photograph, pointing out that it differs from unmediated sight by its rectangular frame, its uniform sharpness from edge to edge, its depth of field, and its stillness, all of which undermine its mimetic claims (505); nevertheless, the photograph's apparent realism sustains the effectiveness of the codes and conventions generated by its rhetoric, that is, by the choice of subject, point of view, lighting, composition, and so on, not to mention the alterations and manipulations performed during the printing process. As Barthes points out, "The denoted image naturalizes the symbolic message, it makes 'innocent' the very dense (especially in advertising) semantic artifice of connotation" (qtd. in Shawcross 6).[7] This attention to connoted meaning, which Barthes calls "myth" (and others "ideology"), provides the insight necessary for taking the semiotic study of photography into the realm of cultural critique. In his own *Mythologies*, Barthes challenges the reader to investigate the "ideological abuse" hidden in "the decorative display of *what-goes-without-saying*" (11).

In recent American cultural iconography involving photographs, a number of Americanists have drawn upon Barthesian semiotics to analyze both the visible and invisible codes at work within specific photographs, making them meaningful within specific economic, political, and social systems. Alan Trachtenberg has pioneered Americanist work in this area, and his *Reading American Photographs* (1989) shows how Mathew Brady, Timothy O'Sullivan, Alfred Stieglitz, Lewis Hines, and Walker Evans constructed photographic images—of "illustrious Americans," slaves, criminals, Civil War scenes, the West, New York City life, the 1930s depression—that were shaped by and helped to shape American history. Other recent studies, by Peter Hales and Timothy Sweet, have presented similar findings; Hales, showing how the photographs of William Henry Jackson were made (and altered and manipulated) to construct commercial images of the "West" and the "Indian"; Sweet, showing how Alexander Gardner and George Barnard, among others, used photography to construct pastoral images that naturalized the massive violence and death of the Civil War. More recently, Judith Fryer Davidov in *Women's Camera Work* (1998) has extended Trachtenberg's work, challenging his focus on male photographers and his conception of American history as "a kind of unified whole" (23).[8] Davidov provides accounts of a network of women photographers, including Gertrude Käsebier, Imogen Cunningham, Dorothea Lange, and Laura Gilpin, and shows how they used photographic images in personal, gendered ways to contribute to the construction of Americanness and otherness.

One of Barthes's key theoretical concepts, the "polysemic" character of the photographic image, has proved central to American cultural iconography. The "floating chain of significance, underlying the signifiers of an image" (qtd. in Sukula 7) discloses how the photograph, by itself, presents only possibilities of meaning, yielding specific semantic outcomes through its placement within particular discourse systems.[9] Trachtenberg, in his essay here, demonstrates Nathaniel Hawthorne's fascination with and understanding of the complex relation to the real that the new technology of daguerreotypy claimed, as well as the polysemic character of the daguerreotype itself. Trachtenberg shows that Hawthorne uses the daguerreotype to elaborate and reflect upon his own art, specifically upon the meaning, the political and historical possibilities, of Romance as a literary form. For Hawthorne, daguerreotypy, like his own romance, works to capture images of an old order passing away yet also becomes implicated in an emergent market-centered commodity culture. In Trachtenberg's reading, *The House of the Seven Gables* communicates the semiotic truth Hawthorne understood and conveyed, that the interpretation of images (and characters) depends not upon their reference to some external truth or reality but upon their role within particular narratives, which endow them with meaning.

Bryan Taylor, whose essay here on nuclear iconography likewise takes a semiotic approach to the image/texts he examines, shows how photographs of "nuclear subjects" can be used to legitimate particular narratives of nuclear reality. Focusing on two volumes of documentary photographs, Robert Del Tredici's *At Work in the Fields of the Bomb* (1987) and Carole Gallagher's *American Ground Zero: The Secret Nuclear War* (1993), Taylor shows how both challenge official nuclear images and popular narratives that have aestheticized the nuclear mushroom cloud and "disappeared" its victims and their radiated bodies. The Del Tredici volume provides an unofficial counterrealism through interviews and photos of nuclear-weapons production sites, while Gallagher's volume uses a "deconstructive pastiche" featuring the disintegrating bodies of downwind sufferers. Of particular interest to Taylor are the self-reflexive moves of both authors, as they call attention to the constructedness of their images. He interprets such moves as signs of the authors' ambivalence toward their medium; their image/texts encode the "real," not the real. Such is the secret, transparent to semiotics, that official narratives keep and subversive ones tell.[10]

Since the 1970s, a semiotic perspective has informed the study of images within the field of American art history, as well as within the history of photography, but here Erwin Panofsky and Ernest Gombrich, rather than Roland Barthes, have been the primary intellectual sources. In the early decades of the twentieth century, iconography, as practiced in art history, involved the careful description and classification of the subject matter and motifs of images. During the 1930s, however, a group of art historians who emigrated from Germany and Austria during the rise of Nazism revolutionized this work and established an interdisciplinary, intercultural approach to the field (see Cassidy). Aby Warburg founded this group, but its most influential member was Panofsky, whose considerable knowledge of art history was matched by his knowledge of literature, philosophy, and religion. Drawing upon Ernst Cassirer's idea of "symbolic values," Panofsky gave iconography—which Warburg had renamed "iconology"—interpretive power, by studying the "intrinsic meanings" of works of art and explaining their origins in "essential tendencies of the human mind" (41); "the discovery and interpretation of these 'symbolical' values," Panofsky writes, "(which are often unknown to the artist himself and may even emphatically differ from what he consciously intended to express) is the object of what we may call 'iconology' as opposed to 'iconography' "(31).

The semiotic emphasis in Panofsky's work, especially in his *Studies in Iconology* (1939), received implicit support from E. F. Gombrich's landmark *Art and Illusion* (1956), which argued for the importance of the "linguistics of the visual image" (9). For Gombrich (at least in this book), artistic conventions were the main determinants of constructed visual images, although in his later writings, he emphasized nature as the source of such images and the key to their interpretation,[11] leaving his work open to the charge—made by Nelson Goodman, Norman Bryson, and others—that it fails to treat the culturally and historically determined character of representation.[12]

Panofsky's "iconology" has also been criticized for its lack of historical and political awareness, even as Panofsky and Gombrich have provided the theoretical foundation for the American cultural iconography to emerge from the field of art history in the 1970s and early 1980s.[13] In her groundbreaking *American Painting of the Nineteenth Century* (1969) and her *Nature and Culture* (1980), Barbara Novak sought to write cultural art history that probed the "*iconological* roots" (*Nature and Culture* vii) of images such as mountains, rocks, clouds, plants, axes, trains, and human figures of nineteenth-century American paintings. In this endeavor, she drew upon Gombrich's emphasis upon artistic conventions and Panofsky's emphasis upon placing images within contemporary religious, philosophical, and aesthetic contexts in order to arrive at their meanings. A similar approach governs other 1980s studies of the American landscape, such as Elizabeth McKinsey's *Niagara Falls: Icon of the American Sublime* (1985) and John Wilmerding's edition *American Light: The Luminist Movement, 1850–1875* (1989), both of which focus primarily upon stylistics, aesthetics, and the history of ideas, not social or political matters.[14]

As Keith Moxey has pointed out with reference to Panofsky's theoretical approach, "the politics of iconology is to claim that it has no politics" ("Politics" 31), and W.J.T. Mitchell in a series of books has made the same point, arguing for the study of images as contested forms of mediation linked to ideology. "The notion of ideology," he points out, "is rooted in the concept of imagery, and reenacts the ancient struggles of iconoclasm, idolatry, and fetishism" (*Iconology* 4). In his own recent work, Mitchell has applied his theory to some specific cultural formations (the last two chapters of his *Picture Theory* [1994], for example, analyze the staged political violence of Spike Lee's *Do the Right Thing*, Oliver Stone's *JFK*, and CNN's coverage of the Gulf War). A recent collection of art historical essays edited by David C. Miller, *American Iconology* (1993), also uses Mitchell's revised conception of iconology as a "touchstone" (2), even if most of the essays within it apply traditional semiotics to the paintings, themes, and movements they explore. Exceptions are Sarah Burns's essay on the commodification of nineteenth-century American art ("The Price of Beauty") and Miller's theoretical "Introduction" and "Afterword," which seek to establish the role of images within "the dominant masculinist and nationalist ideology" (17) of nineteenth-century America.

2

Although a number of art historians remain committed to semiotics and close readings of works of fine art, many, like Mitchell, Burns, and Miller, have turned, during the late 1980s and 1990s, to representational images and analyzed their ideological implications by means of European marxist cultural theory.[15] The constitutive power of representation and the meaningfulness of absences within representation are two of the more important concepts derived from marxist theory, in particular from the work of Louis Althusser and Pierre Macherey, as filtered through the British cultural studies movement. Although Marx himself had little to say about representation, Althusser, in a celebrated essay, defined ideology as "a representation of the imaginary relationship of individuals to their real conditions of existence" (162) and inspired criticism devoted to revealing the ideological constructedness of representations previously accepted as natural and real. In *A Theory of Literary Production* (1978; orig. pub. 1966), Macherey proposed a reading practice based upon the idea that certain historical actualities omitted from a literary representation, because of their alterity to the ideological project of the text, make themselves known at points of contradiction, rupture, or silence in the work; these points mark the return of a repressed, unconscious historical context embodied within the text as a whole, thus revealing the limits of ideology and the conditions of its production within a history of struggle and conflict.[16]

In the 1970s and early 1980s, Althusser's and Macherey's theoretical ideas began to inform the work of a number of British art historians, who imported them into the cultural studies of Richard Hoggart and Raymond Williams and argued for art as a social and political practice engaged in the production and reproduction of ideology by means of representation. The iconography of rural scenes figured prominently in this criticism; Williams's *The Country and the City* (1972) and John Berger's *Ways of Seeing* (1972) marked the beginning of a sustained marxist critique of the picturesque and pastoral traditions of English literature and art, whose images of a serene and innocent English countryside were shown to erase or mask sociopolitical divisions and conflicts. This critique was developed and expanded in art historical studies of the British landscape tradition (see Barrell, Solkin, and Bermingham), which in turn informed the approaches of a number of Americanist studies of the late 1980s and 1990s, where British interest in class conflict and cultural hegemony became Americanized through attention to nationalism, imperialism, sexism, racism, and xenophobia. Within American studies, interest in marxist theory from the 1940s through the 1970s was limited and ambivalent, perhaps because, as Michael Denning has suggested, the focus on American uniqueness "prevented the emergence of a more general 'cultural studies,' and tended to ignore non-American theoretical paradigms" (360). A few Americanists, such as Carolyn Porter, Michael T. Gilmore, and Michael Rogin (*Subversive Genealogy*), revealed the interpretative potential of marxist concepts through their work, and of course Fredric Jameson's *The Political Unconscious* (1981) provided an influential model for marxist interpretation. Not until the mid-1980s, with the appearance of *Ideology and Classic American Literature* (1986), edited by Sacvan Bercovitch and Myra Jehlen, did marxist concepts begin to have a dominant influence upon American cultural iconography, where they have been used primarily to analyze images of the American landscape and their ideological implications.

This critical interest in the American landscape arises from the important cultural fact that American national identity has been long linked to representations of natural scenes, especially those produced by nineteenth-century writers and artists. As Cecelia Tichi points out in her essay here, recent critical inquiry has desacralized the concept of the United States as "nature's nation," now considered "ideolotry." Sarah Burns's *Pastoral Inventions* (1989), the collections *The West as America* (1991) and *Discovered Lands, Invented Pasts* (1992), Vivien Green Fryd's *Art and Empire* (1992), Angela Miller's *The Empire of the Eye* (1993), and Alex Nemerov's *Frederic Remington and Turn-of-the-Century America* (1995) are just a few of the more important studies that critique the relations between images of the American landscape and American cultural politics. In *The Empire of the Eye*, for example, Angela Miller focuses upon the landscape paintings of Thomas Cole and others of the New York School and uncovers the uncertainties and tensions involved in this art's engagement with American nationalism and westward expansionism. Similarly, *The West as America*, based on the controversial Smithsonian exhibit of the same title, looks at images of the frontier, the ideologies they purvey, and the social and political realities they mask, such as the Mexican War, white destruction of Indian tribal life, and native-born fears of a growing immigrant population.[17] These fears are the repressed content of paintings such as Frederic Remington's *Fight for the Water Hole*, as Alex Nemerov's essay in the collection points out ("Doing the 'Old America' "). Nemerov's own book, *Frederic Remington and Turn-of-the-Century America*, expands on this study and shows how

Remington's images of cowboys and Indians, so often considered documentary, were shaped by and helped shape turn-of-the-century American culture, especially its theories of social evolution, misogynistic masculinity, fears of immigration, and the crisis of "Anglo-Saxon" identity.

This cultural context is the same one that has been of interest to Cecelia Tichi in her series of major contributions to American cultural iconography. Her *Shifting Gears* (1987), for example, draws upon a multitude of visual images of the period as it examines technological change between 1890 and 1930 and its effects on American literature and art. In her essay here, Tichi turns to a wide range of nineteenth-century texts and images to elucidate the mechanistic, "arterial," industrial metaphors surrounding the emergence of Yellowstone Park and the geyser "Old Faithful" as icons of American tourist wonderment and sites of national, geopolitical identity. Tichi shows that representations of the Yellowstone geyser region, which in middle-class travelers' accounts becomes a volcanic hell, may well express unconscious political anxieties about the strikes, riots, and social disorder of industrial America in the 1880s.

Tichi's pioneering work in American cultural iconography, coupled with the influence of her feminist contemporaries such as Nina Baym, Martha Banta, and Jane Tompkins, inspired a cluster of books appearing in the late 1980s and 1990s that draw upon the theoretical perspectives of semiotics and marxism to engage various feminist issues, especially the construction of gender. Making use of the opportunity provided by the interdisciplinarity of American studies and the demystification of a male-dominated canon of "great" literature, these studies devote new attention to a range of symbolic practices and iconographic formations. Banta's own monumental *Imaging American Women* (1987), for example, not only categorizes and characterizes countless visual and verbal representations of women between 1876 and 1918, but also explores the meanings and values they "impose" upon the culture. Like Jane Tompkins in *Sensational Designs* (1985), she focuses not upon artistic merit but rather upon the cultural work of these images, which most often function to regulate feminine identity and control social unrest. Jean Fagan Yellin's *Women and Sisters* (1989), in a more focused feminist study, examines the iconography of the antislavery feminists and traces the encoding and recoding of their central emblem, the kneeling female slave, concluding that the appropriation of this oppositional representation by a dominant patriarchal elite is paradigmatic within American history. And a complementary study, Joy Kasson's *Marble Queens and Captives* (1990), examines the role of nineteenth-century ideal sculpture, especially representations of nude women under duress—chained, dead, and dying—which Kasson links to widespread contemporary anxiety about the family, sexuality, and gender identity. These feminist studies of nineteenth-century cultural iconography have their counterpart in feminist studies of twentieth-century cultural formations, especially Hollywood films, which have been analyzed primarily by means of semiotics and psychoanalytic theory.

3

During the 1990s, concepts from psychoanalytic theory became more and more prevalent in American cultural iconography in general, often being combined with semiotic, marxist, and feminist perspectives. Given Althusser's indebtedness to Lacan, and Macherey's indebtedness to Freud, plus the attempt within British cultural studies in the 1980s to create out of Althusserian marxism and Lacanian psychoanalysis a mix known as British poststructuralism (see Easthope 73), it is perhaps not surprising that American cultural studies has drawn upon psychoanalytic theory to explore the role of representations in the construction of subjectivities, both individual and national. Freud, of course, has had a long-standing influence upon studies of American authors and literary works, and during the late 1970s and early 1980s a Freudian perspective informed a number of major historical studies, including those by George Forgie, Jay Fliegelman, and Michael Rogin (*Fathers and Children* and *Subversive Genealogy*). Rogin's most recent psychohistorical explorations into American culture of the twentieth century, as well as his association with the journal *Representations*, have been especially important in the development of American cultural iconography. His *"Ronald Reagan," the Movie: and Other Episodes in Political Demonology* (1987) and *Blackface, White Noise* (1996) draw upon images from movies and films for evidence of the national dream-life that he sees structuring American political identity. For Rogin, images of demonic others, such as "the Indian cannibal, the black rapist, the papal whore of Babylon, the monster-hydra United States Bank, the demon rum, the bomb-throwing anarchist, the many-tentacled Communist conspiracy, the agents of international terrorism" (*"Ronald Reagan"* xiii), are a consistent, repressed feature of American sociopolitical history. Similarly, Eric Lott has combined Freudian psychoanalytic theory with marxist cultural critique in his acclaimed *Love and Theft: Blackface Minstrelsy and the American Working Class* (1993). For Lott, images of "blackness" serve to repress not only a demonic other but also white desire for and identification with that other, at least on the part of nineteenth-century white, male, working-class viewers. The minstrel show, Lott argues, not only produced "blackness" as an inauthentic cultural commodity, but also revealed white obsession with and racial dread of black (male) bodies (6).

Provocative feminist complements to Rogin's and Lott's psychohistorical studies of the nation's sexualized dream-life have been provided by Lauren Berlant and Shirley Samuels, who have probed the relations between images of the female body and American nation building. In her *The Anatomy of National Fantasy* (1991) and *The Queen of America Goes to Washington City* (1997), Berlant shows how national images, monuments, sites, and narratives have been used to construct what she calls, following Lacan, the "National Symbolic." In Lacanian theory, of course, it is language that initiates the child into the Symbolic Order, distancing him or her from the Real, that inaccessible holistic realm, repressed in our conscious adult life. Within the realm of the Symbolic, we become "spoken by" language (rather than merely speaking it), such that language structures and represents the Real, mediating our access to it. Applying Lacanian theory to her study of America's "traditional icons," such as the Statue of Liberty, Berlant argues that they "provide an alphabet for a collective consciousness or national subjectivity; through the National Symbolic the historical nation aspires to achieve the inevitability or status of natural law, a birthright" (*Anatomy* 20). In *The Queen of America Goes to Washington City*, Berlant extends her iconographic studies into the late twentieth century to show how various idealized images and narratives constructed by a conservative politics fraught with contradiction are used to structure American citizenship. One of her key examples is the image of the fetus produced by the pro-life movement, which generates an infantile model of ideal citizenship by erasing the body of the woman altogether and appropriating the magical aura of reproduction to the image itself (83–144).

Given that the woman's body has historically been used to image American national identity (see Corbeiller and Warner), this erasure may seem surprising; however, it accords with the observations of Marina Warner (xx, 277), Lynn Hunt (82–83), and Anne McClintock (354), who have variously explored how the presence of the female figure in political iconography derives not from female influence in politics but rather from its absence. In *Romances of the Republic* (1996), Shirley Samuels reveals the latent hostility toward women's bodies that American nation building involves, as she examines allegorical eighteenth-century political cartoons and discusses the disturbing symbolic violence—dismemberings, beheadings, rapes—inflicted upon female figures representing national identities. Whereas Berlant has focused upon the ways in which cultural hegemony successfully dominates the National Symbolic, Samuels attends to the ambiguities, stresses, and ambivalences within it. In her essay here she shows how race, sexuality, and miscegenation were repressed presences in the construction of American national identity between the Revolution and the Civil War. Focusing on two political cartoons, and Stephen Girard's will and autobiography, along with Stowe's *Uncle Tom's Cabin*, she reveals the racial unconscious that haunts white America—that is, the repressed racial Other embodied within the nation at birth, which cannot be totally forgotten, removed, or severed from it.

Dennis Berthold's essay here also treats the construction of national identity and the violence toward women found in the Medusan iconography used to represent and resolve those political tensions rending the country in the nineteenth century. Berthold focuses on representations of the Italian revolutionary Garibaldi, who, as the type of the self-restrained warrior, a "Washington of Italy," became a cultural icon modeling republican virtue for nineteenth-century Americans and appearing to resolve the contradictory appeals of revolution and order, warfare and peace. The "Garibaldi-mania" that swept the country captured the attention of Herman Melville, who, Berthold shows, found in this figure a means to critique the modern process of image making and to concatenate his own complex, shifting, and conflicted political outlooks. For Melville, Garibaldi as cultural icon is "both revolutionary and conservative, an apostle of both individual liberation and of patriarchal authority who reminds Americans—or at least Melville—that revolution is acceptable when its violence is turned against an obvious Other."

The use of psychoanalytical theory as a means of understanding the role of representational images in the construction of sexual, racial, and national identities has entered American cultural iconography not only directly, as in the work of Berlant, Samuels, and Berthold, but also indirectly through the feminist film theory that first arose in England in the 1970s and 1980s, primarily in the British journal *Screen*, and that soon influenced American cultural studies. This theory, first presented by Laura Mulvey and then developed by other scholars such as Mary Ann Doane, Annette Kuhn, and Teresa De Lauretis, draws upon Freud's concepts of scopophilia and fetishism and Lacan's concepts of the mirror image and identification to show how the film apparatus and cinematic codes of representation construct images of woman "cut to the measure of desire" (Mulvey 25). During the 1980s, certain aspects of this psychoanalytic model were debated, particularly the nature of female spectatorship and the role of narrative in the construction of subjectivity. Today film theory remains heavily invested in semiotics, psychoanalysis, and feminism, but recently it has also turned to cultural studies, identity politics, and subaltern studies (see Bordwell). A key theoretical problem that has emerged in this turn concerns how formalist study of cinematic codes may be linked with political and historical actualities. For example, how do cinematic representations of women and racial others, given their conventionality, connect to the lives of actual people? One answer, discussed by De Lauretis, emerges from the semiotic theories of Peirce, who points out that although the workings of the semiotic system remain closed, with no access to reality except through forms of mediation, both the original construction of signs and their later understanding by interpreters in terms of other signs, called "interpretants," provide a link to history. As De Lauretis explains, the concepts of interpretant and unlimited semiosis "bridge the gap between discourse and reality, between the sign and its referent (the empirical object to which the sign refers); and so they usher in a theory of meaning as a continual cultural production that is not only susceptible of ideological transformation, but materially based in historical change" (172; see also Moxey, *Practice* 29–40).

Since the late 1980s, studies of the cinema have become more and more engaged with historical issues involving race, sexuality, and gender (see, in particular, Gaines; Dyer, *Heavenly Bodies*; Doane 209–48; and Kaplan). The links between female sexuality and "blackness," among gayness, "blackness," and the feminine, and between "blackness" and "whiteness" have all received sustained attention, especially within the Western symbolic system.[18] Doane, for example, shows that Freud's use of the term "dark continent" to signify female sexuality draws upon a colonial discourse that "equated the African woman and the African continent—the conquest of the former signified the successful appropriation of the latter" (213–14). In films such as *Birth of a Nation* (1915), *King Kong* (1933), and *Blonde Venus* (1932), "the cinema as an institution," Doane argues, "would embrace the colonialist project and reinscribe its terms within its uniquely optical narrative logic" (214). Similarly, Richard Dyer has studied the iconographic identification of gay men with femmes fatales and of both with an iconography of luxury and decadence in film noir (*The Matter of Images* 52–72). He has also pointed out the feminization of black men in Hollywood movies, which "constantly puts them into 'feminine' positions, that is, places them structurally . . . in the same positions as women typically occupy" (*Heavenly Bodies* 116–17).

In her *American Anatomies: Theorizing Race and Gender* (1995), Robyn Wiegman has argued that the mutilation of racial Others, especially black males, in American history can be construed as a form of feminization, a reaction to the threat of masculine sameness (90). Interweaving theoretical meditations on the psychological interrelations between race and gender within American cultural history with empirical studies of specific racial iconographies, Wiegman shows how the interracial "buddy" movies of the 1980s and 1990s under the guise of liberalism actually reconfigure white racial supremacy by "defying the legacy of emasculation that attends black male representation, while recasting white masculinity as disempowered and embattled marginality itself." Thus, "in an ironic twist, incorporation of the black male into the reign of the visual that characterizes commodity culture becomes a mechanism through which the history of racism among men is revised and denied" (15).[19]

Eric Lott has also focused upon American film as part of his extended study of the psychological and political interrelations between the construction of whiteness and racialized images of "blackness" within American cultural history, and in his essay here on film noir, he emphasizes the irony that this genre, devoted to exposing white pathology, relies on race "to convey that pathology" and in effect erects "a *cordon sanitaire* around the circle of corruption" it seeks to penetrate. Films such as *Double Indemnity* (1944), *A Double Life* (1948), and *In a Lonely Place* (1950), Lott shows, use black figures to signify and control impure energies within their narratives and, indirectly, within the surrounding culture. The films' chiaroscuro effects, their "darkened frames and darkened lives," are used to assuage fears of the blacks, Chicanos, and Asians who lived on the margins of 1940s American society and threatened white national identity through their growing political power and participation in urban unrest. Although film noir has often been associated with leftist ideals, Lott argues that the intensity of racializing imaging within it, "overdetermined by a climate of felt social decline," harmonized left-liberal perceptions with center-right ones, both of which imagined "white selves cast into a nightmarish world of otherness and racial aliens."

4

One finds in complex studies such as Lott's the influence of theoretical perspectives not only from semiotics, marxism, and psychoanalysis but also from Foucauldian poststructuralism as focused through the lens of postcolonial theory. Although Foucault's writings show little interest in ideology, which he found "difficult to make use of" (118), their emphases upon the "eye of power," the surveillance and control of the dangerous classes, and the constitutive power of discursive formations have all helped shape a number of recent iconographic studies, especially those interrogating representations of whiteness and racialized Others. The scholarly attention recently devoted to the role of representation within U.S. imperialism at home and abroad has been one important consequence of postcolonial adaptations of Foucauldian concepts. As Lott elsewhere points out, "the connection between internal and international is intimate. If national esteem in racial matters is related to international prestige—the ability to wield power among foreign races—it is also (or therefore) the case that representations of national racial difference often provide displaced maps for international ones" ("White Like Me" 476).[20]

Among postcolonial theorists, Edward Said and Homi Bhabha have provided the most influential concepts for examining representations of racial difference linking national racism and imperialism. Said's *Orientalism*

(1978), the foundational text for postcolonial studies, shows how the "Orient" was a discursive formation produced by European culture, and how vision can displace history at sites where imperial eyes view colonial others panoptically, producing colonial subjects and stereotypes (240). These visual formations, Said has argued, can be overcome "through the alternative use of visual media (such as photography)" "to tell other stories than the official sequential or ideological ones produced by institutions of power." Using as an example Malek Alloula's *The Colonial Harem* (1986), Said points out that "the pictorial capture of colonized people by colonizer, which signifies power," can be reinscribed by those seeing their own fragmented history in the pictures ("Opponents, Audiences" 158). The imperial gaze can be turned back upon itself, in other words, through the creation of verbal-visual texts that recontextualize images and endow them with new, resistant meanings.

Having devoted much of his theoretical attention to the attempt by oppressed racial Others to negotiate domination through mimicry, hybridity, and sly civility, Bhabha has also pondered the role of vision in the colonial encounter and sought to problematize images of racial Others by directing attention away from the racist codes and conventions within them and toward the complex processes by which they come into existence and do their cultural work. Bhabha agrees that indeed the creation and perpetuation of stereotypes legitimate the injustice, violence, or oppression inflicted upon the putative referents of the images, but goes on to argue that "to understand the productivity of colonial power it is crucial to construct its regime of truth, not to subject its representations to a normalizing judgement. Only then does it become possible to understand the *productive* ambivalence of the object of colonial discourse—that 'otherness' which is at once an object of desire and derision, an articulation of difference contained within the fantasy of origin and identity" (67).

These Foucauldian and postcolonial perspectives have galvanized a number of recent examples of American cultural iconography, including Henry Louis Gates's study of images of the "New Negro," Brian Wallis's study of the slave daguerreotypes of Louis Agassiz, and Kirk Savage's study of the iconography of African Americans in national monuments, all of which expose and resist racist representations from the past and reinscribe them within new counterhistories.[21] In this collection, the essays by Maurice Wallace, Jenny Franchot, and José Limón make major contributions to this revisionism by studying the role of the visual in subject formation. Wallace's essay tells the unfamiliar history of several African-American men's efforts to "make themselves" through the iconic representational apparatus of black Freemasonry during the Revolutionary and Federalist eras. Specifically, he shows that portraits of founder Prince Hall and leading member Martin Delany provided alternatives to the "typical" images found in eighteenth-century slave advertisements and empowered those whose subjecthood they helped to construct. Ironically, as Wallace points out, the revered portrait of Prince Hall, father of Black Freemasonry, was, in fact, an engraving of a white man holding "papers" in a Federalist or "founding" pose. African-American men thus invented themselves iconically through military and Masonic dress and pose, yet their models of masculinity, "made in America," had beneficial historical effects, providing black Freemasons with cohesiveness, self-discipline, seclusion, and a glorious new ancestry based upon Afrocentric Egyptology.

In her *Roads to Rome* (1994), Jenny Franchot has argued that in the early centuries of American history, Catholicism became Protestantism's Other, the " 'foreign faith' lodged at the heart of American Christendom" (xviii), and that the emotional ambivalence Catholicism provoked became foundational for Poe, Melville, and Hawthorne, among others. In her essay here, Franchot uses postcolonial conceptions of othering to explore religion itself as an Other to modernism. For Franchot, national racism and imperialism are connected through efforts to sever and dismember the Other and repress its re-membering. "Imperial formation and bodily dismemberment or disfigurement are linked narratives," she points out, yet Franchot's essay makes possible the re-membering and re-collection of images, persons, and histories that American imperial whiteness had previously repressed. She focuses upon the sacred iconography that within the growing secularized culture of the post–Civil War period was reduced to iconic fragments, using as examples an engraving of the Virgin Mary, tangled in seaweed, that washes to shore in Harriet Beecher Stowe's *Minister's Wooing* (1859) and the small sculpted arm of a murdered slave, a voudou artifact that appears in George Washington Cable's *Grandissimes* (1880). These, she shows, exerted an anxiety that had to be overcome, through violence if necessary. Cable's novel in particular, she concludes, "bids us reflect on how the religious Other is commemorated as figure of both the criminal and the quaint—a process of miniaturization essential to the construction of an expansionist national identity out of theological ruin and racialviolence."

Drawing upon Bhabha's concept of ambivalence and using the films *High Noon* (1952) and *Lone Star* (1996) as representative texts, Limón examines the clash of Mexican and Anglo cultures in the quasi-colonial Southwest from the late nineteenth century to the present. Focusing on the iconography surrounding a set of racial stereotypes—the Anglo cowboy, the desirable Mexican senorita, the degenerate Mexican male, the prim Anglo woman, and, later, the Latin lover—he argues that these images do not necessarily intensify domination; rather, the represented sexual desire for the racial Other destabilizes the colonial enterprise and finally, as suggested through the sexualized kinship presented in *Lone Star*, leads to its end.

Limón questions the degree of mimesis involved in these promising developments yet references his own experience and recent sociological research to support his conclusion that art in this case reflects life.

Limón's essay and those of our other contributors are far richer and more complex than this sketch of their arguments and theoretical backgrounds can show. Nevertheless, perhaps this brief description can serve as a usable guide for the reader to the large, diverse, and rapidly developing area of cultural criticism represented by this volume. For all of their many different emphases and purposes, these essays exemplify an emergent form of interdisciplinary study and an important new trend in American cultural criticism. Their sophisticated analyses of representational images, especially as such images help construct a sense of American collectivity and participate in the politics of racialized gender and sexuality, make clear the centrality of cultural iconography to an understanding of our national past and present. As a growing number of teachers of American literature and American cultural studies now perceive, to ignore the specifics of visual culture, out of respect for disciplinary boundaries or in deference to the textual, risks missing the rich and complex ways America and Americans are constituted.

NOTES

1. For narratives about the development of British cultural studies, see Easthope; Hall, "Cultural Studies"; and During.

2. Fredric Jameson has identified the "transformation of reality into images" as a distinguishing feature of postmodern culture ("Postmodernism" 125), and as photography, television, film, video, and various computer technologies accelerate the production of images for mass consumption, we see more evidence of a Baudrillardean simulacrum, a world of images floating free from the real, which has disappeared from sight (see Baudrillard). One significant instance of this "murder of the real"(5), as Baudrillard has called it, occurred during the 1991 Persian Gulf War, when television viewers became entranced by the video-game-like images produced by the Pentagon and the networks. Dead and damaged bodies were rendered not just invisible but nonexistent by the simulacrum of war. For astute accounts of this obscenity, see Mitchell (*Picture Theory* 397–405), Franklin, Norris, and Ross.

3. For a definition of this project, see Mitchell ("What Is Visual Culture?"); for multiple perspectives on its viability and significance, see "Visual Culture Questionnaire." Key contributions to its development include Mitchell (*Iconology*), Jenks, and Brennan and Martin.

4. The Protestant iconoclasm that the Puritans brought with them to America, which derived from Calvin's conception that Protestant sacramental rites and Catholic visual art were competing icons, resulted in figurative and actual violence. By substituting living images for live art, Calvin "collapsed the distinction between art and life, just as the iconoclasts did when they perceived themselves as persecuted art

objects" (Kibbey 45); consequently, the Puritans sought to destroy—by beheading, defacing, and burning—not just offending images but also human beings whose material images, whose physical characteristics, differed from their own. The Puritan extermination of the Pequot Indians, like the extreme prejudice against Catholics and antinomian women was iconoclastic.

5. For a historical account of the secularization of the visual, see Jay (43–45).

6. For an account of Barthes's changing views of photography, see Shawcross.

7. A related consideration in reading photographs, as Lee Clark Mitchell has pointed out, is that "any photographer has a more or less hidden agenda, involving at a minimum certain simple economic considerations. To be aware of those considerations is to address a set of similarly simple questions whenever faced with a photograph worth serious attention. For whom is the photographer working or to whom is he planning to sell his image? What is the audience meant to see, and at the same time, not to see?" (xiii).

8. Drawing inspiration from Cindy Sherman's *History Portraits* (1989) (staged photographs of Sherman in the costumes and poses of iconographical subjects from art history), Davidov observes that this female photographer "invites us to view institutions of patriarchal power—History, Truth, Art—as social and historical constructions open to revision. Understanding this, we are at liberty to imagine other stories—sub-versions—that might be recovered" (18).

9. Sekula, an influential American semiotician and photographer in the socialist tradition, has provided an extended discussion of how discursive contexts determine the meanings of photographic images (3–21).

10. Other prominent iconographic studies that focus on the relation between photographs and American cultural history include Lee Clark Mitchell, Wexler, Folsom, Buscombe, Williams, and Dorst.

11. Drawing upon animal behavior studies, Gombrich fashioned a resemblance theory of representation, in which human responses to images depend upon a heuristic process involving biological needs, psychological expectations, and cultural habituation; the "search for meaning" ("Illusion and Art" 213) proceeds by trial and error as the viewer seeks confirmation of the truth of his or her interpretation. For a discussion of the shifts in Gombrich's position, see Mitchell (*Iconology* 75–94).

12. Mitchell has also pointed out that "the 'nature' implicit in Gombrich's theory of the image is . . . a particular historical formation, an ideology associated with the rise of modern science and the emergence of capitalist economies in Western Europe in the last four hundred years" (*Iconology* 90).

13. Because Panofsky's iconological level of interpretation, indebted to Kantian idealism, involves the use of what he calls "synthetic intuition" to gain insight into the essential tendencies of the visual image, it generally ignores economic, political, and social actualities. As Christin Hasenmueller has pointed out, iconology is "a variant of the 'history of ideas,' " and questions remain as to "whether it is *necessarily* a historical concept" (297). More harshly, Christopher S. Wood has observed, "Iconology, in the end, has not proved an especially useful hermeneutic of culture. What it tells us about a culture is usually tautological (something like: this was the kind of culture that could have produced this work)" (24).

14. As Wanda Corn pointed out in 1988, one reason for art history's conservatism is that "the museum—not the university—traditionally has been the primary sponsor of scholarly work, and, until fairly recently, the main source of employment for those wanting to work in the American field. . . . [T]he museum's standard approach to scholarship, that of cataloging, describing, and venerating the artist and the work, has dominated American art studies, even when pursued by nonmuseum scholars" (193).

15. While the traditional "sister arts" criticism of some thirty years ago—which focused on issues of aesthetics and treated painters and writers together—occasionally resurfaces in fine collections (such as Sten's), more often it is theorized and problematized through the vocabulary of semiotics and psychoanalysis (as in Wolf, *Romantic Re-Vision*, and Fried). Most of the American cultural iconography to emerge from art history does not appear in such "sister arts" criticism, however, but in the more interdisciplinary cultural studies of the 1980s and 1990s (for example, Daniels, Truettner and Wallach, Burns, Davis, and Blanchard).

Members of the Yale faculty have influenced much of the cultural iconography emerging from the field of art history in recent years. Jules Prown and Bryan Wolf, in particular, have brought new ideological concerns to the fore within the traditionally conservative practice of art history. At the beginning of the 1980s, a semiotic and formalist perspective governed their writings; Wolf's *Romantic Re-Vision* is devoted to close readings of works of art, and Prown's "Mind and Matter" shows only slight interest in politics and history. Both authors, however, have become more and more committed to cultural critique with the passage of time (See Wolf's "All the World's a Code" and "The Labor of Seeing" and Prown's "Introduction" to *Discovered Lands, Invented Pasts*). The latter even becomes polemical as it connects the treatment of Native Americans to the treatment of "Jews in Nazi-occupied Europe" (xiii).

16. For an excellent summary of the contributions of neomarxist theorists to the concept of ideology, see Jehlen; for the unusual argument that in America "we have no ideology," only "rhetorics" (xxii), see Fisher.

17. Several Republican senators and a group of conservative columnists accused *The West as America* exhibit of "trashing" American history and advancing a Marxist political agenda; for an engaged account of the controversy, see Foner and Wiener.

18. For a survey of recent scholarship on whiteness, see Fishkin. For an astute theoretical and empirical treatment of the representation of whiteness by white people in Western visual culture, see Dyer (*White*).

19. For important related studies of images of blacks in the context of British and American imperialism, see Gilman (especially chap. 3, "The Hottentot and the Prostitute: Toward an Iconography of Female Sexuality"), Pieterse, and McClintock.

20. Walter Benn Michaels ("The Souls of White Folk" and "Race into Culture") has argued that the racism of internal oppression should not necessarily be identified with the racism of American imperialism in the Philippines, given the anti-imperialism of many American racists. The study of American imperialism and its symbolic practices has become, as Janice Radway has pointed out, a new focus for American studies. In her 1998 "Presidential Address" to the American Studies Asso-

ciation, Radway argues that "this turn to the question of American imperialism, both domestically and internationally realized, is not only important but potentially transformative of the field of American studies itself" (8). The collection *Cultures of United States Imperialism* provides strong evidence of this development, as well as of the role of American cultural iconography within it. Its essays by Vincente L. Rafael and Donna Haraway, for example, show the use of photographic images as a means of possession, surveillance, and control—of natives and nature, respectively. For related accounts of photography as a means of surveillance and a tool of British imperialism, see Tagg (66–102) and Ryan; for the role of painting in British imperialism, see Tobin.

21. For other iconographic projects that have the same revisionist intention, see Honour, Boime, McElroy, Golden, and Doss.

WORKS CITED

Althusser, Louis. "Ideology and Ideological State Apparatuses (Notes towards an Investigation)." *Lenin and Philosophy*. Trans. Ben Brewster. London: New Left Books, 1971. 127–86.

Banta, Martha. *Imaging American Women: Idea and Ideals in Cultural History*. New York: Columbia UP, 1987.

Barrell, John. *The Dark Side of the Landscape: The Rural Poor in English Painting, 1730–1840*. Cambridge: Cambridge UP, 1980.

Barthes, Roland. *Mythologies*. Selected and trans. Annette Lavers. New York: Hill and Wang, 1972.

———. "The Photographic Message." *Image, Music, Text*. Trans. Stephen Heath. New York: Hill, 1977.

Baudrillard, Jean. *Simulacra and Simulation*. Trans. Sheila Faria Glaser. Ann Arbor: U of Michigan P, 1994.

Bercovitch, Sacvan, and Myra Jehlen, eds. *Ideology and Classic American Literature*. Cambridge: Cambridge UP, 1986.

Berlant, Lauren. *The Anatomy of National Fantasy: Hawthorne, Utopia, and Everyday Life*. Chicago: U of Chicago P, 1991.

———. *The Queen of America Goes to Washington City: Essays on Sex and Citizenship*. Durham: Duke UP, 1997.

Bermingham, Ann. *Landscape and Ideology: The English Rustic Tradition, 1740–1860*. Berkeley: U of California P, 1986.

Bhabha, Homi K. *The Location of Culture*. New York: Routledge, 1994.

Blanchard, Mary Warner. *Oscar Wilde's America: Counterculture in the Gilded Age*. New Haven: Yale UP, 1998.

Boime, Albert. *The Art of Exclusion: Representing Blacks in the Nineteenth Century*. Washington, D.C.: Smithsonian Institution P, 1990.

Bordwell, David. "Contemporary Film Studies and the Vicissitudes of Grand Theory." *Post-Theory: Reconstructing Film Studies*. Ed. Bordwell and Noel Carroll. Madison: U of Wisconsin P, 1996. 3–36.

Brennan, Teresa, and Martin Jay, eds. *Vision in Context: Historical and Contemporary Perspectives on Sight.* New York: Routledge, 1996.

Bryson, Norman. *Vision and Painting: The Logic of the Gaze.* New Haven: Yale UP, 1983.

Burns, Sarah. *Inventing the Modern Artist: Art and Culture in Gilded Age America.* New Haven: Yale UP, 1996.

———. *Pastoral Inventions.* Philadelphia: Temple UP, 1989.

———. "The Price of Beauty: Art, Commerce, and the Late Nineteenth-Century American Studio Interior." *American Iconology.* Ed. Miller. 209–38.

Buscombe, Edward. "Inventing Monument Valley: Nineteenth-Century Landscape Photography and the Western Film." *Fugitive Images: From Photography to Video.* Ed. Patrice Petro. Bloomington: Indiana UP, 1995. 87–108.

Cassidy, Brendan. "Introduction: Iconography, Texts, and Audiences." *Iconography at the Crossroads: Papers from the Colloquium Sponsored by the Index of Christian Art. . . .* Ed. Cassidy. Princeton: Department of Art and Archaeology, Princeton University, 1993. 3–15.

Corbeiller, Clare le. "Miss America and Her Sisters: Personifications of the Four Parts of the World." *Metropolitan Museum Bulletin*, nos. 19 20 (1960): 209–23.

Corn, Wanda. "Coming of Age: Historical Scholarship in American Art." *Art Bulletin* June 1988: 188–207.

Cultures of United States Imperialism. Ed. Amy Kaplan and Donald E. Pease. Durham: Duke UP, 1993.

Daniels, Stephen. *Landscape Imagery and National Identity in England and the United States.* Princeton: Princeton UP, 1993.

Davidov, Judith Fryer. *Women's Camera Work: Self/Body/Other in American Visual Culture.* Durham: Duke UP, 1998.

Davis, John. *Encountering the Holy Land in Nineteenth-Century American Art and Culture.* Princeton: Princeton UP, 1996.

De Lauretis, Teresa. *Alice Doesn't: Feminism, Semiotics, Cinema.* Bloomington: Indiana UP, 1989.

Denning, Michael. " 'The Special American Conditions': Marxism and American Studies." *American Quarterly* 38 (1986): 356–80.

Discovered Lands, Invented Pasts. New Haven: Yale UP, 1992.

Doane, Mary Ann. *Femmes Fatales: Feminism, Film Theory, Psychoanalysis.* New York: Routledge, 1991.

Dorst, John D. *Looking West.* Philadelphia: U of Pennsylvania P, 1999.

Doss, Erika. "Imaging the Panthers: Representing Black Power and Masculinity, 1960s–1990s." *Prospects* 23 (1998): 483–516.

During, Simon. "Introduction." *The Cultural Studies Reader.* Ed. Simon During. London and New York: Routledge, 1993. 1–25.

Dyer, Richard. *Heavenly Bodies: Film Stars and Society.* Basingstoke: Macmillan, 1986.

———. *The Matter of Images: Essays on Representations.* London and New York: Routledge, 1993.

———. *White.* New York and London: Routledge, 1997.

Easthope, Anthony. *Literary into Cultural Studies.* London: Routledge, 1991.

Fisher, Philip. "Introduction." *The New American Studies: Essays from "Representations."* Ed. Fisher. Berkeley: U of California P, 1991. vii–xxii.

Fishkin, Shelley Fisher. "Interrogating 'Whiteness,' Complicating 'Blackness': Remapping American Culture." *American Quarterly* 47 (September 1995): 428–66.

Fliegelman, Jay. *Prodigals and Pilgrims: The American Revolution against Patriarchal Authority, 1750–1800.* New York: Cambridge UP, 1982.

Folsom, Ed. *Walt Whitman's Native Representations.* Cambridge: Cambridge UP, 1994.

Foner, Eric, and Jon Wiener. "Fighting for the West." *Nation* (July 29/August 5, 1991): 163–66.

Forgie, George. *Patricide in the House Divided: A Psychological Interpretation of Lincoln and His Age.* New York: Norton, 1979.

Foucault, Michel. *Power/Knowledge: Selected Interviews and Other Writings, 1972–1977.* Ed. Colin Gordon. Trans. Colin Gordon et al. New York: Pantheon, 1980.

Franchot, Jenny. *Roads to Rome: The Antebellum Protestant Encounter with Catholicism.* Berkeley: U of California P, 1994.

Franklin, H. Bruce. "From Realism to Virtual Reality: Images of America's Wars." *Georgia Review* 48 (1994): 47–64.

Fried, Michael. *Realism, Writing, Disfiguration: On Thomas Eakins and Stephen Crane.* Chicago: U of Chicago P, 1987.

Fryd, Vivien Green. *Art and Empire: The Politics of Ethnicity in the United States Capitol, 1815–1860.* New Haven and London: Yale UP, 1992.

Gaines, Jane. "White Privilege and Looking Relations: Race and Gender in Feminist Film Theory." *Screen* 29 (Autumn 1988): 12–27.

Gates, Henry Louis, Jr. "The Trope of a New Negro and the Reconstruction of the Image of the Black." *Representations* 24 (Fall 1988): 129–55.

Gilman, Sander L. *Difference and Pathology: Stereotypes of Sexuality, Race, and Madness.* Ithaca: Cornell UP, 1985.

Gilmore, Michael T. *American Romanticism and the Marketplace.* Chicago: U of Chicago P, 1985.

Golden, Thelma, ed. *Black Male: Representations of Masculinity in Contemporary American Art.* New York: Whitney Museum of American Art, 1994.

Gombrich, Ernest. *Art and Illusion: A Study in the Psychology of Pictorial Representation.* Princeton: Princeton UP, 1956.

———. "Illusion and Art." *Illusion in Nature and Art.* Ed. R. L. Gregory and Gombrich. New York: Scribner's, 1973. 193–243.

Goodman, Nelson. *Languages of Art: An Approach to a Theory of Symbols.* Indianapolis: Hackett, 1976.

Hales, Peter. *William Henry Jackson and the Transformation of the American Landscape.* Philadelphia: Temple UP, 1988.

Hall, Stuart. "Cultural Studies and Its Theoretical Legacies." *Cultural Studies.* Ed. Lawrence Grossberg, Cary Nelson, and Paula Treichler. London and New York: Routledge, 1992. 277–86.

———. "Gramsci's Relevance for the Study of Race and Ethnicity." *Journal of Communication Inquiry* 10 (1986): 5–27.

Haraway, Donna. "Teddy Bear Patriarchy: Taxidermy in the Garden of Eden, New York City, 1908–1936." *Cultures of United States Imperialism.* 237–91.

Hasenmueller, Christin. "Panofsky, Iconography, and Semiotics." *Journal of Aesthetics and Art Criticism* 36 (Spring 1978): 289–301.

Honour, Hugh. *From the American Revolution to World War I*. Houston: Menil Foundation, 1989. Vol. 4 of *The Image of the Black in Western Art*. 4 vols. 1976–89.

Hunt, Lynn. *The Family Romance of the French Revolution*. Berkeley: U of California P, 1992.

Jameson, Fredric. *The Political Unconscious*. London: Methuen, 1981.

———. "Postmodernism and Consumer Society." *The Anti-Aesthetic: Essays on Postmodern Culture*. Ed. Hal Foster. Seattle: Bay, 1983. 111–25.

Jay, Martin. *Downcast Eyes: The Denigration of Vision in Twentieth-Century French Thought*. Berkeley: U of California P, 1993. 43–45.

Jehlen, Myra. "Introduction." *Ideology and Classic American Literature*. Ed. Bercovitch and Jehlen. 1–18.

Jenks, Chris, ed. *Visual Culture*. New York: Routledge, 1995.

Kaplan, E. Ann. *Looking for the Other: Feminism, Film, and the Imperial Gaze*. New York and London: Routledge, 1997.

Kasson, Joy S. *Marble Queens and Captives: Women in Nineteenth-Century American Sculpture*. New Haven and London: Yale UP, 1990.

Kibbey, Ann. *The Interpretation of Material Shapes in Puritanism: A Study of Rhetoric, Prejudice, and Violence*. Cambridge Studies in American Literature and Culture 14. Cambridge: Cambridge UP, 1986.

Kuhn, Annette. *Women's Pictures: Feminism and Cinema*. London: Routledge & Kegan Paul, 1982.

Lott, Eric. *Love and Theft: Blackface Minstrelsy and the American Working Class*. New York: Oxford UP, 1993.

———. "White Like Me: Racial Cross-Dressing and the Construction of American Whiteness." *Cultures of United States Imperialism*. 474–495.

McClintock, Anne. *Imperial Leather: Race, Gender, and Sexuality in the Colonial Contest*. New York and London: Routledge, 1995.

McElroy, Guy C. *Facing History: The Black Image in American Art 1710–1940*. San Francisco: Bedford Arts and Corcoran Gallery, 1990.

Macherey, Pierre. *A Theory of Literary Production*. Trans. Geoffrey Wall. Boston: Routledge & Kegan Paul, 1978.

McKinsey, Elizabeth. *Niagara Falls: Icon of the American Sublime*. Cambridge: Cambridge UP, 1985.

Michaels, Walter Benn. "Race into Culture: A Critical Genealogy of Cultural Identity." *Critical Inquiry* 18 (Summer 1992): 655–85.

———. "The Souls of White Folk." *Literature and the Body: Essays on Populations and Persons*. Ed. Elaine Scarry. Baltimore: Johns Hopkins UP, 1988. 185–209.

Miller, Angela. *The Empire of the Eye: Landscape Representation and American Cultural Politics, 1825–1875*. Ithaca and London: Cornell UP, 1993.

Miller, David C., ed. *American Iconology: New Approaches to Nineteenth-Century Art and Literature*. New Haven: Yale UP, 1993.

Mitchell, Lee Clark. "The Photograph and the American Indian." *The Photograph and the American Indian*. Ed. Alfred L. Bush and Mitchell. Princeton: Princeton UP, 1994. xi–xxvi.

Mitchell, W.J.T. *Iconology: Image, Text, Ideology*. Chicago: U of Chicago P, 1986.

———. *Picture Theory: Essays on Verbal and Visual Representation*. Chicago: U of Chicago P, 1994.

———. "What Is Visual Culture?" *Meaning in the Visual Arts: Views from the Outside, A Centennial Commemoration of Erwin Panofsky (1892–1968)*. Ed. Irving Lavin. Princeton: Institute for Advanced Study, 1995. 207–17.

Moxey, Keith. "The Politics of Iconology." *Iconography at the Crossroads: Papers from the Colloquium Sponsored by the Index of Christian Art*. Ed. Cassidy. 27–31.

———. *The Practice of Theory: Poststructuralism, Cultural Politics, and Art History*. Ithaca: Cornell UP, 1994.

Mulvey, Laura. *Visual and Other Pleasures*. Bloomington: Indiana UP, 1989.

Nemerov, Alex. "Doing the 'Old America': The Image of the American West, 1880–1920." *The West as America*. 285–344.

———. *Frederic Remington and Turn-of-the-Century America*. New Haven and London: Yale UP, 1995.

Norris, Margot. "The (Lethal) Turn of the Twentieth Century: War and Population Control." *Centuries' Ends, Narrative Means*. Ed. Robert Newman. Stanford: Stanford UP, 1996. 151–59.

Novak, Barbara. *American Painting of the Nineteenth Century: Realism, Idealism, and the American Experience*. 2d ed. 1969; New York: Harper & Row, 1979.

———. *Nature and Culture: American Landscape and Painting, 1825–1875*. New York: Oxford UP, 1980.

Panofsky, Erwin. *Meaning in the Visual Arts*. Garden City : Doubleday, 1955.

Peirce, Charles Sanders. *Collected Papers of Charles Sanders Peirce*. Vol. 2. Ed. Charles Hartshorne and Paul Weiss. Cambridge: Belknap P of Harvard UP, 1958.

Pieterse, Jan Nederveen. *White on Black: Images of Africa and Blacks in Western Popular Culture*. New Haven: Yale UP, 1992.

Porter, Carolyn. *Seeing and Being: The Plight of the Participant Observer in Emerson, James, Adams, and Faulkner*. Middletown: Wesleyan UP, 1981.

Prown, Jules David. "Introduction." *Discovered Lands, Invented Pasts*. xi–xv.

———. "Mind and Matter: An Introduction to Material Culture Theory and Method." *Winterthur Portfolio* 17 (Spring 1982): 1–19.

Radway, Janice. "What's in a Name? Presidential Address to the American Studies Association, 20 November, 1998." *American Quarterly* 51 (March 1999): 1–32.

Rafael, Vicente L. "White Love: Surveillance and Nationalist Resistance in the U.S. Colonization of the Philippines." *Cultures of United States Imperialism*. 185–218.

Rogin, Michael. *Blackface, White Noise: Jewish Immigrants in the Hollywood Melting Pot*. Berkeley: U of California P, 1996.

———. *Fathers and Children: Andrew Jackson and the Subjugation of the American Indian*. New York: Random House, 1976.

———. *"Ronald Reagan," the Movie: and Other Episodes in Political Demonology*. Berkeley: U of California P, 1987.

———. *Subversive Genealogy: The Politics and Art of Herman Melville*. New York: Knopf, 1983.

Ross, Andrew. "The Ecology of Images." *Visual Culture: Images and Interpretation.* Ed. Norman Bryson, Michael Ann Holly, and Keith Moxey. Hanover: Wesleyan UP, 1994. 325–46.

Ryan, James R. *Picturing Empire: Photography and the Visualization of the British Empire.* Chicago: U of Chicago P, 1997.

Said, Edward W. "Opponents, Audiences, Constituencies and Community." *The Anti-Aesthetic: Essays on Postmodern Culture.* Ed. Hal Foster. Seattle: Bay, 1983. 135–59.

———. *Orientalism.* New York: Random House, 1978.

Samuels, Shirley. *Romances of the Republic: Women, the Family, and Violence.* New York: Oxford UP, 1996.

Savage, Kirk. *Standing Soldiers, Kneeling Slaves: Race, War, and Monument in Nineteenth-Century America.* Princeton: Princeton UP, 1997

Sekula, Allan. *Photography against the Grain: Essays and Photo Works 1973–1983.* Halifax: The P of the Nova Scotia College of Art and Design, 1984.

Shawcross, Nancy M. *Roland Barthes on Photography.* Gainesville: UP of Florida, 1997.

Snyder, Joel. "Picturing Vision." *Critical Inquiry* 6 (1980): 499–526.

Solkin, David H. *Richard Wilson: The Landscape of Reaction.* London: Tate Gallery, 1982.

Sten, Christopher, ed. *Savage Eye: Melville and the Visual Arts.* Kent: Kent State UP, 1991.

Sweet, Timothy. *Traces of War: Poetry, Photography, and the Crisis of the Union.* Baltimore and London: Johns Hopkins UP, 1990.

Tagg, John. *The Burden of Representation: Essays on Photographies and Histories.* Amherst: U of Massachusetts P, 1988.

Tichi, Cecelia. *Shifting Gears: Technology, Literature, Culture in Modernist America.* Chapel Hill: North Carolina UP, 1987.

Tobin, Beth Fowkes. *Picturing Imperial Power: Colonial Subjects in Eighteenth-Century British Painting.* Durham: Duke UP, 1999.

Trachtenberg, Alan. *Reading American Photographs: Images as History, Mathew Brady to Walker Evans.* New York: Hill and Wang, 1989.

Truettner, William H., and Alan Wallach, eds. *Thomas Cole: Landscape into History.* New Haven: Yale UP; Washington, D.C.: National Museum of American Art, 1994.

"Visual Culture Questionnaire." *October* 77 (Summer 1996): 25–70.

Wallis, Brian. "Black Bodies, White Science: Louis Agassiz's Slave Daguerreotypes." *American Art* 9 (Summer 1995): 38–61.

Warner, Marina. *Monuments and Maidens: The Allegory of the Female Form.* New York: Atheneum, 1985.

The West as America: Reinterpreting Images of the Frontier, 1820–1920. Ed. William H. Truettner. Washington, D.C., and London: Smithsonian Institution P, 1991.

Wexler, Laura. "Black and White in Color: American Photographs at the Turn of the Century." *Prospects* 13 (1988): 341–90.

Wiegman, Robyn. *American Anatomies: Theorizing Race and Gender.* Durham: Duke UP, 1995.

Williams, Susan S. *Confounding Images: Photography and Portraiture in Antebellum American Fiction*. Philadelphia: U of Pennsylvania P, 1997.

Wilmerding, John, ed. *American Light: The Luminist Movement, 1850–1875*. Princeton: Princeton UP and the National Gallery of Art, 1989.

Wolf, Bryan Jay. "All the World's a Code: Art and Ideology in Nineteenth-Century American Painting." *Art Journal* 44 (Winter 1984): 328–33.

———. "The Labor of Seeing: Pragmatism, Ideology, and Gender in Winslow Homer's *The Morning Bell*." *Prospects* 17 (1992): 273–318.

———. *Romantic Re-Vision: Culture and Consciousness in Nineteenth-Century American Painting and Literature*. Chicago: U of Chicago P, 1982.

Wood, Christopher S. Introduction. *Perspective as Symbolic Form*. By Erwin Panofsky. Trans. Wood. New York: Zone, 1991. 7–24.

Yellin, Jean Fagan. *Women and Sisters: The Antislavery Feminists in American Culture*. New Haven and London: Yale UP, 1989.

Part One

BETWEEN IMAGE AND NARRATIVE:
FIGURING AMERICAN COLLECTIVITY

Seeing and Believing: Hawthorne's Reflections on the Daguerreotype in *The House of the Seven Gables*

ALAN TRACHTENBERG

1

"I don't much like pictures of that sort—they are so hard and stern; besides dodging away from the eye, and trying to escape altogether. They are conscious of looking very unamiable, I suppose, and therefore hate to be seen. . . . I don't wish to see it any more" (91–92). Phoebe's unease with image effects of the sort produced by daguerreotypes invokes an early moment in the career of photography in America, a moment of shudder, suspicion, and refusal (see also Trachtenberg, "Mirror" and "Photography"). This particular instance occurs in Nathaniel Hawthorne's *The House of the Seven Gables* (1851), a narrative in which daguerreotypes figure consequentially both in the plot and in the literary theory internalized as a major theme within the fiction. For if the narrative launches itself in the preface as an argument on behalf of "Romance" over "Novel," the figurative rhetoric by which Hawthorne embodies that distinction, so crucial to his undertaking, draws on the same daguerrean effects to which Phoebe reacts. Sharing features of both "Novel" and "Romance," of science and magic, of modernity and tradition, the daguerreotype plays a strategic role in the narrative as an emblem of the ambiguity that the tale will affirm as the superior mark of "Romance"—if not exactly "Romance" itself, at least a major narrative resource for defining and apprehending what that term means.

A writer of novels, the "Author" explains in the preface, "is presumed to aim at a very minute fidelity, not merely to the possible, but to the probable and ordinary course of man's experience" (1). Too glaring to miss, the analogy of novel writing to photography seems confirmed by the mimetic intentions of both. But Hawthorne's description of the latitude of the romancer—the allowable deviations from a strictly faithful mimesis—also evokes photography, particularly daguerreotypy: the romancer "may so manage his atmospherical medium as to bring out or mellow the lights and deepen and enrich the shadows of the picture" (1).[1] The literary distinction between two kinds of mimesis—one strictly adherent to an imitation of the probable and the ordinary, the other less constrained and freer to deploy atmospheric effects—corresponds to a distinction already well formulated in theories of photography at the time, between merely mechanical and self-consciously artistic uses of the new medium.[2] While "minute fidelity" seems incontrovertibly to associate photography with "Novel," with its recurring imagery of light and mist and shadow, the preface subtly recruits the daguerreotype for a key role in the definition of "Romance" that the narrative will unfold.

Two sentences are especially important. "The point of view in which this Tale comes under the Romantic definition, lies in the attempt to connect a by-gone time with the very Present that is flitting away from us" (2). The present flits away just as does the picture on the mirrorlike surface of a daguerreotype. But how are we to take "connect," especially in light of the rejection of "very minute fidelity"? Further on, the "Author" warns against reading the tale as a too literal picture of an actual place and says that such a reading "exposes the Romance to an inflexible and exceedingly dangerous species of criticism, by bringing his [the author's] fancy-pictures almost into positive contact with the realities of the moment" (3). How are we to understand the difference between dangerous "positive contact" and presumably benign "connect"? We are teased into imagining another mode of fidelity to "Present," to "realities of the moment"—that is, the mode of "Romance," which defines itself not by an absolute difference from "Novel" nor by a rejection of mimesis but by the positing of another kind of mimesis, atmospheric, shadowed, faithful to that which flits away: a kind of mimesis that the narrative will apprehend with the help of its ambiguous and problematic daguerreotypes.[3]

A present that flits away, fancy-pictures which might be brought "almost" into "positive contact" with "realit[y]," portraits that dodge the eye and try to escape (to escape detection?)—Hawthorne's figures play nicely on what by 1851 had become a fairly common experience: that apparent trick of the mirrored metallic face of the daguerreotype image, seeming at once here and gone, a positive and a negative, substance and shadow. What one sees, shadow or image, or indeed one's own visage flashed back from the mirrored surface, depends on how one holds the palm-sized cased image, at what angle and in what light. The image materializes before one's eyes as if out of its own shadows. Because of the daguerreotype's peculiar construction, built up, as one recent expert explains, through accumulated surface granules rather than suspended in an emulsion (as in paper prints), what is required for the image to seem legible—or, as they said at the time, to "come to life"—is a specific triangulation of viewer, image, and light.[4]

In the face of such contingency and instability of seeing, no wonder that some like Phoebe felt disconcerted by the experience. Phoebe's outcry and the suggestive language of the preface signal how deeply engaged this narrative is with daguerrean seeing, its ambiguities of affect and, I shall argue, ambivalences of purpose. How are we to understand, for example, the motives and purposes of the novel's ardent daguerreotypist, Holgrave? "I misuse Heaven's blessed sunshine by tracing out human features, through its agency" (46), the young man confesses to Hepzibah. Surely we want to read "misuse" as coyly self-ironic, a nicely turned disclaimer of anything irregular in his craft. Is not his practice of daguerreotypy a sign of Holgrave's most appealing traits—his experimental bent, his adventuresomeness, his facility with modern tools? To be sure. But Phoebe personifies the sun's purest rays, and Holgrave comes close to misusing her; her feminine innocence we are surely meant to take as the novel's least controvertible value; in the end it is what saves Holgrave from himself. Our smile at "misuse" fades into a deeper, more shadowed concern when we learn of Holgrave's secret purpose of revenge against the Pyncheons in whose house he presently resides. Is he tenant or spy? In any case he resides in disguise, perhaps even from himself. Might not the craft he practices in the deep recesses of the old mansion as well as in his public rooms in the town be viewed as a purposefully atavistic regression to the witchcraft of his ancestors, the original Maules from whom Colonel Pyncheon, founder of the family, had stolen the land for his estate and house two hundred years earlier?

Etching his text with strokes of ambiguity and dubiety, Hawthorne draws widely on figural terms from the popular discourse of the daguerreotype circulating in the print culture of the 1840s and early 1850s (see Trachtenberg, "Mirror" and "Photography"). He draws on that gothicized discourse not for the sake of local allusions alone but as a vehicle of his deepest intentions in the romance, which are to probe the implications of the new order of things of which photography serves as the auspicious type. Alternative views of the daguerreotype portrait, of the autoptic process of apparently unmediated seeing and believing that the camera putatively represents, and of the physiognomic principles of portraits as such serve the tale's ulterior purposes. To be sure, a narrative more of picture than action, of tableaux than plot, of gothic device than dialogic interaction, *The House of the Seven Gables* leaves its largest questions unsettled, its complexities and complications aborted by the quick fix of a hastily arranged fairy-tale ending in which Holgrave seems to abandon daguerreotypy (this is not clear), along with his resentment and radical politics (this is clear), for pastoral squiredom. It is as if, Walter Benn Michaels provocatively suggests, the daguerreotype of the dead Judge Pyncheon releases them all from both the burden of a weighty "Past" and the instabilities of a flitting "Present," frees them altogether from "Novel" to spend their days within the stone-protected realm of "Romance" (Michaels 95–101). Whatever authorial purposes account for the novel's odd ending, it reflects in part on daguerrean visibility, on photography's cultural work within a society rapidly undergoing unsettling change toward market-centered urban capitalism. No wonder Melville found in the narrative an "intense feeling of the visable truth," meaning by that, he wrote to Hawthorne, "the apprehension of the absolute condition of present things as they strike the eye"(124).

2

Hawthorne focuses his inquiry into means and ends of the daguerreotype on the figure of his hero. At present Holgrave lives as an itinerant daguerreotypist, a fact that seems at first marginal to the main action of the narrative, which in summary resembles popular Gothic melodramas: a decaying old house, an ancient crime, a family curse, a thirst for revenge. The story centers on Judge Jaffrey Pyncheon's effort to extract from his cousin Clifford, just released from a lengthy unjust imprisonment, information about a missing family deed to lands in Maine. The Judge had framed Clifford, giving false evidence that convicted his cousin of the murder of their wealthy uncle. Jaffrey's treachery and his greed make him seem an avatar of the original seventeenth-century Pyncheon, founder of the once magnificent, now decaying House of the Seven Gables. Two descendants whose decrepitude matches that of the ancient house occupy the dwelling: the penurious Hepzibah, whose rather helpless try at selling groceries in a wing of the house opens the action of the novel, and her sadly ruined brother Clifford. They are joined by their sprightly country cousin Phoebe and the ambiguous tenant, the young daguerreotypist with alarmingly radical views on the sinfulness of inherited property and other social conventions. It will emerge that the young man has counterfeited his identity, for he is none other than a descendant of the Matthew Maule from whom the original Pyncheon had wrested the parcel of land on which the house sits. That legalized theft followed Maule's conviction on charges of witchcraft, a false accusation which provoked Maule's wrathful curse from the gallows that the lying, overreaching Pyncheon will drink blood. The stern old man's sudden death in a paroxysm the very day his house was completed (Maule's son Thomas was the chief carpenter) seemed to fulfill Maule's curse, the curse of the dispossessed and the resentful.

By legend the curse persists: virtually every generation has seen a Pyncheon who resembled the hard, unbending founder, even to the point of dying suddenly with a gurgling sound in his throat. The present Judge is the latest avatar and the final one, for Holgrave's camera will show beyond cavil that his death was natural after all, the result of an inherited ailment. The curse lifted, Clifford exonerated, Phoebe and Holgrave married—the entire cast of characters, including the old retainer Uncle Venner, betake themselves to the Judge's country estate, now restored to rightful heirs, the newly wed and redeemed descendants of both Maule and Pyncheon. With harmony between the antagonistic families (a distinctly class antagonism) finally achieved, the story closes happily as Hepzibah, out of the largesse of her newly recovered wealth and social station, dispenses silver coin to the town "urchin."

Like many readers, D. H. Lawrence puzzled over this curious tale of sinful fathers, vengeful sons, and compliant daughters in a bizarrely modern world: "The Dark Old Fathers. The Beloved Wishy-Washy Sons. The Photography Business. ? ? ?' (104). As far as the plot goes, only the final evidentiary picture of the Judge's death makes a difference, as a kind of messenger from the gods. But Hawthorne has his purposes, slyly insinuated in the daguerrean figures already quoted from the preface. The fixed picture that preserves what flits away had been a popular trope in the photographic trade for more than a decade: "Seize the shadow ere the substance fade." "Fancy-pictures" and "flitting" suggest that Hawthorne in some manner saw his own text as bearing a resemblance to the daguerrean image and its uncanny effects. One recent critic remarks that the narrative itself might be read as a "flickering" apparitional, here-again, gone-again daguerreotype portrait (Davidson 697). The fact that Holgrave is also an author (his name can be read as self-written) carries the suggestion further of a metadiscourse on the art of narrative. Does Holgrave's daguerreotypy serve as a heuristic analogy to Hawthorne's writing of romance?

It is significant in this regard that Holgrave's daguerreotypes appear within a political universe, a world threatened by both past and future, by inherited corruption founded upon illegitimate class privilege, and by the discordant energies of modernity, the railroad, the telegraph, market society. Moreover, associated at once with sorcery through the Maule eye of Holgrave and with modern mechanical instruments of change, Holgrave's daguerreotypes combine elements of past and present, of tradition and change, of magical and rational systems of knowledge. The narrator situates the products of Holgrave's equivocal craft within a radiating web of implication.

It is noteworthy, then, that the first daguerreotype presented to a viewer in the narrative is a failed image, one that misses its intention: a dour picture of the Judge which so displeases Phoebe that she turns away. The exchange occurs, not incidentally, in the Pyncheon garden near the bubbling waters of Maule's Well. The picture was "intended to be engraved," Holgrave explains, presumably for the Judge's use in his campaign for governor.[5] What seems to ruin the image is the incorrigible hardness of the Judge's physiognomy:

> Now, the remarkable point is, that the original wears, to the world's eye—and, for aught I know, to his most intimate friends—an exceedingly pleasant countenance, indicative of benevolence, openness of heart, sunny good humor, and other praiseworthy qualities of that cast. The sun, as you see, tells quite another story.... Here we have the man, sly, subtle, hard, imperious, and, withal, cold as ice. Look at that eye! Would you like to be at its mercy? At that mouth! Could it ever smile? And yet, if you could only see the benign smile of the original! It is so much the more unfortunate, as he is a public character of some eminence, and the likeness was intended to be engraved. (92)

Holgrave's explanation of the failure, often taken as an unequivocal endorsement on the author's part as well as his hero's, of the new medium, echoes the Enlightenment rationalist ideology embedded within popular commentary on photography. Yet it will prove to be every bit as equivocal as the young Holgrave-Maule himself: "There is a wonderful insight in heaven's broad and simple sunshine," he explains to Phoebe. "While we give it credit only for depicting the merest surface, it actually brings out the secret character with a truth that no painter would ever venture upon, even could he detect it" (91). Knowing that the self-authored Holgrave himself travels under a false sign, that he too harbors a "secret character," is enough warning for us to hold these words at some distance. Is his mention of "secret character," like his present disguised tenancy in the house of his family's dispossession, a tactical move toward his own inherited interest in exposing the Pyncheons' illegitimacy and destroying them? Like the actual pictures he makes—three are mentioned: two portraits of the dubious Judge Pyncheon (one after his death), and another we never see directly, of Uncle Venner, the town's storyteller and down-home philosopher—Holgrave's words about his craft are freighted with implications eventually to be drawn forth.

Other readers have shared D. H. Lawrence's suspicion of something secretive and covert about the novel. "It is . . . full of all sorts of deep intentions . . . certain complicated purposes" (97), remarked Henry James, adding that what Hawthorne evidently "designed to represent was not the struggle between an old society and a new . . . but simply . . . the shrinkage and extinction of a family" (102). If not "struggle" between the old and new, then at least, as Frank Kermode nicely puts it, the narrative registers "a transition from one structure of society, and one system of belief and knowledge, to another" (429). James notes cogently that the characters "are all figures rather than characters—they are all pictures rather than persons" (99). In the "history of retribution for the sin of long ago" (41), as the narrator describes his tale, Holgrave, who had taken up the daguerrean line "with the careless alacrity of an adventurer" (177), plays a kind of avenging angel, not with a sword but a camera or, better, a certain kind of eye that adapts itself with alacrity (less careless than he admits) to the daguerrean mode of vision. Holgrave's "deep, thoughtful, all-observant eyes" (156), the Maule "family eye" (156) in which "there was now-and-then an expression, not sinister, but questionable" (156), are there to witness the final act of what he conceives as a drama: "Providence . . . sends me only as a privileged and meet spectator" (217). Author, actor, and privileged audience—his role is foretold in the shadowy, teasing way in which the past repeats itself in the world of the narrative. He is the Maule "descendant" whom Hepzibah imagines seeing her fall from lady to hucksteress as "the fulfillment of his worst wishes" (ironically so, for he is also "her only friend") (46). He represents the "posterity of Matthew Maule" who, through "a sort of mesmeric process," can make the "inner region" of the family looking glass come "all alive with the departed Pyncheons; not as they had shown themselves to the world, nor in their better and happier hours, but as doing over again some deed of sin, or in the crisis of life's bitterest sorrow" (21), as he may indeed have made the Judge look in the failed daguerreotype.

"They are all types, to the author's mind," writes James, "of something general, of something that is bound up with the history, at large, of families and individuals" (99). Like each of the principal characters, Holgrave is both himself and not himself, a person and a type, a figure in his own right and a figure in an ancient, repetitive drama. Indeed, the inner life of the plot shapes itself around the need Holgrave feels most acutely to resolve the ambiguity of identity he shares with the Pyncheons: at once themselves and copies of ancient originals "doing over again some deed of sin."

Thus within the drama of the romance Holgrave's often cited words about the sun's "wonderful insight" appear to the reader (if not to Phoebe) as double-edged, covert, shadowed. Can he mean that the sun, sheer material light, does in fact possess an "insight"? Or that he, descendant of the wronged Maules and privy to the ancestral gift of witchcraft (their power to torment bestowed on them by the projected guilt of their oppressors), already knows the "secret" written on the "merest surface" of Judge Pyncheon's self-betraying face and knows craftily how to bring it out? Is the sun aligned with the "Black Arts" Hepzibah affectionately suspects him of (84)?[6] The pedagogy he offers to Phoebe in the garden next to Maule's Well is a lesson not so much on the superiority of photography to painting as on a larger matter related to the "complicated purposes" of the romance: the unreliability of appearances, of representations altogether. Can we believe what we see, the "merest surface" of things and people, crafted surfaces such as paintings, maps, even mirrors, and especially the appearances put on by such public benefactors as the capitalist, politician, and horticulturalist Jaffrey Pyncheon, whose public face is all smiles and benignity? Is there a trustworthy way of seeing through surfaces, interpreting them as signs of something not seen, a "secret character," an invisible writing?

Hawthorne deepens and complicates the issue by raising yet another question about that "character" beneath the Judge's smiling exterior disclosed by the sun, a question about its origins. Is the Judge's character his own, or is it merely a copy of his ancestor's, a replay, like his death, of an inherited infirmity? If he is indeed only a copy of an ancient original, then the "secret" part of his "character" signifies something different from simple hypocrisy or duplicity. The "truth" the sun "brings out" may be hidden from the Judge himself. It lies in his history, a family history of illegitimate class privilege and abrogated power, and particularly of the use of established authority to lend an official seal to the original theft of Maule's land. It is in the Pyncheon interest to keep that origin secret, to repress its threatening truth, and when repression becomes habitual, it produces a secretiveness that no longer understands what it hides or why. What the sun reveals through Holgrave's failed daguerreotype, then, is not the Judge's ineptitude in maintaining an affable facade before the camera but his alienation from his own "character." What the sun reveals, in short, is not just something to be glimpsed beneath a facade, something merely visible, but something to be interpreted. A visibility incomplete in itself, the daguerrean image Holgrave offers to Phoebe's eyes is in search of an explanatory narrative.

3

Near the heart of the plot lies a document, "a folded sheet of parchment" (316) hidden behind the ancestral portrait of the first Pyncheon. "Signed with the hieroglyphics of several Indian sagamores," this "ancient deed" (316), which Jaffrey is desperate to lay his hands on, represents the legislative "grant" on which the original Pyncheon based his "claims" against the "right" of Matthew Maule to possess what, "with his own toil, he had hewn out of the primeval forest, to be his garden-ground and homestead" (7). This mere piece of paper, these undecipherable scrawls in a language no one remembers, recall the "recondite documents" (19) Bartleby labors to copy in Melville's "story of Wall Street" (13), or the scraps of paper Ike McCaslin puzzles over in the commissary in Faulkner's "The Bear." Hawthorne represents as an American version of original sin an originating act of ruthless theft the knowledge of which calls into question all constituted authority.[7] What the Judge's "secret character" hides even from himself is the fact that his historical being arises from a crime, his ancestor's deed against "natural right" disguised as a legitimate "claim" in an undecipherable legislative "deed." "Deed"—the conflation of act and word places a lexical pun at the heart of the original sin: the deed (act) of displacing the Lockean "right" to ownership of the products of one's labor with "claims" based upon a cryptic deed (word) written by distant legislators or even more distant sagamores. "Secret character" behind "merest appearance" revives the pun on "deed," signifying at once character as accumulated acts (the Judge's personal sin against Clifford) and character as a written inscription (the Judge's figural reenactment of the first Pyncheon's crime).

Only by restoring this history, which requires a new way of thinking about the relation between self and past, can Holgrave render his daguerreotype of the Judge legible as revelation of hidden truth. The light of the sun alone cannot suffice, contrary to the claims of Holgrave's compeers in the real world of commercial portrait photography. Working photographers proffered visibility as their commodity, the sun their warranty of reliable truth.

In a moral climate in which citizens felt anxious about "character," eager to trust the facades projected in images of men holding public trust yet distrustful of their own eagerness, photographers offered their goods as a social good, a guide to virtue. For was not character readily discernible in the face? And did not the daguerreotype provide the republic with its most foolproof means of discerning character?[8]

By allowing Holgrave a set of words that seem so in accord with this popular republican ideology of the image, Hawthorne slyly encourages the reader to lower his or her guard. The issue turns on the ambiguity within another key word: "character" as what is true about a person, "character" as an assumed role, such as the public face put on by the Judge, or indeed that performed by the contemporary Maule in his "character" as Holgrave, daguerreotypist. In that drama Holgrave performs as both author and actor: "[I]n this long drama of wrong and retribution, I represent the old wizard" (316). This confession holds the crux of the matter: the conflict between character as a set of moral traits engraved within and visible without, and character as a performed role in a scripted drama. Changing occupations like so many roles, "putting off one exterior, and snatching up another, to be soon shifted for a third," without ever altering the "inner most man" (177), Holgrave is the figure within whom tension between self and role most overtly plays itself out. At stake is whether he will remain a "type," in the sense of a foreordained copy, or become a free historical agent, a self in historical time, free to script his own roles.

Hawthorne formulates Holgrave's inner conflict as that between a commitment to historical time and one to eschatological time and represents the conflict as an issue of interpretation. How are we to understand the failed daguerreotype of Judge Pyncheon? Not one of those photographers Walter Benjamin calls "illiterate," who "cannot read his own pictures"

(215), Holgrave knows (it is, we might say, his secret knowledge) that the meaning of the daguerreotype cannot rest in the unsupported image alone but resides only within a particular system of meaning. The system activated by his words to Phoebe is a rather bland but nonetheless distinct version of Christian typology, in which secrets are foreknown by providence. In Hawthorne's half-serious, half-skeptical use of the typological method of interpretation, "secret character" refers to a residue of prophecy uttered in the past: Maule's curse. The face, then, is an inscription that can be known only by reference to something antecedent to itself. The serious side of Hawthorne's typological method says that the secret of faces lies in the fact that they are really copies of absent originals. The skeptical side says that the original is not so much an absent figure (the portrait of the ancestral Pyncheon to whom the Judge bears an uncanny resemblance, or the lost deed) but a continuing process, an ongoing history. Judge Pyncheon is either a pure figural reflex of a determining original sin or a free historical agent responsible for his own badness, his own corruption.

Her shuddering initial reaction to the daguerreotype of the Judge initiates Phoebe into typological explanation. "I know the face" she cries, "for its stern eye has been following me about, all day. It is my Puritan ancestor, who hangs yonder in the parlor" (92). That misidentification is her first lesson; the uncanny resemblance brought out by the daguerreotype points her directly to the typological source of her uncle's "secret character": "It is certainly very like the old portrait" (92). The process begun in the garden continues when Phoebe encounters the Judge face-to-face; beneath his sunny exterior she recognizes the "hard, stern, relentless look" of "the original of the miniature [the daguerreotype]" (119). As she notes in a recurrence of the uncanny, the "original," the face before her, copies the features of the ancestor whose portrait in its antique, faded condition "brought out" the "indirect character of the man" (58). The ancient portrait strikes her as a "prophecy" (119) of the modern man, and in her "fancies" (124) that in the living Judge "the original Puritan" (120) stood before her, she gives a start (124). Thus the process of interpretation inaugurated by Holgrave teaches Phoebe a lesson essential to the system of meaning that Hawthorne takes as his object of investigation, one in which material substance of today seems to cast shadows of yesterday.

The process of interpreting the first daguerreotype culminates in the final taking of a likeness, the death portrait that will prove, typologically speaking, that in effect the good Judge had been dead all along, "fixed" as only the dead can be in an unalterable "character": "Death is so genuine a fact that it excludes falsehood, or betrays its emptiness" (310; see Michaels 100–101). For the reading instigated by Holgrave in the garden begins the torturous process of converting the Judge into a scapegoat, to be ritually slain by the camera. On the disclosure of his death everything else depends in this narrative of magical consummations. Both magical and political, Holgrave's reading of the Judge's image, of the Judge himself as an image, dissolves corrupt public authority by disclosing the corpse, the rotten "deed" decaying just behind the elegant facade. Holgrave's is that "sadly gifted eye" whose knowing look "melts into thin air" the "tall and stately edifice" the Judge had constructed for the "public eye" (229). The narrative elaborates this architectural figure. The Judge's self is like a marble palace constructed of "the big, heavy, solid unrealities" of wealth and power and "public honors," its windows "the most transparent of plate-glass," its dome open to the sky (229). The architectural figure recalls nothing so much as one of the era's novel creations, a mercantile shop posing as a neoclassical palace, while its stateliness recalls the original appearance of the House of the Seven Gables itself: "There is something so massive, stable, and almost irresistibly imposing, in the exterior presentment of established rank and great possessions, that their very existence seems to give them a right to exist; at least, so excellent a counterfeit of right, that few poor and humble men have moral force enough to question it, even in their secret minds" (25).[9] The political point of Holgrave's hermeneutics becomes clear: to penetrate "exterior presentment" in order to disclose the "counterfeit of right" it claims for itself.

Holgrave's lesson in the reading of the daguerreotype (both typological and historicist) sheds light, moreover, on the role of picturing as such within the texture of the book. The preponderance of looking, seeing, gazing, scrutinizing—for example, "To know Judge Pyncheon, was to see him at that moment" (129)—declares the reading of images (reading in the sense of comprehending the look of things and persons) as a core issue in the narrative. Often the verb is made explicit: Clifford "reads" Phoebe, "as he would a sweet and simple story" (142); Holgrave too "fancied that he could look through Phoebe, and all around her, and could read her off like a page of a child's story-book" (182). People stand to each other as texts, transparently legible or guardedly cryptic. There are texts within texts, not only figurative storybooks and the "legend" of Alice Pyncheon composed by Holgrave but a host of pictures: "quaint figures" (11) ornamenting the exterior of the house; "pictures of Indians and wild beasts grotesquely illuminat[ing]" (33) the map of the legendary Pyncheon territories in Maine; "grotesque figures of man, bird, and beast" painted over the old tea set, "in a world of their own" (77); and the gingerbread figures of animals and "the renowned Jim Crow" (50). Some are ephemeral, vanishing as quickly as they are seen: the "continually shifting apparition of quaint figures, vanishing too suddenly to be definable," of Maule's Well (88) and the "brilliant fantasies" that depict the world "in hues bright as imagination" on the "nothing" surface of Clifford's soap bubbles (171). And, of course, there are the most prominent pictures: the ancient portrait of the founding ancestor, the Malbone miniature of Clifford that Hepzibah cherishes, and the daguerreotypes of the Judge. How does one read images of the world, the world deflected into image? The question of visuality as cognition lies athwart the entire narrative.

Indeed, the narrator introduces the larger question at the outset: "The aspect of the venerable mansion has always affected me like a human countenance, bearing the traces not merely of outward storm and sunshine, but expressive, also of the long lapse of mortal life, and accompanying vicissitudes, that have passed within. Were these to be worthily recounted, they would form a narrative of no small interest and instruction, and possessing, moreover, a certain remarkable unity, which might almost seem the result of artistic arrangement" (5).

Interpretation appears here at the outset not just as a correlation of outer trace and inward life but as "narrative" with its own laws and codes of "arrangement." Here is the method of "Romance" promised in the preface, the method that presumes a relation between outer and inner as inherently ambiguous. Is the narrative true or only a plausible guess, governed equally by the desire for "unity" and by reference to actual fact or document? Indeed, as it proceeds, the narrative more and more adduces what it calls "tradition" against "written record," a polarizing of modes of telling that becomes part of a diagrammatic structure of oppositions: on one hand, public records, official, "cold, formal, and empty words" (122); on the other, "the private and domestic view" (122), homely truths, gossip, rumor, chimney-corner tradition. Parallel to this contrast, substantially between writing and speech, is "the vast discrepancy between portraits intended for engraving, and the pencil-sketches that pass from hand to hand, behind the original's back" (122). (Holgrave's daguerreotype, recall, was indeed "intended for engraving," but the measure of its failure was its resemblance to a satiric pencil-sketch view of the Judge.) A corresponding opposition in the schema of personae has the Judge, the archpublic figure, set in polar opposition to Uncle Venner, the book's gossip, who mediates between the sphere of women (he makes daily rounds in the town from kitchen to kitchen) and of men: the Judge, who takes "his idea of himself from what purports to be his image, as reflected in the mirror of public opinion" (232), and the Uncle, the "man of patches" (155) whose wardrobe consists of throwaways, "a miscellaneous old gentleman, partly himself, but, in good measure, somebody else" (62).

How are we to understand Holgrave's art of daguerreotypy within this structure of oppositions? The daguerreotype occupies a paradoxical position. The narrative comes down on the side of tradition, gossip, and pencil-sketches, linked through Uncle Venner and Phoebe to an older village culture, a republican culture founded on community and consensus. The old ways survive into and provide a perspective upon a present characterized by two localized but intense images of change: Hepzibah's fantasy of a "panorama, representing the great thoroughfare of a city" (48), and the railroad-car vista of Hepzibah and Clifford, during their mad flight from the threatening Judge, of "the world racing past" (256). The latter is more nightmarish and metaphysical, as Clifford discourses crazily in the rattling car on electricity as "an almost spiritual medium" (264), on the blessings of the railroad and the insubstantiality of real estate. The scene is a severe gloss on the deceptively milder "fluctuating waves of our social life" (38) by which the narrator had introduced Hepzibah's reopening of the shop. If that moment of transformation of a patrician into a plebian hints at the upheavals of the Panic of 1837 and its aftermath, the effects of the railroad ride seem momentous: villages "swallowed by an earthquake"; meeting-house spires "seemed set adrift from their foundations"; the "hills glided away." "Everything was unfixed from its age-long rest, and moving at whirlwind speed" (256). Something even more calamitous awaits the time-stricken couple at "a solitary way-station": an abandoned church "in a dismal state of ruin and decay . . . a great rift through the main-body of the edifice"; a farmhouse black with age, "relics of a wood-pile" near the door (266), gruesome icons of the new mechanical civilization that unfixes everything and bequeaths a wasted godless landscape.

Hepzibah's earlier fantasy in her shop depicts an equally new landscape of modernity but one obverse to the ruinous scene: prosperous mercantile capitalism confidently enjoying its high commercial stage. In place of the riven church, glittering shops; in place of the eye of God, a mirror: "Groceries, toyshops, dry-goods stores, with their immense panes of plate-glass, their gorgeous fixtures, their vast and complete assortments of merchandize, in which fortunes have been invested; and those noble mirrors at the farther end of each establishment, doubling all this wealth by a brightly burnished vista of unrealities! . . . this splendid bazaar, with a multitude of perfumed and glossy salesmen, smirking, smiling, bowing, and measuring out the goods!" (48). The very figure of Broadway, the fantasy reenacts a world of goods and shoppers doubled by mirrors into unrealities (who can tell the copy from the original?), just as goods double or reduplicate themselves in the guise of their invisible agency, money. The mirror of unrealities leaps out as the apt emblem of commodity culture, the very agent of reproduction, transforming substance into image in a process that itself mirrors the apparent magic whereby money vanishes into goods and reappears as profit. The mystery of such market transactions arises, as Marx famously pointed out in his formulation of "commodity fetishism" (71–83), through the effacement of all signs of labor by which goods might be recognized and known as the investment of toil. Condensed in Hepzibah's fantasy lies the historical secret of the Judge—not only of his wealth garnered from the "crime" of appropriation in the capitalist market but his "public character" raised by a trick of mirrors into an edifice resembling a commercial emporium disguised as a domed, neoclassical palace. The Judge sees himself only in the mirror of his market self, takes the "unrealities" of doubled wealth as the truth of his being.

Can we doubt Hawthorne's purpose in these alternating views of modern change: a kaleidoscopic view of the old countryside, unfixed, ruined, deprived of God; a panoramic view of the new city as a marketplace with no perspective outside itself, only an internal mirror doubling its surfaces into "unrealities"? Widely separated in the narrative, the two views form a composite dialectical image less of a "struggle between an old society and a new" than of an already accomplished victory of new over old. If the new has no substance, in the old sense of solid reality, the old has no resources, except the resources of "Romance," which imagine the persistence of the older republic of rural virtue in the shadowed regions of the new society.

Recall the ending of the romance: the happy resolution, following the fortuitous demise of the Judge, of the ancient quarrel between Maule and Pyncheon. Holgrave gives up his Maule eye, quits photography, retires with Phoebe and the others to a country estate, a house of stone—the "lapse of years . . . adding venerableness to its original beauty"—while the inhabitants "might have altered the interior" as they wish (314). Withdrawing behind protective walls, the group forms, in Holgrave's anticipatory image, a magic circle against the threat of a political economy that reproduces the world as image-commodities. The happy ending evokes another political economy, transmuted by "Romance" from archaic practice into imaginative value, a critical (even if defenseless and rearguard) perspective upon the new society.

Consider Phoebe, who represents the Pyncheon line melded into the folkways of the old New England countryside. She enters the narrative just as Hepzibah ventures into modernity by opening her shop, as if elicited magically as an antidote to the threatening mirrored panorama of the city market. Consider the village market Phoebe re-creates in her management of the Pyncheon shop. With her first customer, an old woman who "was probably the very last person in town, who still kept the time-honored spinning-wheel in constant revolution" (78), she barters her goods for homemade yarn as the two voices "mingl[e] in one twisted thread of talk" (79). With her "gift of practical arrangement," her "natural magic" (71), she makes her own goods, such as yeast, beer, cakes, and breads, instinctively following Uncle Venner's old "golden maxims": "Give no credit! . . . Never take paper-money! Look well to your change! Ring the silver on the four-pound weight! Shove back all English half-pence and base copper-tokens, such as are very plenty about town! At your leisure hours, knit children's woollen socks and mittens! Brew your own yeast, and make your own ginger-beer!" (65–66).

Can it be only a coincidence that Venner's mention of silver and copper links his "golden maxims" surreptitiously to Holgrave's daguerreotypes, images made on silver-plated copper and often "fixed with pure chloride of gold, so that it is impossible that the pictures can fade for ages" (McLees 18)? No matter how oblique, the allusion clarifies brilliantly the paradoxical predicament of the daguerreotype within the text: its association on one side with all the unsettling elements of modernity and, on the other, with traditional modes of figurative cognition and social exchange. Associated with an eye that makes edifices melt away, with forces that unfix, the daguerreotype not only fixes the fleeting image but also fixes it as a "secret character," something solid and definite beneath the Judge's insubstantial surface of smiling munificence. It partakes of the invasive technologies of modern life, the public "gaze" Hepzibah fears, the "eye-witnesses" who report to the Judge on "the secrets of your interior" (236), and represents the black or Maule side of Holgrave's own analytic eye. Yet it is also allied with the solid coin of Venner's maxims against the fluid paper wealth of the Judge, his investments, speculations, membership on corporate boards. If the Judge's edifice of appearances resembles money and what Marx called its all-confounding powers, the daguerreotype redeems paper (or the outmoded, debased copper) into the hard species of silver and gold. If, as popular writers at the time claimed, "character . . . [is] a kind of capital," "like an accumulating fund, constantly increasing in value" (qtd. in Halttunen 47), then Holgrave's silver-plated image drives out false currency and its unrealities.

No wonder, then, that the narrative's third daguerreotype is of none other than Judge Pyncheon's foil, the good Uncle Venner himself. "[A]s a mark of friendship and approbation, he readily consented to afford the young man his countenance in the way of his profession—not metaphorically, be it understood—but literally, by allowing a daguerreotype of his face, so familiar to the town,—to be exhibited at the entrance of Holgrave's studio" (157). Here again Hawthorne evokes a common practice of the daguerrean trade, a display of wares to tempt the public into the rooms upstairs. The familiarity of the face would make good bait. But there is a symbolic aspect to the linkage between the young and the old man afforded by the exhibition, heightened all the more by the fact that we never see the actual image. Like the analogy between maxims of gold and silver and the materiality of the daguerreotype, its absence renders Venner's picture all the more potent as a kind of amulet. To grasp the implications of Venner's face as advertised trope for Holgrave's daguerrean practice, we need to look more closely at the old "patched philosopher"—and his relevance to the typological theory of character at issue in the narrative.

According to the typological view, characters are not free to choose their destinies; Holgrave must behave as a wizard and Judge Pyncheon as a greedy hypocrite. But Hawthorne allows Holgrave a will to change; he endows him with an inviolable "innermost man." He has nothing to hide, only something hidden within himself he needs to ferret out and overcome. The process of coming to himself, a process enacted in the historical time of the narrative, requires that he exorcise the ghost haunting the house, a ghost in the form of that very typological system that prophesies Maule to be Maule and Pyncheon Pyncheon, and by which Holgrave-Maule must expose and exorcize the corrupt Judge. Jaffrey must die that Holgrave be free. The need is ontological: as long as a representative of the old, tyrannical system of representation lives, the cyclic drama continues. And the camera proves just the right instrument of execution. First, it raises the old legend by revealing the Judge's typological "character" beneath his surface appearance. Second, in the death portrait it turns around and disproves the legend by revealing the death to be of natural causes. In each case the camera's report is meaningful only by interpretation: in the first instance, the old typological account of why the Judge is evil; in the second, a "scientific" account that accords with a view of the Judge as a historical creature, with a view of history as process rather than cycle.

In the end Holgrave abandons the camera, or so we assume, as he enters his estate as a country squire. The modern instrument has served his purpose of a deconstructive politics, of exposure and exorcism. By itself, he has shown, the camera has no theory of character, no independent ideology; it serves the discursive needs of its practitioners and clients. It either provides the compliant mirror images the Judge desires and lives by, or subverts those images, allowing inner corruption to show through surface displays of virtue. Is there an alternative to these two versions of character —one doomed to repeat the past, the other doomed to live always in the eye of others? An answer lies with "wise Uncle Venner," who presides over the fairy-tale ending, is seen last as the curtain falls, and whose replica exhibited at the entrance to Holgrave's studio holds the key to the daguerreotype's equivocal place in this tale of many equivocations.

Venner condenses an alternative theory of society and character. As "immemorial personage," "patriarch," the "familiar" of the "circle" of families he visits daily, he stands (even too obviously) for continuity, the redemptive folk memory; he is the secular "clergyman," venerable and venerated, whose liturgy is gossip, story, and maxim. He welcomes Holgrave into the storytelling circle as a "familiar." And by exhibiting Venner's image at the entrance to his studio, Holgrave declares his allegiance to continuity, sympathy, communal sustenance, and a theory of character consistent with Venner's "miscellaneous" appearance, his wardrobe of ill-assorted hand-me-downs. "[P]artly himself, but, in good measure, somebody else," Venner is neither entirely self-made (like Holgrave in his adventuring phase) nor other-made (like the Judge). He appears as both a copy and an original, whose patched exterior at once discloses and conceals his inner truth. One can imagine his daguerreotype portrait only as a perfectly equivocal construction; hanging by the door, the portrait declares Holgrave's studio to be, like "Romance" itself, the very place of equivocation, where "merest surfaces" lose their self-sufficiency and seek their meanings in communal narratives, such as Venner's sustaining stories.

To save himself from himself Holgrave must slay the scapegoat, surrogate of the bad father, and replace him with a good father, the venerable Venner. Venner saves the young man from the radical implications of his youthful politics, from the dangerous illusion that programmatic politics can effectively shape the tides of change. In the end, a historicist view of history proves too difficult to encompass, the railroad ride of Clifford and Hepzibah too menacing to be sustained. In Hawthorne's method of romance, as James recognized, this point cannot be made in narrative action; it can only be supplied as an authorial observation. Thus the narrator interpolates a remark regarding Holgrave's revolutionary hatred of the past: "His error lay, in supposing that this age, more than any past or future one, is destined to see the tattered garments of Antiquity exchanged for a new suit, instead of gradually renewing themselves by patchwork" (180). Venner is a walking theory of social change as slow accretion rather than sudden irruption or the imposition of rationalist utopia. He leads the survivors to a recomposed middle landscape, in which the values of an economy based on barter and solid coin are transmuted into values of true exchange among familiars, well protected by solid stone walls. And significantly, some degree of social deference is restored: Hepzibah distributes her largesse, providing Uncle Venner himself a cabin on the edge of the property. Thus the anxiety of visibility is tempered by an imaginary restoration of rank.

The meaning of the ending may lie precisely in its unbelievability, its transformation of an already defeated culture (the republican ideal, associated with Andrew Jackson, of an exchange economy among producers and small shopkeepers in a market free of manipulation by banks) into a permanent value. A lost vision of entrepreneurial, petit bourgeois social relations elevated into a historical impossibility, the dream of a restored "circle": only its impossibility, Hawthorne has us realize, endows the ending with the redemptive power of "Romance." Hawthorne proposes "Romance" as a power to preserve a lost idea of a republic of virtue, at the expense, we must note, of imagining a historical action that might resolve the modern version of the Maule-Pyncheon class conflict. The marriage of Maule and Pyncheon accomplishes what the daguerreotype by itself cannot: it wishes away the nemesis of the modern market, a monied class of investors, speculators, and manipulators.

Hawthorne's view of the daguerreotype seems in the end as equivocal as the political vision of the text as a whole. The popular ideology assumed (or desired) a transparent relation between face and character, between expression and truth. It endowed the mirror image with power to stir emulation, to provide models of visible virtue, to preserve the presence of the missing and the dead ("It is as if the subject of a daguerreotype is in some sense already dead," writes Michaels [100]). In the godless labyrinth of the marketplace, the mirror might serve as a way back toward familiar paths but only within typological narratives in which physiognomy doubles as psychology. Without such narratives, Hawthorne understood, photography threatened to let loose additional ambiguities, confusions between copies and originals. By questioning popular assumptions about the medium, by casting a skeptical eye on the claims of a photographic power independent of self-reflective structures of meaning, Hawthorne represents photography as a new political mode of seeing with unforeseen consequences. Confronting the "visable truth" of his age, in Melville's words, "the absolute condition of present things as they strike the eye," Hawthorne recognizes in the modern engine of visibility a new version of the old challenge of seeing to believing.

NOTES

1. Cathy N. Davidson makes a similar observation about the rhetoric of "Romance" in the preface, but where I see Hawthorne as locating the daguerreotype in a suggestively ambiguous site between "Novel" and "Romance," she argues that "Hawthorne adopts a photographic metaphor not to support the realistic novel but to describe the romance" (686). This leads her to argue, without explaining the apparent inconsistency, that "Holgrave's claims for the ultimate truth of the daguerreotype" contrast with Hawthorne's "enlisting" of the daguerreotype on the side of "Romance" (687). As I try to show, if we recognize the equivocal status of photography already present in the preface, we can avoid what I see as the mistake of taking Holgrave's claims at face value.

2. Richard Rudisill's *Mirror Image: The Influence of the Daguerreotype on American Society* (1971) remains the most complete and historically coherent account of intellectual, literary, and popular conceptions of the daguerreotype in the United States. Robert Taft's *Photography and the American Scene* provides an indispensable narrative of the appearance of the daguerreotype in America and its commercial development.

3. Although I concur in general with Walter Benn Michaels's argument about ideological freight carried by the term "Romance" in the text, it is my view that at stake is not mimesis as such but alternative modes of mimesis, and that by force of its association (not an absolute one) between "Romance" and the daguerreotype, the former needs to be seen not as antimimetic but something like antipositivist.

4. Susan Barger writes: "In effect, seeing the image is dependent upon the unique viewing geometry made up of the viewer, the daguerreotype, and the illumination source" (114). See also M. Susan Barger and William B. White, *The Daguerreotype: Nineteenth-Century Technology and Modern Science* (1991).

5. In *Reading American Photographs* (chap. 1), I discuss the theory and the practice of the public emulatory daguerreotype portrait, especially those "intended to be engraved."

6. Associations of daguerreotypy with alchemy abounded in the 1840s and 1850s, for obvious reasons. McLees attributed the origins of the medium to the experiments of "the Alchemic philosophers" (5).

7. The missing deed, with its inscriptions of Indian "hieroglyphics," of course addresses the issue of real estate and "title," which Michaels has shown persuasively informs the narrative and extends the horizon of conflict back to the first transactions between Europeans and native inhabitants, antecedent to the Maule-Pyncheon conflict. Might we not imagine an appropriate decipherment of those hieroglyphics to be a denial of the validity of European concepts of property and ownership altogether? The few references in the text to Indians hint that matters prior to and deeper than the class conflict between the two European families might be at issue in the tale.

8. So thought Marcus Aurelius Root, who wrote that in the power of the face to express inner character, and in the daguerreotype to capture that expression, "lies a valuable security for social order, insuring, as it does, that men shall ultimately be known for what they are" (43–44). The famed Boston daguerreotypist Albert Sands Southworth, sometimes taken by critics as a prototype for Holgrave, offered an interesting variation on this theme, one that veers toward the Hawthornian notion of "Romance." He argued that the power of penetration beneath surfaces belonged not to the mechanical medium but to the "genius" of the true artist. "Conscious of something besides the mere physical, in every object in nature," the true artist will feel "the soul of the subject itself." With these preternatural abilities in play, something emanates from the camera as forcefully as the light-borne impressions that enter it. "The whole character of the sitter is to [be] read at first sight." At the same time, "defects are to be separated from natural and possible perfections. . . . Nature is not at all to be represented as it is, but as it ought to be, and might possibly have been" (321–22).

9. Spann quotes an 1846 account of the new A. T. Stewart clothing shop on Broadway: "The main entrance opens into a rotunda of oblong shape, extending the whole width of the building, and lighted by a dome seventy feet in circumference. The ceilings and sidewalls, are painted in fresco, each panel representing some emblem of commerce. Immediately opposite the main entrance, . . . commences a flight of stairs which lead to a gallery running around the rotunda. This gallery is for the ladies to promenade upon" (97). Hawthorne's narrative "connects"

with the "Present" in part by drawing figurative allusions from such self-mirroring, self-referential places of spectacle as the proto–department stores of the 1840s and their largely female clientele-audience.

WORKS CITED

Barger, M. Susan. "Robert Cornelius and the Science of Daguerreotypy." *Robert Cornelius: Portraits from the Dawn of Photography: An Exhibition at the National Portrait Gallery. . . .* Ed. William F. Stapp et al. Washington, D.C.: Smithsonian Institution, 1983. 111–28.

Benjamin, Walter. "A Short History of Photography." *Classic Essays on Photography.* Ed. Alan Trachtenberg. New Haven: Leete's Island, 1980.

Davidson, Cathy N. "Photographs of the Dead: Sherman, Daguerre, Hawthorne." *South Atlantic Quarterly* 89 (1990): 667–701.

Halttunen, Karen. *Confidence Men and Painted Women: A Study of Middle-Class Culture in America 1830–1870.* New Haven: Yale UP, 1982.

Hawthorne, Nathaniel. *The House of the Seven Gables.* Vol. 2 of *The Centenary Edition of the Works of Nathaniel Hawthorne.* Ed. William Charvat et al. Columbus: Ohio State UP, 1965.

James, Henry. *Hawthorne.* 1879. Ithaca: Cornell UP, 1967.

Kermode, Frank. "Hawthorne's Modernity." *Partisan Review* 41 (1974): 428–41.

Lawrence, D. H. *Studies in Classic American Literature.* 1923. New York: Viking, 1964.

McLees, James E. *Elements of Photography. . . .* 1855. Rochester: International Museum of Photography at the George Eastman House, 1974.

Marx, Karl. *Capital: A Critique of Political Economy.* Ed. Frederick Engels. Vol. 1. 3d ed. Trans. Samuel Moore and Edward Aveling. New York: International, 1967.

Melville, Herman. "Bartleby, the Scrivener." *The Piazza Tales and Other Prose Pieces.* 1839–60. Evanston: Northwestern UP; Chicago: The Newberry Library, 1987. 13–45.

———. "To Nathaniel Hawthorne." April 16, 1851. Letter 83 in *The Letters of Herman Melville.* Ed. Merrell R. Davis and William H. Gilman. New Haven: Yale UP, 1960. 123–25.

Michaels, Walter Benn. *The Gold Standard and the Logic of Naturalism.* Berkeley: U of California P, 1987.

Root, Marcus Aurelius. *The Camera and the Pencil: Or, The Heliographic Art.* 1864. Pawlet: Helios, 1971.

Rudisill, Richard. *Mirror Image: The Influence of Daguerreotype on American Society.* Albuquerque: U of New Mexico P, 1971.

Southworth, Albert Sands. "An Address to the National Photographic Association of the United States." *Philadelphia Photographer* October 1871: 320.

Spann, Edward K. *The New Metropolis: New York City, 1840–1857.* New York: Columbia UP, 1981.

Taft, Robert. *Photography and the American Scene: A Social History, 1839–1889.* New York: Macmillan, 1938.

Trachtenberg, Alan. "Mirror in the Marketplace: American Responses to the Daguerreotype." *The Daguerreotype: A Sesquicentennial Celebration.* Ed. John Wood. Iowa City: U of Iowa P, 1989. 60–73.

———. "Photography: The Emergence of a Keyword." *Photography in Nineteenth-Century America.* Ed. Martha A. Sandweiss. New York: Abrams, 1991. 16–47.

———. *Reading American Photographs: Images as History, Mathew Brady to Walker Evans.* New York: Noonday-Hill, 1989.

CHAPTER 2

Nuclear Pictures and Metapictures

BRYAN C. TAYLOR

DURING the early 1980s literary theory and cultural politics conspired to create a fledgling interdisciplinary project known as "nuclear criticism." This project formed in reaction to renewed Cold War tensions surrounding events such as the Soviet invasion of Afghanistan and to a flood of popular-cultural texts that projected the consequences of nuclear war (such as "the republic of insects and grass" described by Jonathan Schell [3–96]). Scholars working in this genre are uniquely concerned with how language and images shape the public experience of nuclear weapons.[1] Their work treats several sites of nuclear culture, such as the "nukespeak" used by government officials and journalists to depict nuclear weapons as objects of public policy, the organizational cultures in which nuclear weapons are designed and manufactured, and the popular films, novels, and television programs through which postwar culture has assimilated the daunting "fact" of nuclear weapons (see respectively, e.g., Chilton; Gusterson, *Nuclear Rites*; and Brians).

There are at least three recurring themes in this body of critical work. One involves the largely symbolic status of nuclear-weapons phenomena. Critics have been energized by Jacques Derrida's insight that because full-scale nuclear war has not happened yet (and would annihilate discourse if it did), it is "fabulously textual" (23). The bomb exists largely in the projections and simulations (such as computer war-games) of competing nuclear interests. While this argument sidesteps the bomb's historical materiality for groups such as the Japanese *hibakusha* (bombing survivors), it evokes the paradoxical *hyper*reality of Mutually Assured Destruction (MAD). In this Cold War policy, nuclear weapons are performances of nationalist resolve whose overriding purpose is to defer their own becoming—to never be "used." As a result, much of nuclear discourse—both official and critical—is produced from an asymptotic, apocalyptic vantage point. It views the present from a future-anterior moment that cannot occur without narrative and existential rupture.

Another recurring theme involves theorizing nuclear culture as a dialogic site of struggle between conflicting and interanimating discourses (e.g., those of technical rationality and feminist spirituality), each seeking authority over the meaning and consequence of nuclear weapons (see Taylor, "Politics"). Viewed from this perspective, nuclear texts embody and organize these competing discourses through ideological narratives that privilege the legitimacy and inevitability of certain social arrangements and marginalize and repress their alternatives. Overdetermined and polysemic, these texts circulate among various interpretive communities as "events in a play of discourses whose concerns are power, virtue, the ends of society, and the nature of reality" (Smith 15).

A third theme involves the role of nuclear criticism in the ongoing narrativization of nuclear reality. Nuclear critics generally agree that while the potential consequences of nuclear weapons defy discourse, it is only through discourse that the weapons acquire their value and utility. Because these critics believe discourse that legitimates and rehearses nuclear war to be dangerous, they argue that criticism should intervene for a number of purposes. These include historicizing the production and accommodation of nuclear hegemony, exposing its ambiguities and contradictions, restoring to public consciousness what it has repressed, providing alternative narratives of the nuclear future, and energizing democratic participation in nuclear policy making (see Shapiro).[2]

In this essay I analyze a pair of texts that potentially facilitate these progressive relations between nuclear authorities and citizens. They are volumes of photographs taken during the 1980s and early 1990s by two members of the Atomic Photographers' Guild: Robert Del Tredici and Carole Gallagher. Organized in 1986 by Del Tredici, this international group includes both art- and documentary-photographers who depict the widely dispersed but historically connected figures, locations, events, institutions, and technologies contributing to "the nuclear condition." These photographers share "a documentary bent and a hunger for unseen evidence . . . an eye for innuendo, a taste for paradox and the ability to walk among conspiracies and phantoms" (Del Tredici, "Trinity" 9). Their images have been widely circulated in official, mainstream, and antinuclear publications, and have contributed to the process by which late- (and now post-) Cold War generations have visually assimilated the Bomb (see, e.g., "Fifty Years," Lehman, and *Closing the Circle*).

This process has been relatively neglected by nuclear criticism, and one of my purposes here is to extend knowledge of how visual codes operate in photography to reproduce nuclear subjectivity. I am not saying that nuclear criticism has neglected visual media per se. There exist bodies of criticism, for example, of nuclear art and nuclear cinema (see respectively, e.g., Farrell and Broderick). Much of this film criticism is revealing, however, in its emphasis on narrative elements (such as the cultural anxieties that nuclear films appear to express) over uniquely visual codes. This anti-iconographic bias is likely due to the predominance of literary theory in seminal nuclear-critical works that have "read" linguistic operations in official and marginalized discourses. David Dowling, for example, compresses this bias, in the form of a manifesto: "The power of the bomb is ruled by the power of the *word*, and only by continual de-construction of the *word* will we avoid the destruction of the world" (208; emphasis added).[3]

Alternatively, a nuclear-critical iconology would acknowledge that cultural subjects are constituted through both reading *and* viewing practices, and would historicize the apparatus through which nuclear weapons have been photographed in American culture. It would analyze the interaction of visual and verbal codes (such as captions) in these photographs, the uses to which they have been put in various cultural contexts, and their consequences for existing power relations between nuclear authorities and citizens. One recent example of this type of critical work is Peter Hales's oppositional reading of photographs taken by U.S. government agents during their appropriation of lands in Tennessee, Washington, and New Mexico for the wartime development of nuclear weapons (*Atomic Spaces*). In these images of rural peoples, ecosystems, and folkways, Hales finds a painful history of *intra*national suffering, displacement, and resistance to an imperialist Manhattan Project, otherwise obscured in its euphemistic and technical records.

Scholars who indirectly contribute to nuclear-critical iconology include H. Bruce Franklin and Alan Trachtenberg, who trace how photography has served to condemn, romanticize, and fetishize war for popular audiences within different historical periods. The violence of war, these scholars agree, exacts costs for the human body that, when depicted photographically, threaten to overwhelm the adequacy of systems of signification and morality. Such photographs become evidence in ongoing cultural debates about the nature, outcome, and consequence of war (e.g., as a tragedy, defeat, or triumph). Used in this way, images reproduce and transform ideologies such as nationalism and patriarchy that support war. Neither scholar, however, addresses the topic of *nuclear* war, which presumably complicates this process through differences in scale and consequence.

Other critics are more direct in their considerations of nuclear-cultural iconography. Several reviewers, for example, have considered the recent landscape photography of nuclear-weapons production and testing sites by Peter Goin and Richard Misrach. These reviews debate the ability of these sublime images to evoke the "invisible" cellular qualities of environmental disaster and innovatively to challenge viewers' common sense (see, e.g., Covino and Solnit). In an essay marking the fiftieth anniversary of Hiroshima, Jeremy Millar historicizes the relationship between nuclear and photographic technologies. He clarifies the often-ironic role played by photography in scientific discoveries of radioactivity (and its somatic effects) and in the objectification of enemy territory as a prerequisite for strategic bombing. Peter B. Hales ("The Atomic Sublime") and Peggy Rosenthal, further, examine the symbolism of the nuclear mushroom cloud. Hales describes how popular assimilation of the mushroom cloud during the postwar period was mediated through a "coercive economy of meanings" (9) mixing nature worship, patriotism, and religious righteousness. Militaristic interests, he argues, tightly controlled this process by carefully screening and briefing witnesses to nuclear tests and by promoting mythological frames for interpreting their explosions that obscured human accountability for nuclear effects on victims' bodies (e.g., by characterizing their clouds as the product of supernatural forces). These seminal narratives defined through revelation the nature of the wartime nuclear "secret" and have powerfully shaped contemporary understanding of the nuclear object. Rosenthal's survey of meanings of the mushroom cloud in Cold War–era imagery concludes that it condenses a variety of nuclear motives: "In its remarkable receptivity to projections upon it of even vaguely congruent images, whether fetus or phallus or smiling face, brain or tree or globe, the mushroom cloud projects back the array of human responses to all that it stands for: responses of pride, parochial possessiveness, creative resistance, denial, [and] despair" (88).

One enduring topic in nuclear-cultural iconography involves the politically incendiary object of the irradiated body. Hugh Gusterson ("Nuclear War") discusses the formidable problem that images of actual nuclear casualties (e.g., Japanese sailors sickened by radioactive fallout from a 1954 nuclear test) pose for government officials hoping to maintain a nominally consenting and resolute citizenry. Because these morbid bodies create anxiety for the live bodies that may yet join them, they are typically "disappeared" from technical projections and from representations of nuclear-weapons effects. Robert Jay Lifton and Greg Mitchell's recent history of *Hiroshima in America* documents how footage of Japanese casualties and survivors was typically confiscated, censored, and classified by American Occupation forces. "From the very start," they conclude, "the visual record of the atomic bombing would be limited to structural effects, while the human dimension would be evaded or ignored" (59). M. K. Johnson analyzes how the denotations and connotations of indexical signs of the nuclear body can be ideologically fixed such that, for example, Japanese bombing victims depicted in a 1945 issue of *Life* magazine were equated with and "explained" by images of American soldiers wounded at Pearl Harbor. Such equivalencies inhibit moral reflection about the eradication of distinctions between civilians and combatants in total warfare, a condition brought to its conclusion in the cities-as-hostages logic of MAD.

These arguments establish that nuclear iconography is a highly charged field of political struggle between dominant and marginalized cultural interests practicing various aesthetic strategies to legitimate their narratives of nuclear reality. Photography forms one medium through which American citizens have historically negotiated the significance of nuclear-weapons technologies and institutions and their consequences. Inevitably, the conservative realism promoted by militaristic and nationalistic interests has influenced artistic and documentary photographs of nuclear bodies and the institutions that create those bodies. Abigail Solomon-Godeau, for example, notes at least two different aesthetics in documentary photographs of the U.S. nuclear-weapons production complex. One she finds to be naively ahistorical and sentimental, arguing that it depicts the nuclear threat as an abstract (and thus inevitable) feature of the human condition. The other aesthetic is more critical and depicts the specific manifestations of labor, technology, and (ir)rationality that sustain nuclear weapons (rev. of *Our Lives, Our Children*).

I am concerned here with the operations of this second, more politicized aesthetic in the photography of Del Tredici and Gallagher, focusing on how their work recovers invisible, institutionalized "nuclear power" so that it can be disrupted. To this end, I analyze below the specific, formal strategies that create this politicized aesthetic. In each case, I argue, the work of these artists reflects two distinctly *different* strategies. The first is a progressive, documentary realism that restores to public memory "actual" nuclear objects which have been obscured and repressed. This depiction of concrete scenes, events, practices, and agents forms a sort of "counter-realism" that subverts the monologic authority of nuclear orthodoxy by restoring the integrity of nuclear history. The second strategy involves a politically reflexive, "deconstructive pastiche" (Solomon-Godeau, *Photography* 100) that takes as its object the very nature of nuclear representation (see also Nichols, *Representing Reality* 56–75). The "metapictures" (Mitchell chap.2) created in this strategy destabilize the authority of hegemonic nuclear images and narratives by contrasting them with their unofficial counterparts (e.g., photographs of traveling fallout clouds taken by area residents that belie official claims as to the on-site "containment" of radiation from nuclear testing). These images frequently reflect the use of montage, simulation, repetition, and irony. Collectively, these techniques disrupt the passivity of viewers and implicate them in the evaluation of nuclear representations. In each body of work, however, this antirealist strategy potentially works at cross-purposes to documentary realism, and I will attempt a reading of their relationship that, if not resolving their apparent contradiction, reframes its political effectiveness.

ROBERT DEL TREDICI: REORGANIZING THE BOMB

The title of Del Tredici's 1987 volume, *At Work in the Fields of the Bomb*, suggests his goal of depicting the industrial sites and professional practices that create U.S. nuclear weapons. The volume forms the culmination of a six-year project whose purpose, Del Tredici explains, was to assemble "a body of basic words and images" enabling the American public to view "the nuclear arsenal at its source" (ix). Potentially, this discourse offers "the collective imagination something accurate and graphic to hang onto as it strives to come to terms with the Bomb's reality" (ix): "the deep and silent impact that its mass-production surely must be having" ("Trinity" 8). Del Tredici traveled around the world photographing key sites of nuclear-weapons production and interviewing various figures involved in manufacturing their components, planning their use, researching their biological effects, and protesting their existence. The resulting text consists of over one hundred black-and-white photographs with accompanying "field notes" and interview transcripts. These elements are integrated to clarify phenomena traditionally cloaked by official secrecy and public denial: the structure, process, and consequence of nuclear-weapons organization.

I use the term *organization* here in two ways to indicate both the *actual* laboratories, materials-production facilities, assembly plants, and test sites of nuclear-weapons production and also the *discursive processes* through which raw materials, technology, and human labor are rationally "managed" to accomplish this end. Del Tredici's images and interviews recover the material and symbolic dimensions of this work. They detail its characteristic features and routines, and its signficance for the soldiers, workers, civil defense planners, health professionals, peace activists, and ordinary citizens who have historically performed and been affected by these routines. The text depicts these organizations as symbolic sites of conflict among multiple voices struggling to legitimate and challenge conventional procedures for protecting worker health and public safety and for using nuclear weapons. Ultimately, this novelistic juxtaposition serves to criticize the obsessive, technical rationality that pervades these organizations, and that enforces nuclear secrecy and performativity.[4]

One example of novelistic discourse in the volume involves an extended sequence of images and narratives that critically configures the spatial and temporal dimensions of nuclear-weapons organization.[5] This sequence comprises twenty-one photographs that depict the process by which uranium is mined, refined, and assembled with other manufactured components to produce finished U.S. nuclear warheads. This montage both mimics and disrupts the actual dimensions of this process in real time and space.

It is the mimicry that is distinctive here: while Del Tredici's images are realistic, they are typically assembled in sequences that disrupt the conventions of linear time and simple cause-and-effect relationships. Instead, themes and topics recur unpredictably as formal illustrations of the text's central theme: the tension between cultural forgetting and uncontrollable, dreamlike eruptions of lived nuclear history.

Characteristically, then, this sequence begins with its ending: an aerial view of the Amarillo, Texas, Pantex facility where U.S. weapons are assembled in their final stage. It is the following image of a bleak, desolate Canadian mine pit from which uranium ore is extracted (the caption states that "radiation in the pit can be 7,000 times higher than normal background levels" [#13]) that signals the convergence of narrative sequence and industrial process.[6] The next five images depict the Fernald, Ohio, "Feed Materials Production Center," where powdered uranium concentrate from the mine is subsequently converted first into salt crystals and then into metal ingots. One image, "Sampling the Derby" (#18), depicts a middle-aged white female worker wearing safety glasses, overalls, gloves, and a cap, gathering shavings from a uranium ingot for laboratory testing (see fig. 2.1). The caption describes the levels of penetrating beta and gamma radioactivity in this procedure and suggests that the woman's health is at risk. The morbidity of this possibility and of the potential extended consequences of her work make the flower she wears in her hair ("because it is the week before Christmas") seem both ironic and poignant.

The sequence proceeds to depict the further refinement of uranium metal in processes conducted at Fernald and at a separate plant in Ashtabula, Ohio. During this phase of the sequence, in his interview with the Ashtabula plant manager, Del Tredici challenges the man's claim that his employees are not endangered by radioactivity with probing questions about the health risks posed by their inhalation of airborne uranium oxide (136–38). In combination with other depictions in the volume of sick and dying workers, this discourse suggests that nuclear workers are vulnerable to exploitation by management, which retains expert control over the official standards by which health risks are defined, and protection enforced.

Following this image, the sequence of industrial process is unexpectedly interrupted by a portrait of Dr. Thomas Mancuso, a former health consultant to the U.S. government (#26). Del Tredici reveals that after fourteen years of study, Mancuso concluded that levels of acceptable radiation in nuclear plants were too high by a factor of ten, and that repeated exposure to even low levels of radiation significantly increased the risk of cancer for workers (138–41). In the portrait Mancuso is lit eerily from below (see fig. 2.2): the mood of the scene is ominous. In recalling his sudden dismissal by the government and the mysterious destruction of his data, Mancuso concludes that officials have systematically underrepresented levels of risk

Fig. 2.1. "Sampling the Derby." Photograph by Robert Del Tredici. By arrangement with HarperCollins Publishers.

posed to nuclear workers in order to avoid paying compensation for their subsequent illness and death.

The next image resumes depiction of the industrial process with another aerial view, this time of the South Carolina "Savannah River Plant," where refined uranium metal is converted into plutonium and tritium for nuclear warheads. Del Tredici's interview with the plant's public relations manager reveals an astonishing degree of compartmentalization: "We don't have anything to do here with the actual fabrication of weaponry. And from my perspective, I make a very conscious effort to know as little about that end of the nuclear defense program as possible. . . . I don't have a *need to know*" (141). This image is followed by yet another interruption of the sequence (now recognizable as commentary) from scientist William Lawless, who resigned in 1983 from his post as manager of the plant's nuclear waste disposal program after he was prevented from releasing a report criticizing its practices. Lawless describes the U.S. nuclear-weapons complex as a "closed system" that moralizes dissent as treason, and willfully endangers its workers and surrounding communities by suppressing data about radioactive contamination (141–44).

After images of the Savannah River Plant's administration building, an uncovered waste ditch, a radicalized local farmer, and a plant worker who was fired after contracting a rare cancer associated with radiation exposure,

Fig. 2.2. "Dr. Thomas Mancuso." Photograph by Robert Del Tredici. By arrangement with HarperCollins Publishers.

the thematic connections defining this sequence dissipate. It reflects, however, a textual strategy of juxtaposing both official and marginalized voices in a manner that challenges dominant nuclear rationality by ensuring that its pronouncements of certainty do not go unquestioned, and that oppositional interests are not silenced. Additionally, the images restore to cultural consciousness an actual industrial process that is dispersed in space and time, whose connections have been obscured by secrecy and rationalization, and which has generally been repressed by nuclear citizens. Nuclear weapons are *counter*organized by the text in a manner that critiques their routine production. The viewer-reader[7] is challenged to impose narrative logic on this symbolic *re*production, and assumes increased reponsibility for its meaning.

This progressive documentary realism, in which Del Tredici recovers the suppressed "facts" of nuclear history to inspire reform, is in turn mediated by the presence of a second, more postmodern aesthetic. This competing aesthetic is indicated by moments of rupture and irony where Del Tredici takes nuclear representation itself as his subject, and evaluates the discursive strategies by which the Bomb is conventionally made real to audiences. As in the industrial-process sequence, this aesthetic contrasts official and unofficial accounts in a way that denaturalizes the former and

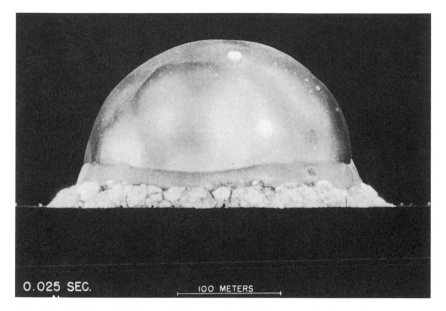

0.025 SEC.   100 METERS

Fig. 2.3. "Trinity: 5:30 A.M., July 16, 1945." Photograph by Berlyn Brixner. By arrangement with HarperCollins Publishers.

privileges the latter. In the process, however, it deconstructs nuclear weapons as *effects* (not referents) of competing discourses (including Del Tredici's) and invites ethical reflection about this very process.

One example involves two sets of images and the voices that speak about them. The images are entitled "Trinity: 5:30 AM, July 16, 1945" (#99) and "Hiroshima, August 6, 1945" (#100). They are set on two facing pages that, unlike others in the volume, are black. This contrast is dramatic, and brackets the images in a mood of negation and mourning.

The "Trinity" photo depicts the world's first atomic explosion, detonated by Los Alamos scientists in the New Mexico desert. In this image taken by Berlyn Brixner, the event's "official photographer," a giant sphere of superheated gas and dust rises from the ground (see fig. 2.3). Frozen in its rapid expansion against the night sky, it appears almost completely smooth and solid. Only its puffy hem of boiling earth suggests the devastation that it both contains and also promises as a simulation of the Nagasaki yet to come.[8] In his interview with Brixner, Del Tredici establishes rapport with a fellow professional, quizzing him about his equipment and his composition of the shot. Brixner recalls that his main worry was that the fireball would expand beyond the camera frame, spoiling the image. "You sound like a true photographer," responds Del Tredici, "taken by the visual

Fig. 2.4. "Hiroshima, August 6, 1945." Photograph by Yoshito Matsushige. By arrangement with HarperCollins Publishers.

quality of it" (185). This description acquires irony as Brixner discloses that he has since had no second thoughts about Hiroshima or Nagasaki ("that was simply the price of war" [186]), and complains that he has not received adequate credit as the sole "author" of these widely reproduced images. "Photos by Brixner," he says proudly. "That's right, every one of them" (187).

Del Tredici contrasts Brixner's proprietary interest in his work, and his artistic detachment from its connotations, with the "opposing" images of Hiroshima and the personal narrative of their author, Yoshito Matsushige. Of these five photographs, two show the interiors of buildings with collapsed walls, broken and scattered glass, and the jagged frames of doors and furniture stuck at unnatural angles. Two of the other images show a gathering of people on the sidewalk outside a destroyed building. All of the surrounding buildings are also destroyed; a cloud of dust and smoke rises into the air behind them. Some of the figures are without clothes, which have apparently been burned and shredded in the nuclear blast. Their scorched hair stands out wildly from their heads, giving them a feral appearance (see fig. 2.4). In the fifth image a uniformed man with a bandage on his head sits at a table, writing on a slip of paper, before a line of people. In the foreground, a man holds his hand to his head. Behind the man at the table, a woman breathes through a scarf wrapped over her mouth. In all of these images, no one is looking at the camera. Lifton and Mitchell's commentary is apposite: "There are no corpses in these photographs, yet they capture the horror of the atomic bomb far better than images of blackened trees or twisted girders. That is because [their subjects] . . . are still experiencing the bomb itself. The weapon has not finished with them or their city" (61).

In his interview with Del Tredici, Matsushige reflects on the circumstances and the cost of recording these images. As a Japanese army reporter and newspaper photographer, he guessed immediately that the blast had not been caused by "an ordinary bomb," and that "it was time to go to work" recording the aftermath (187). Yet when he confronted the crowds of dead and suffering victims, his professionalism posed a terrible dilemma. "When I saw them I realized I had to take a picture, and I tried to push the shutter, but I couldn't. It was so terrible. The people were pathetic. I had to wait" (188). When asked why he took only five photographs that day, Matsushige explains, "Before I became a professional cameraman, I had been just an ordinary person" (187). He was able to overcome his revulsion at the scene only by asserting, "I am a professional cameraman, so I have to take pictures." Despite this rationalization, he found that he was unable to "push the shutter a second time without crying" and so turned away first from the bodies presented in fig. 2.3 (students from a girls' high school, he reveals) and then later from victims boiled in a swimming pool and a busload of charred bodies. All of these scenes were "too terrible to take a picture of" (188).

In this contrast between Brixner and Matsushige, Del Tredici constructs an ethical reflection on the politics of professional photography and of nuclear representation in general. Brixner stands in as the subject of an official, positivist aesthetic devoted to the technical, refined, and safely remote documentation of nuclear destruction. This aesthetic, argues Carol Cohn, offers a vantage that privileges the fantasy narrative of the invulnerable user (and not the victim) of nuclear weapons. So framed, the Trinity explosion appears both awesome and abstract, providing sublime data of both current and future nuclear performances. Matsushige's aesthetic, alternatively, is one of distressing nuclear effects and restores what is vanished in Brixner's aesthetic by tracing Trinity's historical consequence. In this nuclear aftermath, we see the breakdown of nuclear-professional objectivity. Photography becomes an additional violation of the dead and dying, stripping whatever dignity remains to them to define and own their suffering. Matsushige's account confirms that photographic realism can be overwhelmed by excessive images of nuclear death that expose its affective contingencies and repressions. But the postnuclear camera can, in the absence of its physical destruction, still record, and its images can endure to circulate as critical counterrealism, with unpredictable effects.

"SIGNIFYING HUSKS": CAROLE GALLAGHER
AND THE DOWNWINDERS

Gallagher's 1993 volume, *American Ground Zero: The Secret Nuclear War*, grows out of her decade-long, quasi-ethnographic immersion in the culture of workers, military veterans, and local residents who have been affected by radioactive fallout from U.S. nuclear-weapons tests conducted between 1951 and 1992 at the Nevada Test Site.[9] For several decades these "downwinders" have claimed that this fallout (especially that from above-ground testing conducted between 1951 and 1963) has contributed to their excessive rates of illness, birth defects, and death, and they have sought legal redress and federal compensation for their losses. These efforts have been largely unsuccessful. Although Congress has recently passed legislation compensating narrowly qualified applicants from these groups, the U.S. government has historically rejected claims of responsibility for downwinder suffering by invoking immunity from prosecution of its policy decisions and by employing sophisticated epidemiological arguments that invalidate claims of a direct, causal relationship between radiation exposure and subsequent illness.[10]

The more than one hundred black-and-white images, edited personal narratives, and excerpted historical texts collected in Gallagher's volume create a compelling turn in an ongoing cultural conversation regarding the costs of nuclear-weapons development. As discussed above, this conversation has increasingly revolved around representations of nuclear bodies— the subjects who have been affected in this process. During the recent fiftieth anniversary of Hiroshima, this repressed symbolic body erupted increasingly into cultural consciousness. Media reports, for example, detailed secret Cold War radiation experiments conducted by nuclear-medical authorities on vulnerable human subjects without their informed consent. Images of these victims (including pregnant women, cancer patients, and mentally retarded children) circulated widely in the news media as an elegaic intertext suggesting violated innocence and the betrayal of public trust (see fig. 2.5). Images of Hiroshima victims, additionally, have haunted the debate surrounding exhibition of the *Enola Gay* aircraft in the Smithsonian National Air and Space Museum: acknowledgment of these victims formed one pivot of acrimony among veterans' groups, curators, and consulting historians (see Taylor, "The Bodies of August"). Gallagher's text replies to scientific and reactionary political discourses that would suppress or minimize the suffering of the nuclear body. Recoded in Gallagher's work as a situated, reflective, and expressive subject, the downwinder body realizes its subversive potential to restore to public consciousness a lunar signified of official discourse (Nichols, "Getting to Know You"; Taylor, "Shooting

Fig. 2.5. "The Face of HP-3." Front cover of the *Bulletin of the Atomic Scientists* (March/April 1994) showing the photograph of a youthful Eda Charlton, who later became an unwitting subject in secret government medical experiments involving the injection of plutonium into her body. By arrangement with the Educational Foundation for Nuclear Science.

Downwind"). By combining the indexical quality of the photograph with the authenticity of personal narrative, Gallagher deploys a counterrealism that potentially convinces viewers of the negligence and liability of nuclear officials in contributing to downwinder illness and death.

Gallagher's text reflects three strategies that create this effect. The first strategy involves recovering what is arguably suppressed by the official realisms of nuclear policy and science: the bodily experience of pain and illness that defies language but also grounds human community. Gallagher documents through her images and interviews the forms of experience that are associated with downwinder conditions, such as stoicism, grief, and

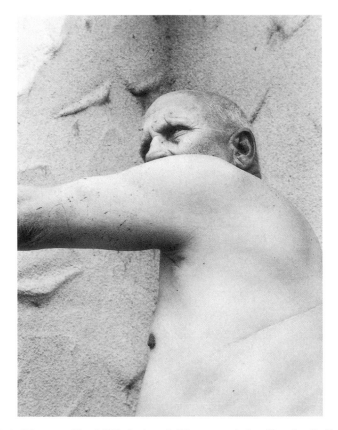

Fig. 2.6. "Reason Fred Warheime." Photograph by Carole Gallagher. By arrangement with the artist.

crippling depression. She records the texture of the disintegrating body in mortal pain: its slow and inexorable consumption by cancer; its violation by medical procedures that slice, scrape, and amputate. This engagement with the concrete, truth-unto-itself of downwind subjectivity invites—at the least—reconsideration of hegemonic narratives of nuclear risk.

One image, "Reason Fred Warheime" (72–75; see fig. 2.6) demonstrates this first strategy. Shot from below, it shows the naked head and torso of an older, white male, leaning with both hands against what appears to be a stone wall. This pose exposes the man's left side and a long sickle-shaped scar running from his shoulder blade underneath his arm and across his rib cage toward his sternum. The endpoints of this wicked scar are not visible. The man's head is turned back over his left shoulder toward an implied spectator. His facial expression suggests pain and defiance: the scar is proffered as a badge of suffering. Gallagher's interview with the man reveals that the scar is the result of an operation conducted to remove a malignant lung tumor. His narrative suggests that this cancer was caused by cumulative exposure to radiation: he participated in the immediate postwar occupation of Nagasaki by the U.S. Army and served in military maneuvers at the Nevada Test Site. There he was commanded to march within two hunderd yards of "ground zero" following a nuclear explosion (from whose fallout the soldiers suffered skin burns and vomiting). His hair and teeth fell out by the time he was twenty-eight. By age thirty, he suffered from radiation cataracts, osteoporosis, and muscle deterioration.

In addition to documenting these qualities of embodied experience, Gallagher's text also repairs a specific effect of epidemiological discourse. When epidemiology encodes downwinder subjects as scientific data, it severs them from their connections to relatives, neighbors, friends, coworkers, and fellow church members. Alternatively, Gallagher's work recovers the integrity of what was apparently assaulted by fallout: *relationships* that created cherished forms of downwinder community and family, and grounded individual biographies. As a result, Gallagher suggests, downwinder illnesses and deaths are tragic beyond their destruction of mortal subjects. In their wake these events leave painful emotions of guilt and grief for "survivors" (who may also read in them their own impending fate). It is this sacred existence for each other, and its violation, that Gallagher attempts to restore as a context for ethical evaluation of nuclear-weapons development.

This strategy is suggested by an image and interview, entitled "Diana Lee Woosley and LaVerl Snyder" (120–23; see fig. 2.7). The image shows two white women seated close together on a wooden porch bench, looking directly at the camera. The older, dark-haired woman shown on the right is smiling faintly and extends her right arm around the shoulder of the other, smaller and younger woman. In turn, this woman rests her left hand in the older woman's lap and clasps her hand. Both women are dressed casually and display the tender familiarity of mother and daughter (even their feet are entwined). The serenity of this domestic scene is distorted, however, by the deep shadows that frame the pair and by the younger woman's unnaturally swollen face.

Gallagher's interview with the women recounts how their lives have apparently been affected by radioactive fallout. LaVerl Snyder recalls that in 1958, while she was carrying her daughter in the womb, she was exposed to test fallout that caused nausea, burns, and blisters on her skin and led to the loss of her teeth, hair, and finger- and toenails. Her daughter was subsequently delivered prematurely and suffering from cancer, weighing little more than three pounds. At the age of six months, her cancer was treated with crude and unlocalized radiation that deformed her heart, lungs, breasts, and spine. As Diana Lee Woosley aged, she suffered from

Fig. 2.7. "Diana Lee Woosley and LaVerl Snyder." Photograph by Carole Gallagher. By arrangement with the artist.

constant vomiting and congestive heart failure, and underwent traumatic surgical procedures to correct her spinal deformity. Her face, we learn, is swollen from large doses of prednisone, which she must take to combat the diseases that exploit her weakened immune system—a treatment that has itself caused diabetes. Beyond this suffering of their bodies, however, the women have also suffered psychologically. Snyder recalls her grief and horror at the invasive "treatments" her daughter has suffered, and her fervent wish that the government might compensate her for her medical bills ("I'm just talking about helping" [122–23]). Woosley, in turn, has suffered "a lot of marriage problems." Her husband is "probably tired of me being sick, and I understand that" (123). For comfort and inspiration, she says, she turns to *her own* children. Gallagher evokes in this account the social webs that are torn by the biological effects of fallout. By recovering the discourse of survivorship, this strategy opposes official discourses that would objectify the downwinder subject and enable forgetting.

As with Del Tredici's work, however, Gallagher's progressive documentary realism is mediated by a reflexive strategy that potentially contradicts her professional identity as "a blank slate upon which the [downwinder] stories and images could be written" (xxiii). In this second strategy, she employs bricolage to construct an intertextual truth from fragments of various discourses such as the political theories of Erasmus and Frederick Douglass, Dorothea Lange's fifties-era documentary photographs of Utah Mormons, letters from nuclear officials, and the Nuremberg principles. As in Del Tredici's images, this pastiche juxtaposes official and unofficial discourses to subvert the authority of the former and to implicate them in the suffering of nuclear victims. Occasionally, however, Gallagher's strategy exceeds characteristic modes of documentary intertextuality and achieves an ironic and self-conscious deconstruction of nuclear imagery. These ruptures in her counterrealism vary in degree and have a number of potential effects: they open nuclear weapons up to scrutiny as sedimented sites of representation; they confirm the ethical role of representation in constructing their significance; and they motivate a more active and conscious decoding by viewers. It is also possible, however, that they destabilize viewer sympathy for the downwinders by deferring their facticity through representations of representation.

This polysemy becomes apparent when Gallagher traces various manifestations of the mushroom cloud. She includes in her text both metonymic images that depict actual blasts and their subsequent fallout clouds as well as more metaphorical images that *imply* these phenomena and *evoke* their connotations of dread and contamination. One literal image offered early in the text depicts the nuclear test "Shot Priscilla," detonated on June 24, 1957 with an explosive yield of 37,000 tons of TNT (xiii; see fig. 2.8). This image depicts a dark, ominous, twin-capped (and, yes, *phallic*) cloud towering over the roiling desert surface. Mountains in the background provide scale indicating the cloud's immensity. Gallagher's narration suggests its effects: "After witnessing this shot, soldiers returned to [camp] bleeding from the eyes, ears, nose and mouth" (xii).

Because it is impossible for Gallagher to track, long after the fact, the behavior of these clouds, she resorts to a variety of intertextual strategies that evoke their effects. One involves using Lange's fifties-era images of this same rural Western population—a strategy that, Ferenc Morton Szasz argues, provides the "before" and "during" that temporally contextualize Gallagher's images as "after." One untitled image[11] shows the front cab of

Fig. 2.8. "Shot Priscilla, 37 Kilotons, June 24, 1957." Photograph by the United States Department of Energy. By arrangement.

a pickup truck containing an adult man, and a young boy and girl (310; see fig. 2.9). These figures are all looking forward, out toward an object beyond the left edge of the photograph, which is cloaked in shadow. Their expressions are barely visible through the windshield's grime, but the girl's large, round eyes and her opened mouth suggest a state of concern. This ominous mood is reinforced by the mound of hay that the group is hauling in the bed of the truck. It billows out behind and above the cab like a cloud threatening to engulf them.

A second strategy involves Gallagher's incorporation of unofficial photographs of the mushroom and fallout clouds taken by downwinders them-

Fig. 2.9. "Untitled." Photograph by Dorothea Lange. By arrangement with the Dorothea Lange Collection, The Oakland Museum of California.

selves: the indexical facticity of these images supports their accompanying narratives about the clouds' effects. One appears in Gallagher's photograph "Martha Bordoli Laird" (114–19; see fig. 2.10). Here, a white middle-aged woman stands in a dimly lit shed, surrounded by a graphic analogue of human mortality: hanging deer carcasses. She holds up two pictures for the camera. The first shows a group of smiling young children and an older woman posed in front of the doorway of a schoolhouse. The second image—which partially covers the first—shows a black cloud descending on a small, isolated cluster of buildings.

The positioning of these two prop photographs in Gallagher's image functions to deny official accounts that minimized the existence and effects of the fallout clouds. It also signals the events related in the woman's narrative. Three of the children in the first photograph are her own. One has died from leukemia and the other two suffer radiation-related illnesses. This intertextual strategy reflects a recurring motif whereby Gallagher's subjects offer up images of their deceased loved ones for the camera, and for the viewer. Such poses evoke the occult power of photography to preserve its subject for the viewer in "an arena of sentiment bounded by nostalgia on one end and hysteria on the other" (Sekula 94). They also reflexively

Fig. 2.10. "Martha Bordoli Laird." Photograph by Carole Gallagher. By arrangement with the artist.

position the viewers of Gallagher's images in relation to these downwinder survivors. Just as these subjects hold up images of their cherished losses, Gallagher holds *them* up for the viewer to register their grief and vulnerability (some of Gallagher's subjects did in fact die between the taking of their photographs and the publication of the volume). Viewers are structurally invited to act toward Gallagher's subjects as they themselves act toward the subjects of *their own* photographs.

A third strategy used by Gallagher to prove her argument in the absence of more immediate documentation is to metaphorically evoke the clouds as an uncanny, enduring presence in the downwinders' cultural landscape. "Eugene and Francis Spendlove," for example, are shaded by a tree whose blooming branches form a by-now-familiar shape (190–92; see fig. 2.11). "Cuba Lyle," similarly, suggests childhood innocence "menaced" by an ominous, rising mound that is composed precisely behind and above the foreground figure so that it appears to be advancing unnoticed, "pressing" down on him, and "blocking" his potential "growth" (166–69; see fig. 2.12).

That Gallagher is playing here with the mushroom cloud's clichéd iconography should by now be apparent and is confirmed in her image "Ted Przygucki" (64–67; see fig. 2.13). A middle-aged white man faces the camera holding up an official military photograph of a nuclear test that shows a rising mushroom cloud being advanced upon by a group of soldiers. The small metal screen in the man's throat suggests that he has lost his "voice": the prop image in turn "speaks" for his history as an atomic veteran who witnessed twenty-two test explosions. Gallagher's placement of this photograph in the pose, however, suggests a wry commentary on the intertextual relationships between radiation and different types of photography.

Fig. 2.11. "Eugene and Francis Spendlove." Photograph by Carole Gallagher. By arrangement with the artist.

To trace this intertext, we must remember that documentary photography is inherently associated with radiation since it captures the spectrum of visible light reflected by its subject. More specifically, X-ray radiation is used by medical authorities in conjunction with photographic technology to diagnose the interior truth of ill and injured bodies (a region that, the downwinders report, was steadfastly ignored by local nuclear authorities, who instead measured external, "penetrating" beta- and gamma-type radiation, and who downplayed the health risks for downwinders posed by alpha-radiation ingested through their breathing, eating, and drinking contaminated materials). Because X-rays are known to pose health risks to developing fetuses, were used in the secret Cold War radiation experiments discussed above, and were also dispersed by exploding nuclear bombs (atomic veterans have reported viewing through closed lids the bones in their hands covering their eyes), they cannot be completely detached from connotations of nuclear war, violation, and downwinder illness. This conflation of destruction and recording leads critic Jeremy Millar, in reading the grotesque "shadows" of carbonized Hiroshima victims etched onto buildings, to describe that blast as "the world's largest photograph" (33).

In posing her subject in this fashion, with the photograph held close and centered on his chest, Gallagher is exploiting the amorality and intertextuality of this phenomenon. Her own photograph forms a sort of punning

Fig. 2.12. "Cuba Lyle." Photograph by Carole Gallagher. By arrangement with the artist.

ethical X-ray that reframes the prop official image *as if it were an X-ray plate revealing the suppressed truth of Przygucki's irradiated interior.* Her image manipulates the photograph's denotation (nuclear blast) and its connotation (radioactive fallout) to confirm that the relationship established in the man's narrative between his exposure to radiation ("a lot of dust and ashes would get on us after the shot" [66]) and his subsequent illness ("my teeth fell out about 1956" [66]) is one of cause. Index is appropriated as symbol.

This image confirms the twin impulses in Gallagher's work toward a progressive documentary realism that recovers the hidden history of downwinder suffering, and a deconstructive pastiche that self-consciously juxtaposes discourses to produce truth-as-effect. While these aesthetics are alternately complementary and competitive, they potentially contribute to an ethically heightened meditation by viewers on the discursive manufacture of nuclear history and culture.

CONCLUSION: THE EPISTEMOLOGY OF FALLOUT

What conclusions, then, may we draw about the different aesthetics displayed in the work of these artists and their productivity in the evolving post–Cold War culture? Two claims seem apparent.

Fig. 2.13. "Ted Przygucki." Photograph by Carole Gallagher. By arrangement with the artist.

First, the tension between these two aesthetics does not appear to have troubled most commentators. Reviewers have largely upheld the volumes as exemplars of the first aesthetic—progressive documentary realism—and have not engaged their ironic and self-implicating tendencies (see Szasz for an exception). Evaluated within this framework, the texts have generated both preferred and oppositional readings. Vince Leo, for example, praises the neutrality displayed in Del Tredici's work: "There is no ideological ax to grind. There is simply one clearly stated fact after another" (18). Empowered with these alternative "facts," Leo concludes, viewers can "redirect" evolving nuclear history (18) and dispel a pernicious illusion promoted by nuclear deterrence: that the frightening symbolism of nuclear weapons has succeeded in preventing their materiality. Alternatively, Leo argues, Del Tredici's work clarifies that, because their production has poisoned the environment and has harmed workers and citizens, "nuclear weapons pose a crisis for our civilization *even if they are never used*" (18). Elsewhere, Reg Saner has echoed this claim that nuclear photography depicts ecologically *haunted* sites: "Once we've done with *it*, radioactive waste hasn't done with *us*. Not by an eon" (147).

Gallagher's text has become a minor cause célèbre among proponents of documentary and scientific realisms. Perhaps because her work challenges epidemiological findings, some reviewers apply positivist criteria to evaluate its validity. Some of the resulting readings are sympathetic and favor verisimilitude: "*American Ground Zero* does not constitute legal or scientific proof of anything. But given the machinations of lawyers and the duplicities of nuclear scientists recounted herein, what it does provide is far more important—human testimony pervasive and damning enough for anyone to understand" (Frick 10). Other readings are not sympathetic, however, and favor scientific criteria such as representative sampling and experimental controls: "[The photographs and narratives] are all anecdotal and don't prove anything" (Powers 121). Gallagher anticipates and defends against this criticism in the volume by including the endorsement of an independent epidemiologist (332–33) and by providing a large number of images and narratives that relentlessly support her claim. These strategies create unpredictable consequences, however: readers may reject this rhetoric of quantity as too long or too depressing. Even if they are compelled by the images, they may interpret them through an ideological code of individualism that encourages sympathy for downwinder subjects and diverts attention from the workings of nuclear institutions. Gallagher attempts to prevent this critical deferral by supplementing the images with verbal discourse, but there is no guarantee that readers will preserve their preferred relationships in the decoding process.

Because of these contingencies mediating the success of progressive documentary realism, we can posit a different reading of deconstructive pastiche in these works that does not minimize it as mere style, anomaly, or flaw. This reading reframes their reflexivity as a manifestation of ambivalence toward the constraints of documentary realism and of desire for a more radical aesthetic offering alternative critical strategies. This reading is supported by Abigail Solomon-Godeau's observation that "the problem confronting any genuinely radical cultural production is not simply a matter of transforming existing forms through the insertion of some new politicized content or subject matter, but rather to intervene on the level of the forms themselves, to disrupt what the forms put in place" (*Photography* 189). In this way, Del Tredici and Gallagher appear to acknowledge that replacing official nuclear certainty with its progressive counterpart may have only limited success (particularly when hegemonic interests are able to control the premises by which their conflict is framed and resolved). Instead, the deconstructive photographs reject nuclear certainty by asserting its formal *opposite*: reflexive images that *evoke and critique through their multistable forms* the oppressive discourses of the nuclear age. Through the contrast created by their forms, these images suggest *how* these discourses have historically effaced their own contingency and distorted the authentic, polyphonic expression of collective nuclear experience. The open-endedness of these images jars their viewers into new levels of participation in—and responsibility for—discursive closure of the nuclear future.

Fig. 2.14. "B-36 Mark 17 H-Bomb Accident (May 22, 1957), 5½ Miles South of Gibson Boulevard, Albuquerque, New Mexico, 1991." Photograph by Patrick Nagatani. By arrangement with the artist.

The potential effects of this postmodern aesthetic become more apparent when we contrast the tentative, ambivalent reflexivity of Del Tredici and Gallagher with the work of their colleague Patrick Nagatani. In his 1991 volume *Nuclear Enchantment*, Nagatani combines the techniques of color-washing and collage with the use of models to create deeply ironic images. His photograph "The Accident" (86; see fig. 2.14), for example, employs pastiche to "re-create" a 1957 incident in which a B-36 bomber dropped a nuclear bomb in a New Mexico field (its nuclear explosive did not detonate). The subject of Nagatani's image, however, is the not the event itself but the process by which viewers may come to know about it. Not surprisingly, there is no official marker of this event at the physical site, and it was not publicized until 1986. Accounts of the event's cause also vary and suggest that "normal accidents" such as these may be inevitable.

To evoke the undecidability of this contested event, Nagatani depicts a figure posed in the New Mexico field, which is covered in snow. The figure is Nagatani himself, bundled in winter clothing, with his face turned away from the camera. In the image Nagatani holds a photograph out in front of his body and appears to be comparing *its* image to the scene in front of him. This prop photograph is the product of an earlier attempt by Nagatani to complete this very project on this very site. It is *itself* a reflexive depiction of Nagatani and his assistants, who are posed in the act of staging the originally planned image. Metaphors, simulations, and photographic references are all densely layered in this prop image. One of Nagatani's assistants is posed in its foreground as if he were a press photographer capturing Nagatani and another assistant (also posed as a photographer) in their preparations to shoot different stagings of the event. These stagings are surreal, however, and involve a reclining nude woman and other female figures in military uniforms gesturing toward a garishly colored plot of ground. Yet another assistant in the foreground is holding up a photograph (appropriately enough, one of Del Tredici's) of the type of bomb dropped by the plane. Apparently unseen by all of these figures is a blurry image of the bomber in question (actually a suspended model of the aircraft), zooming overhead as if it were about to crash. As positioned by the Nagatani who holds up this prop image, its foreground figures gaze across representational levels directly at the viewer, creating a level of self-consciousness that is almost unbearable. In a last fillip, our photographer Nagatani underscores the contingency of "The Accident" by depicting the shadow of his camera falling across his own back.

This complication of relations between photography and the real is so exquisite that it is almost painful to untangle. Yet in depicting the erasure of his team's previous labor by snow and by time (this is the effect created by a comparison of the prop photograph to its "actual" referent), Nagatani also evokes the suppression of the "actual" bombing event by secret military operations (which have since "cleaned up" the site) and by history. These conditions require a critical reinvention of the scene, and this one functions to clarify the sedimented nature of nuclear representation and to problematize the criteria by which viewers may distinguish between "real" and "imaginary" nuclear worlds.

The pictures and metapictures discussed in this essay are historically significant. They suggest how visual codes operated during the late moments of the Cold War to open up and to foreclose possibilities for nuclear subjectivity. They also complicate the evolving trajectory of nuclear history. They may spur viewers to revise official accounts of nuclear history and to reform nuclear institutions. They may sensitize viewers to the ways in which "realistic" nuclear discourses enforce passivity and inhibit reflexivity. They may convert viewers' anxiety about possible nuclear futures into heightened awareness of contemporary nuclear operations.

The unstable textuality of these images, furthermore, resonates with the spasming, post–Cold War, nuclear-critical object, which is currently configured in tensions between old traditions and new crises. Many of the weapons plants photographed by Del Tredici, for example, have since been closed owing to decrepitude and contamination (while the Department of Energy pursues plans to consolidate its operations and to create new facilities for building future weapons). The downwinders photographed by Gallagher continue to die from their illnesses and to lose court battles with the federal government (while findings of Gulf War Syndrome fuel paranoia concerning secret contamination of vulnerable populations by the national-security state). And even as conventional wisdom holds that the Cold War (along with the threat of nuclear holocaust) is over, the proliferation and dispersal of nuclear weapons among "terrorists" and "rogue" states sustain the reactionary apparatus of militarism. These conflicting forces of repetition and change structure the power relations between nuclear-weapons officials and citizens. They also indicate that neither nuclear criticism nor its object is anachronistic (Luckhurst; Ruthven, chap. 4). As a result, we do well to remember that both words *and* images will influence the evolution of nuclear hegemony. Let neither medium be neglected by nuclear criticism.

NOTES

1. While nuclear criticism may or may not constitute a distinct genre of critical practice, nuclear textuality is a topic that cuts across various disciplines practicing literary, rhetorical, and media criticism, as well as discourse-analysis, cultural history, political science, anthropology, and sociology.

2. Ruthven's recent history of the project makes a useful distinction between two critical subgenres: a Nuclear Criticism that embraces Derridean textualism and deconstruction to critique metatheoretically the possibilities of a nuclear-critical discourse; and a more politicized, materialist, and neopragmatic nuclear criticism concerned with intervening in public deliberations about weapons and militarism. While I typically position myself in the latter group, this essay also attempts to bridge the two models.

3. This bias, Hales notes ("The Atomic Sublime," 29 n. 10), is also displayed in the absence of illustrations and photographs in Spencer Weart's (ironically subtitled) *Nuclear Fear: A History of Images.* In this work, Weart defines images not as icons or indexes but psychologically as "mental representation[s] . . . combined with their associated beliefs and feelings" (436). Similarly, Peter Schwenger's *Letter Bomb: Nuclear Holocaust and the Exploding Word* reveals this bias not only in its title but also in its conclusion that because "it is through language . . . that war's aspect of unmaking is removed from a nation's consciousness" (51), the task of nuclear criticism is to theorize a language adequate for progressive nuclear representation.

4. After Bakhtin's description of verbal-ideological de-centering.

5. I am interpreting the images *with* their corresponding notes, grouped separately at the back of the volume, as if they were presented together as a verbal/visual unit. It is not unreasonable to assume that readers usually turn back and forth between the two sets of messages in sequence or at least process them retrospectively as a coherent unit. Since Del Tredici's sequences are often nonlinear, the volume invites negotiated and tactical readings.

6. Photographs in Del Tredici's volume are not paginated. Hereafter, numerals in parentheses preceded by the symbol "#" indicate the number of a photograph as designated within the volume. Quotations taken from captions of unpaginated photographs are cited in similar fashion.

7. As works of photojournalism, *At Work* and *American Ground Zero* require both reading and viewing. I use the term "viewer" to describe moments of textual engagement that primarily involve visual codes, and "reader" to describe those primarily involving verbal codes.

8. The Trinity test confirmed the viability of a plutonium-implosion bomb-design subsequently used on the city of Nagasaki. Trinity has come to stand, however, as a foreshadowing of all uses of all types of nuclear weapons. For this reason, Del Tredici can juxtapose Yoshito Matsushige's images of Hiroshima, which was actually bombed with a uranium-gun device, without fear of inconsistency.

9. For the phrase used in the heading of this section, see Watney 183.

10. For overviews of this history, see Howard Ball, *Justice Downwind: America's Atomic Testing Program in the 1950's* (1986); and Philip Fradkin, *Fallout: An American Nuclear Tragedy* (1989).

11. Gallagher presents the image as untitled. In granting permission for its reproduction, the Oakland Museum refers to this image as "Gunlock, Henry and Gus Bowler Haying, 1953."

WORKS CITED

Bakhtin, M. M. "Discourse in the Novel." *The Dialogic Imagination: Four Essays*. Ed. Michael Holquist. Trans. Caryl Emerson and Holquist. University of Texas Press Slavic Series 1. Austin: U of Texas P Slavic, 1981. 259–422.

Ball, Howard. *Justice Downwind: America's Atomic Testing Program in the 1950's*. New York: Oxford UP, 1986.

Brians, Paul. *Nuclear Holocausts: Atomic War in Fiction, 1895–1984*. Kent: Kent State UP, 1987.

Broderick, Mick. *Nuclear Movies: A Critical Analysis and Filmography of International Feature Length Films Dealing with Experimentation, Aliens, Terrorism, Holocaust, and Other Disaster Scenarios, 1914–1989*. Jefferson: McFarland, 1991.

Chilton, Paul, ed. *Language and the Nuclear Arms Debate: Nukespeak Today*. Dover: Frances Printer, 1985.

Closing the Circle on the Splitting of the Atom. Office of Environmental Management, U.S. Department of Energy: Washington, D.C., 1995.

Cohn, Carol. "Sex and Death in the Rational World of Defense Intellectuals." *Signs* 12 (1987): 687–718.

Covino, Michael. Rev. of *Nuclear Landscapes* by Peter Goin. *Artforum* 30 (1991): 27–28.

Del Tredici, Robert. *At Work in the Fields of the Bomb*. New York: Harper, 1987.

———. "Trinity: Fifty Years After." *Creative Camera* 334 (1995): 8–9.

Derrida, Jacques. "No Apocalypse, Not Now (Full Speed Ahead, Seven Missiles, Seven Missives)." *diacritics* 14 (1984): 20–31.

Dowling, David. *Fictions of Nuclear Disaster.* Iowa City: U of Iowa P, 1987.

Farrell, James T. "Nuclear Friezes: Art and the Bomb from Hiroshima to Three Mile Island." *Twenty/One* 1 (1989): 58–75.

"Fifty Years of Nuclear Testing." *Nuclear Times* 10 (1992): 44–47.

Fradkin, Philip L. *Fallout: An American Nuclear Tragedy.* Tucson: U of Arizona P, 1989.

Franklin, H. Bruce. "From Realism to Virtual Reality: Images of America's Wars." *Georgia Review* 48 (1994): 47–64.

Frick, Thomas. "Sweet Dreams, Nuclear Regulatory Commission." Rev. of *American Ground Zero: The Secret Nuclear War,* by Carole Gallagher. *Los Angeles Times Book Review* 14 July 1993: 10.

Gallagher, Carole. *American Ground Zero: The Secret Nuclear War.* Cambridge: MIT P, 1993.

Goin, Peter. *Nuclear Landscapes.* Baltimore: Johns Hopkins UP, 1991.

Gusterson, Hugh. *Nuclear Rites: A Weapons Laboratory at the End of the Cold War.* Berkeley: U of California P, 1996.

———. "Nuclear War, the Gulf War and the Disappearing Body." *Journal of Urban and Cultural Studies* 2 (1991): 45–55.

Hales, Peter B. *Atomic Spaces: Living on the Manhattan Project.* Urbana: U of Illinois P, 1997.

———. "The Atomic Sublime." *American Studies* 32 (1991): 5–32.

Johnson, M. K. "Symptom, Sign, and Wound: Medical Semiotics and Photographic Representations of Hiroshima." *Semiotica* 98 (1994): 89–107.

Lehman, Susan. "Fallout: The Whistleblower, the Ethicist and the Reporter." *Mirabella* July 1994: 126–31.

Leo, Vince. "The War Game." Rev. of *At Work in the Fields of the Bomb,* by Robert Del Tredici. *Afterimage* 15 (1988): 18–19.

Lifton, Robert Jay, and Greg Mitchell. *Hiroshima in America: Fifty Years of Denial.* New York: Grosset/Putnam, 1995.

Luckhurst, Roger. "Nuclear Criticism: Anachronism and Anachorism." *diacritics* 23 (1993): 89–97.

Millar, Jeremy. "Fatal Trajectories." *Creative Camera* 334 (June/July 1995): 30–33.

Misrach, Richard. *Bravo 20: The Bombing of the American West.* Baltimore: Johns Hopkins UP, 1990.

Mitchell, W.J.T. *Picture Theory: Essays on Verbal and Visual Representation.* Chicago: U of Chicago P, 1994.

Nagatani, Patrick. *Nuclear Enchantment.* Albuquerque: U of New Mexico P, 1991.

Nichols, Bill. " 'Getting to Know You . . .': Knowledge, Power, and the Body." *Theorizing Documentary.* Ed. Michael Renov. AFI Film Readers 6. New York: Routledge, 1993. 174–91.

———. *Representing Reality: Issues and Concepts in Documentary.* Bloomington: Indiana UP, 1991.

Powers, Thomas. "Downwinders: Some Casualties of the Nuclear Age." Rev. of *American Ground Zero: The Secret Nuclear War,* by Carole Gallagher. *Atlantic Monthly* March 1994: 119–24.

Rosenthal, Peggy. "The Nuclear Mushroom Cloud as Cultural Image." *American Literary History* 3 (1991): 63–92.

Ruthven, Ken K. *Nuclear Criticism*. Carlton, Austral.: Melbourne UP, 1993.

Saner, Reg. "Bomb Love: And After?" Rev. of *Nuclear Landscapes*, by Peter Goin and *Bravo 20: The Bombing of the American West*, by Richard Misrach. *Georgia Review* 46 (1992): 144–49.

Schell, Jonathan. *The Fate of the Earth*. New York: Avon, 1982.

Schwenger, Peter. *Letter Bomb: Nuclear Holocaust and the Exploding Word*. Baltimore: Johns Hopkins UP, 1992.

Sekula, Alan. "On the Invention of Photographic Meaning." *Thinking about Photography*. Ed. Victor Burgin. London: Macmillan Education, 1982. 84–109.

Shapiro, Michael J. *Representing World Politics: The Sport/War Intertext—With a Postscript on the Nuclear Question*. Working Paper No. 9. San Diego: U of California Institute of Global Conflict and Cooperation, 1987.

Smith, Jeff. *Unthinking the Unthinkable: Nuclear Weapons and Western Culture*. Bloomington: Indiana UP, 1989.

Solnit, Rebecca. "Unsettling the West: Contemporary American Landscape Photography." *Creative Camera* 319 (1992): 12–23.

Solomon-Godeau, Abigail. *Photography at the Dock: Essays on Photographic History, Institutions and Practices*. Media and Society 4. Minneapolis: U of Minnesota P, 1991.

———. Rev. of *Our Lives, Our Children*, by Robert Adams. *Exposure* 22, no. 3 (Fall 1984): 53–56.

Szasz, Ferenc M. "The Photography of the Atomic Age: A Review Essay." *New Mexico Historical Review* 70 (1995): 77–82.

Taylor, Bryan C. "The Bodies of August: Photographic Realism and Controversy at the National Air and Space Museum." *Rhetoric and Public Affairs* 1 (1998): 331–61.

———. "The Politics of the Nuclear Text: Reading Robert Oppenheimer's *Letters and Reflections*." *Quarterly Journal of Speech* 78 (1992): 429–49.

———. "Shooting Downwind: Depicting the Radiated Body in Epidemiology and Documentary Photography." *Transgressing Scientific Discourses: Communication and the Voice of the Other*. Ed. Michael Huspek and Gary Radford. Albany: State U of New York P, 1997. 289–328.

Trachtenberg, Alan. *Reading American Photographs: Images as History, Mathew Brady to Walker Evans*. New York: Noonday-Hill, 1989.

Watney, Simon. "Photography and AIDS." *The Critical Image: Essays on Contemporary Photography*. Ed. Carol Squiers. Seattle: Bay, 1990. 173–92.

Weart, Spencer R. *Nuclear Fear: A History of Images*. Cambridge: Harvard UP, 1988.

CHAPTER 3

Pittsburgh at Yellowstone: Old Faithful and the Pulse of Industrial America

CECELIA TICHI

YELLOWSTONE National Park became a tourist "Wonderland" only after the 1870s, when a mix of writers, photographers, illustrators, publishers, and corporations, notably the Northern Pacific Railroad, repositioned its public identity from hell-on-earth to what John Muir called "a big whole-some wilderness" (Muir, *Our National Parks* 37). A significant part of Yellowstone's shift from hell-on-earth to a new geophysical identity involved figuration of the human body, as Muir's essay indicates in its doubly gendered terms of "Mother Earth" and of "Nature working . . . like a man." In the latter decades of the century, as Yellowstone and its geyser region became identified as an American Wonderland, texts supporting the newer identity participated in the kinds of figuration proliferating in contemporary essays and narrative.

In part, the bodily terms in texts on Yellowstone operated as a familiarizing stratagem whereby the distant alien land of rocky mountain ranges, erupting geysers, mud volcanoes, boiling springs, and the like, became more conceptually accessible, enticing visitors who would have arrived by rail—5,438 in the summer of 1895, 9,579 in 1899—the increase due largely to the easing of economic conditions following the Panic of 1893 and the heavy promotion in the railroad flyers. (The Northern Pacific printed the words "Yellowstone National Park Route" on each page of its folders.) One visitor of 1887, Francis Sessions, positioned Yellowstone this way: "nearly as large as the state of Connecticut, situated in the heart of the Rocky Mountains, about one thousand miles from St. Paul on the east and about the same from Portland, Oregon, on the west" (Sessions 435).

Sessions's reference to the "heart" of the Rockies fits Muir's reference to "the very heart-joy of earth" in "the wild parks of the West" (282, 1–36). The heart, in fact, is but one of the bodily terms pervasive in the discourse of the new Yellowstone, though attention to the role of figuration of the human body in texts on Yellowstone 1870s–1920s reveals the "double discourse of the natural and the technological" (Seltzer 152). This discourse, especially focused on the geyser Old Faithful, produced an icon of industrial America. To recognize this is also to see the basis on which the geyser area also became a text on the sociocultural disjunctions of the new industrial order.

Prior to a series of explorations beginning in 1869, the Yellowstone area was known as "Colter's Hell," a tall-tale scene of "burning plains, immense lakes, and boiling springs" encountered at first hand by a few white trappers, hunters, and mountaineers dating back to John Colter's foray in the area in 1807–8, when he split off from the Lewis and Clark expedition and ventured into Yellowstone (Kinsey 45–46). Colter was not alone, for another of the first white male explorers of the region, James Bridger, had called it "a place where hell bubbles up" ("Yellowstone Park as a Summer Resort," 248).

Such descriptions fit earlier-nineteenth-century fables of the far West as a Great American Desert including "scenes of barrenness and desolation," of "the most dismal country" riddled with man-eating grizzlies, of "dismal and horrible mountains," of the "desert," of endless plains "on which not a speck of vegetable matter existed" (Lawton-Peebles 224–25). In order for the Yellowstone area to become credible as a national park and tourist "Wonderland," as it was called by the *Helena Daily Herald* in 1872, it was necessary that it be assigned a new public identity.

This was achieved, as we shall see, in part by bodily figuration appearing both in travel and expeditionary texts. But the whole process of Yellowstone's reidentification has been documented as a part of the larger post–Civil War project by which the trans-Mississippi West, heretofore understood to be the Great American Desert, now became a pathway to the "Edenic civilization that would occur as Americans entered the region, settled there, exploited its natural resources, and made the West over in their desired image" (Hales 46–47). In the case of Yellowstone, "Wonderland" replaced the inferno in expeditionary reports by Nathaniel P. Langford (1871) and especially Ferdinand V. Hayden (1872), who extolled the beauty and "magnificent features" of the area (Kinsey 83). These were augmented by guidebooks describing Yellowstone's majesty, beauty, and enchantment, and by travel writing in the following decades in such middle-class magazines as *Harper's New Monthly Magazine*, *Scribner's*, *National Geographic*, and the *Atlantic Monthly*, whose essays recounted personally inspiring visits and beckoned readers to visit the park for health, adventure, and edification. Throughout, one finds a rhetorical strategy using bodily figures to emphasize maternal succor and masculine guardianship.

Yellowstone's new identity was also achieved by visual media, such as the Hayden party's expeditionary photographs by William Henry Jackson. These showed male, shaftlike rock formations and female valleys, along with canyons and waterfalls in compositional terms that "continued the Romantic landscape tradition" (Hales 50). Alan Trachtenberg, discussing the work of Timothy O'Sullivan, another post–Civil War photographer of the West, remarks that such photographs belong to the tradition of landscape art, "landscape" referring to a particular genre of academic painting (128).

But painting also played a major role in establishing the new identity of Yellowstone. The painter Thomas Moran, also with the Hayden group, sketched scenes that provided illustrations for essays in *Scribner's* on "The Wonders of Yellowstone" and for James Richardson's *Wonders of the Yellowstone* (1872). Probably more important, Moran became nationally known for his huge (7 <sc10> 12 feet) oil painting, *The Grand Cañon of the Yellowstone* (1872), which was publicly exhibited in the U.S. Capitol and was instrumental in the creation of the park by an act of Congress signed into law by President Ulysses S. Grant in March 1871, setting the region aside as "a great national park or pleasure ground for the benefit and enjoyment of the people."[1] In the painting, as in a series of his watercolors, Moran's compositional exploitation of arches, towers, rocks, and trees, together with his adaptation of the aesthetic principles of John Ruskin and the painterly techniques of Joseph Mallord William Turner in capturing atmospheric effects and color, largely enabled Moran to translate Yellowstone as a landscape of the American sublime, a response codified earlier in the century in relation to America's first icon of nature, Niagara Falls (Kinsey 20–40; McKinsey 30–36, 99). In Moran's painting, shafts of rock and tree trunks frame a wide deep valley from which a central column of white mist rises skyward. In bodily terms, one recalls Perry Miller's statement on late-nineteenth-century representations of steam as "the pure white jet that fecundates America," inseminating the "body of the continent" (Seltzer 27).

Business, too, was centrally involved in the transformation of Yellowstone from "a place where hell bubbles up" to the new Wonderland. *Scribner's* evidently funded the exhibition of Moran's huge canvas in Clinton Hall on New York's Astor Place, just as it published numerous Moran-illustrated essays on the area, including John Muir's. In addition, executives and financiers of the Northern Pacific Railroad understood the advantages of a sublime, enticing Yellowstone for income generated by passengers, freight, and stockholders (Kinsey 64). Subliminally, at least, that phallic shaft of steamy white mist central to Moran's *The Grand Cañon of the Yellowstone* looked enough like locomotive steam to appeal to such groups. The financier Jay Cooke was instrumental in promotion of the new image of Yellowstone as exemplum of Western grandeur, and after the collapse of his empire in 1873, the reorganized company continued its public-relations campaign on behalf of the area. Joni Louise Kinsey writes of this group of businessmen, artists, and explorers: "Through their collective efforts, [Yellowstone] was transformed from a remote hell on earth into America's wonderland in the public imagination. . . . By 1890 the demonic perceptions of the place . . . were thoroughly transformed. Yellowstone had become, to the eager tourists and the corporations, a wonderland that promised unlimited rewards" (58, 78).

The vocabulary of the human body consistently figured in the transformation of the West and of Yellowstone in particular. One may presuppose that the rock shafts and deep ravines and gorges visually represented in photographs, woodcuts, and oil canvases conveyed a sexualized message of phallic and yonic forms. But an explicit bodily vocabulary can be found in the numerous print texts on Yellowstone. Incongruous as it may seem that texts sustaining the landscape tradition should revert to bodily figuration, the centuries-old practice of delineating geographic traits in bodily terms served the purposes of travel and expeditionary writers, who also followed rhetorical convention from the previous century, such as one typical late-eighteenth-century verse on the American continent, "where Oregon foams along the West, / And seeks the fond Pacific's tranquil breast" (Lawton-Peebles 239; see Kolodny).

Breasts, faces, and the other physical features recurring regularly in the production of Yellowstone-as-Wonderland in middle-class American magazines, 1870s–1920s, for the most part do so in heterosexually normative terms. Cliffs in the park have "perpendicular faces" ("Washburn Expedition" 436). The mountains, like sentinels (presumably male bodies in military posture), "keep watch and ward over this bewilderingly beautiful handiwork of Nature's own" (Armstrong). The object of the sentinels' vigilance is in part the adjectively female Yellowstone Lake, "a beautiful body of water" (though elsewhere, in another text, the lake is depicted as shaped like the wounded hand of a German army veteran [Dale 6]).

Some writers feminized the park in terms of maternal succor, the breast mimicked the breast in shape and the production of a milk-white snow: "The headwaters of the Missouri, Colorado, and Columbia rivers are all suckled here from the same breast of snow," and Lake Yellowstone is "nestled in the bosom of the Rocky Mountains" (Comstock 48, "Washburn Expedition" 489). Late-nineteenth-century texts also codify Yellowstone National Park as a sentient being expressive of feelings. The "mood" of Yellowstone Lake, for instance, "is ever changing." It "laughs" and then turns "angry" ("Washburn Expedition" 490).

John Muir feminizes the park in terms of "Mother Earth" but moves anatomically inside the body when he says that park visitors are "getting in touch with the nerves of Mother Earth" (50, 2). Muir's image is significant for its anatomical internalization, a direction that various writers also followed. In 1893, in *The Significance of the Frontier in American History*,

Frederick Jackson Turner remarked that "civilization in America has followed the arteries made by geology. . . . like the steady growth of a complex nervous system for the originally simple, inert continent" (14–15). Hayden explicitly linked the railroad's utilitarian relation to this geological arterial system: "[T]he multitude of rivers that wind like arteries through the country . . . excavate the avenues for our railroads" (qtd. in Hales 69).

This textual mapping of the area in terms of internal organ systems is significant because it enables the production of certain social meanings that devolve from the traits of those organs, including arterial blood flow and cardiac pulse. The arterial rivers conjoin, in cardiovascular terms, with the heart, and not surprisingly, the April 5, 1873, *Harper's Weekly Magazine* included an article entitled "The Heart of the Continent: The Hot Springs and Geysers of the Yellow Stone Region" (273–74).

The heart-as-center was, of course, a centuries-old convention but gained a certain agency from the dictum of Ralph Waldo Emerson, whose American scholar is not only "the world's eye" but "the world's heart" ("American Scholar" 73). Cardiac vitality is correlatively located at the center of the Emersonian universe: "The heart at the centre of the universe with every throb hurls the flood of happiness into every artery, vein and veinlet, so that the whole system is inundated with the tides of joy" (*Society and Solitude* 306–7). In his essay "The Yellowstone National Park," Muir, the self-proclaimed student and admirer of Emerson, asserted, "The shocks and outbursts of earthquakes, volcanoes, geysers, storms, the pounding of waves, the uprush of sap in plants, each and all tell the orderly love-beats of Nature's heart" (*Our National Parks* 70).

The health of that heart was measured in a pulse manifest by Old Faithful geyser. In his essay on Yellowstone, Muir describes "a hundred geysers," though Old Faithful was, and is to this day, preeminent. Named by Nathaniel P. Langford and Gustavus C. Doane, who had written of the Yellowstone area prior to congressional action establishing the park in 1871, Old Faithful is repeatedly singled out as exemplary.

It is the "most instructive" geyser, wrote Hayden in 1872: "When it is about to make a display, very little preliminary warning is given. There is simply a rush of steam for a moment, and then a column of water shoots up vertically into the air, and by a succession of impulses is apparently held steadily up for the space of fifteen minutes" (175). In 1878, Joseph Le Conte identified the trait—punctual regularity—for which old Faithful is best known. " 'Old Faithful,' " he wrote, "is so called from the frequency and regularity of its eruptions, throws up a column six feet in diameter to the height of 100 to 150 feet *regularly every hour* [italics mine] and plays each time fifteen minutes" (412).

Like Le Conte's, numerous texts from the 1870s cite the unvarying regularity of Old Faithful, always in terms of approval and admiration. It is "the only reliable geyser in the park. You can always bet on seeing him every sixty-five minutes." There has been no "appreciable difference in its eruptions for over thirty years. . . . It always displays the same graceful, slender column. . . . *the* geyser of the park." Old Faithful sets "a noble example to his followers . . . and [is] punctual [as] "a tall, old-fashioned clock." It is "the perfect geyser," the "model geyser. . . . Old Faithful is a friend to every tourist. . . . With the regularity of a clock, he pours out his soul toward heaven every sixty minutes and then sinks back to regain new strength" (Francis 34; Hague, "The Yellowstone National Park" 523; Weed, "Geysers" 294; Rollins 886; Hague, "The Yellowstone National Park" 517; Henderson 164; King 597).

The very name—*Old* Faithful—connotes the cherished, familiar, and dear. The geyser becomes an object of affection because of its very predictability, its punctuality. The hotel beside it would be named the Old Faithful Inn, as if hospitality itself were linked to the geyser, as if it performed intentionally for the visitors who had endured the inconvenience of travel in order to experience what John Sears has called the "sacred places," the sacralized tourist sublime associated throughout the century with such sites as Niagara Falls, Kentucky's Mammoth Cave, Yosemite's sequoias. More than one writer said that the road traveled to the geysers was "dull, dusty, glaring, and disappointing," but if Old Faithful failed to meet expectations, no one but Rudyard Kipling said so in print (Rollins 872). This cherished, sacred Old Faithful is clearly central to Emerson's and Muir's idea of the organic, benevolent heart of the natural world.

Yet texts from the 1870s to the 1920s indicate that the sociocultural definition of Old Faithful changed radically from the version embraced in the rhetoric of Emerson and Muir. Pulse itself becomes a crucial term in this change. Numerous commentators characterized geyser eruptions as pulsations. "*The geyser*," said one writer in 1890, "is a pool of limpid, green water whose surface rises and falls in rhythmic pulsations. . . . [A]t every pulsation, thick white clouds of steam came rolling out." A group in 1882 observed "nine successive pulsations" of the geyser. Many of the "springs . . . rise and fall every second or two . . . with each pulsation, [by] . . . steady impulses, ... regular pulsations" (Weed, "Geysers" 291; "Washburn Expedition" 437; Francis 35; Hayden 163, 174).

The pulse in these statements reverts to the arterial pulse, which in medical history is both mechanistic and organic. Texts such as Muir's ally the geysers' rhythms with those of waterfalls, storms, and avalanches, and thus position them with the rhythms of nature (*Our National Parks* 54). The mechanistic, however, reverts to the many references to the steady, regular, clocklike pulsations and eruptions affirmed in the tributes to Old Faithful quoted above. In regard to Old Faithful, the relation of the organic to the mechanic is neither a binary division nor an antithesis but a conjunction. The geyser operates as nature's own clockworks.

The regularity of Old Faithful's pulse had a crucial connection to the medical history that linked the body to the clock. The arterial pulse had been measured by the clock since the early eighteenth century, when Sir John Floyer published *The Physician's Pulse Watch* (1707), an account of his invention of a mechanical watch with a second hand subsequently standard in timepieces. The sixty-second minute thus became the standard for pulse measurement. Floyer measured patients with "exceeding and deficient pulses," and these he worked to reregulate. Those which beat too fast or too slowly, according to the measurement of the pulse watch, were treated with medical regimens involving heat and cold. Life consists, Floyer theorized, "in the Circulation of blood, and that running too fast or slow, produces most of our Diseases" (Clendening 573–74). The healthy body was that whose pulse throbbed in synchrony with the measurement of the pulse watch.

By the late nineteenth and early twentieth centuries, medical experts agreed that "changes of the pulse are important," and recognized a normative range of healthy pulsations even as they named irregularities or arrhythmias (e.g., "bigeminal and trigeminal pulsations"), separated the arterial from the venal and hepatic pulses, and devised new instruments for measurement, such as the sphygmograph, which showed the pulse in a series of curves (Barwell 89; Osler, *Principles* 650–51). As one specialist wrote in 1902, "The rate of the pulse is the most simple of all signs," and "variations in rhythm are usually readily recognized," though "the timing of the various events in a cardiac revolution . . . can only be acquired by careful practice. . . . with the radial pulse as a standard" (Mackenzie 6, viii).

Old Faithful, as we have seen, was celebrated for its hourly pulse measured radially. It met the standard of the sixty-second minute encapsulated within the sixty-minute hour. Its health was proven by its very regularity over decades.

Yet the pulse regularity of Old Faithful involved more than the apparent synchrony of nature with human horology. Muir tries to adhere to the organic model of the Emersonian "heart at the centre of the universe with every throb hurl[ing] the flood of happiness into every artery, vein and veinlet," but other writers, and even Muir himself, were responding to a new model of the body as machine (see Seltzer, Banta).

As Mark Seltzer has shown in *Bodies and Machines* (1992), ideology was convertible into biology in the late nineteenth and early twentieth centuries, with the previous distinction "between the life process and the machine process" now collapsed (159). This new body-machine conflation is evident, for instance, in the writings of William Osler, the preeminent physician-teacher-researcher at the University of Pennsylvania and the

Johns Hopkins medical school, one of the founders of modern clinical medicine and author of a major, much reprinted medical textbook, *The Principles and Practice of Medicine* (1895). Osler wrote extensively on the cardiovascular system in terms of mechanization and focused on the very kind of privileged white male bodies responsible for the new capitalist economic and industrial system. His patient, a "man of great vigor" who "lived a business life of the greatest possible intensity," the "hustling life of Wall Street," who "regarded himself as 'hard as nails,' " nonetheless failed to realize "that he is a machine" (5).

As such, Osler insists, his heart is a "pump," while the small arteries act as "stopcocks" or "taps" that, stimulated, become "sluice-gates to be open or shut." Each cell is a "factory." Diet should be temperate, says Osler, "food intake just enough to keep the engines running at steady speed" (13).

The physician extends a cardiovascular analogy to an irrigation system with supply pipes, pump, and sluices. Such symptoms as vertigo, headaches, anginal attack, palpitations, and sclerotic arteries are attributable to "difficulty in clearing of ashes and cinder the furnaces which keep up the fires of life in every unit of the bodily frame," as if "the engines are stoked for the Glasgow express . . . but put to work shunting empty trucks in the station yard" (7). Osler worried that the relentless "high pressure" pace of business and the professions (presumably including his own, medicine) gave the bodily "engines no rest," so that bodies at age fifty were "only fit to be scrapped" (8). Osler does compare cardiovascular obstructions to "weedy channels" in the farm fields and urges the patient with high blood pressure to "cultivate his garden," but the garden is technologically structured as a site of agricultural engineering.

Such a mechanistic body as that produced by Osler converges conceptually with the pulse mechanism of Old Faithful. But the repositioning of Yellowstone as the U.S. Wonderland included such technologizing of the body as well as of the material environment that was thought to be correlative with it. The post–Civil War decades not only redefined the body but witnessed the transformation of the Northeast and Midwest into industrial centers. This transformation, too, is important to the specific ways in which bodily identity produced Old Faithful as a bodily icon of industrial America.

The industrializing American scene is acknowledged in Muir's "The Yellowstone National Park" despite the preponderance of pastoral and domestic terms that bid to identify Yellowstone as a designed park on the order of Frederick Law Olmsted's Central Park or Boston's Fenway or Philadelphia's Fairmount Park. Muir's terms are organic, the very mineral formations turned into flowers.

Abruptly, however, Muir invokes a radically different environment as he describes the geyser basin. It is as if "a fierce furnace fire were burning beneath each" geyser, "hissing, throbbing, booming," writes Muir. "Looking down over the forests as you approach [the geysers]," he adds, "you see a multitude of white columns, broad reeking masses, and irregular jets and puffs of misty vapor . . . entangled like smoke . . . suggesting the factories of some busy town" (*Our National Parks* 43).

The factories of some busy town. So the "fierce furnace," the noises of hissing, throbbing, and booming after all recall the industrial landscape thousands of miles east of Yellowstone that, ironically, is the very landscape preserved in its natural splendor from the encroachment of industrialism. The sublime Yellowstone of William Henry Jackson's photographs, of Thomas Moran's huge painting, of the railroad guidebooks and flyers, for that matter of Muir's own crafting, suddenly is challenged by an apparently incongruous, even antithetical, overt image of industrial America.

Comparing the geyser area to "the factories of some busy town," Muir's diction collapses the boundaries between the two worlds of nature's Wonderland and technological industrialism. The writer whose name had become synonymous with naturalism and conservation, with appreciation of wilderness qua wilderness, who speaks of mineral formations as bouquets of flowers, who writes that the geyser visitors "look on, awe-stricken and silent, in devout, worshipful wonder" seems inadvertently to reveal a major disjunction in consciousness (53, 54). The geysers look like a factory, and the most visited site in Yellowstone National Park turns out to be Pittsburgh.

Others, in fact, explicitly named the city identified with steel and coke magnates Andrew Carnegie and Henry Clay Frick in their descriptions of Old Faithful. The "rising smoke and vapor" reminded one writer "of the city of Pittsburgh," and another observed that "a view of the city of Pittsburg [*sic*] from a high point would convey some idea of the appearance of this valley [of geysers and hot springs], except that in the former case the dense black smoke arises in hundreds of columns, instead of the pure white feathery clouds of steam" (Koch 503, Hayden 173). In 1880, S. Weir Mitchell, the physician known for his immobilizing "rest cure" for disordered women, described the area of "mud volcanoes" as comparable to "the exhaust of a steam-engine, and near it from the earth come the rattle and crash and buzz and whirring of a cotton-mill" (701). Significantly, it was another nature writer, John Burroughs, who compared the geyser area to an industrial site when he wrote in 1907 that "as one nears the geyser region, he gets the impression from the columns of steam. . . . that he is approaching an industrial centre" (63).

In part, such comments are utilitarian, measuring wastefulness against a norm of efficient usage. The geysers emit steam "in extravagant prodigality . . . enough steam is wasted here to run all the Western railways" ("Editor's Study" 320). A writer in the *Nation* observed that enough geyser water shot into the air "to run all the factories of Pennsylvania for a week" ("Yellowstone Park as a Summer Resort" 249). Burroughs "disliked to see so much good steam and hot water going to waste" because "whole towns might be warmed by them, and big wheels made to go round" (64).

Technological analogies providing easily accessible lessons to the reading public also show the extent of middle-class familiarity with mechanistic thinking, as when a geologist in 1898 explained that some geysers "have been formed by explosion, like the bursting of a boiler," or when steam vents are said to "keep up a constant pulsating noise like a high-pressure engine on a river steamboat," or when geysers are termed "natural steam-engines," their vapor likened to "the smoke of the . . . locomotive" (Tarr 1575; Hayden 164; Weed, "Geysers" 299; Rollins 883).

Whether used as a utilitarian measure of usage or wastefulness, or as a term of explanation or description, however, these references to machine technology, heavy industry, and the industrial city provide a context in which the bodily identity of Old Faithful becomes clearer. Though Muir grouped geophysical eruptions, wind-and-wave hydraulics, and botanical cycles as the percussive "orderly love-beats of Nature's heart," the industrial context produced a different cardiac model. The clockwork regularity of Old Faithful's pulse, when set within the context of an industrializing America, defines the geyser as an industrial-age bodily icon. If, as Osler argued, a man must realize "that he is a machine," then the geophysical expression of that machine body becomes Old Faithful geyser (Osler, *Collected Papers* 5).

Old Faithful in this sense is a synecdoche of the valorized body of the industrial era—a body understood as a machine whose pulse must be regular as clockwork. It is male, in that the realm of heavy industry was gendered masculine (despite the female operatives in textile mills), and its eruptions encompass the ejaculative in the arterial. Indeed, Muir emphasizes that geysers sometimes erupt for periods of nearly one hour, "standing rigid and erect. . . . seeming so firm and substantial and permanent" (*Our National Parks* 42, 54).

Such expression of male virility is fully consonant with the new industrial ethos of the later nineteenth century, and Old Faithful thus exemplified the ideals of an industrial society organized for maximal rationalized production. Like the railroads and well-run industrial plants, Old Faithful produced on schedule. (One guide to Yellowstone included "Geyser Time Tables," as if the eruptions were naturally scheduled like trains [*Practical Guide to Yellowstone*].) True, Old Faithful's eruptions varied by a few minutes, but the concept of hourly regularity was intact, as the numerous tributes to the geyser as reliable, punctual, regular as a clock all indicate. Old Faithful reassuringly enacted the unvarying, relentless rhythms of an industrial system and thus seemed to be the "American incarnation," in Myra Jehlen's term, of the capitalistic social order of industrial, technological production. Its pulse could be measured by the clock, its very arterial rhythm seeming to be nature's own precocious foreordination of the American modernity manifest in the industrial system.

"Nature's nation" thus was validated by nature's own industrial pulse. The very geophysical heart of America beat the rhythms of mechanization. Those seeing the geyser basin as a version of Pittsburgh or a similar "industrial centre" thus could appreciate Old Faithful as the paradigmatic pulse of that very system. Presumably, those responding with approbation also felt their interests to be well served by the new industrial order. A mutually reinforcing triad emerges—of Osler's Wall Street white male engine, of the industrial environment devised and financed by it, and of the natural expression of the engine pulse of nature's nation at Yellowstone. The three pulses are one, and they were represented by those who gathered in May 1872 to view Moran's Yellowstone painting. As one railroad executive described them, "the press—the literati—the rich people" (Kinsey 73).

Evidently, however, the geyser basin of Yellowstone also aroused anxieties pertinent to the industrial system and thereby to its bodily identity. No other geyser approached Old Faithful in regularity of pulse. Its punctuality was offset by other geysers' "capricious[ness]" and "misbehavior," and some of the geyser names suggest the anxiety evoked by their very irregularity and turbulence: Hurricane, Restless, Spasmodic, Spiteful, Impulsive, Fitful, Spasm (Francis 34; Hague, "The Yellowstone National Park" 523). Against Old Faithful, the very unpredictability of other geysers needs to be engaged, not solely in geophysical terms but, as with Old Faithful, in those of sociocultural issues in late-nineteenth- and early-twentieth-century America.

For Yellowstone's old identity as hell-on-earth was not quite effaced or even entirely repressed despite the vigorous efforts of its post-1870 spokespersons. The continuation of the old infernal identity has less to do with an inadequate campaign on behalf of the new Yellowstone Wonderland than it does with certain contemporary representations of industrial America. Ironically, just at the point when the cohort of photographers, painters, railroad executives, publishers, and the like, collaborated to identify Yellowstone as America's Wonderland, public discourse in the United States was fashioning an infernal identity for industrial America. While the West was newly configured in Edenic terms, the industrial Northeast and Midwest were assigned Yellowstone's old identity as hell-on-earth.

In fact, from the 1860s, fiction writers, journalists, and illustraters presented the new urban industrial order in terms of the infernal. Woodcuts and lithographs, for instance, in *Harper's Weekly Magazine* (November 1, 1873; July 7, 1888) showed tense laborers shoveling coal into beehive coke ovens as flames roil skyward, while other bare-chested workmen tend the fiery furnaces of the iron mill as flames backlight the night sky in a blinding blaze. Writers, too, produced these kinds of infernal images. Rebecca Harding Davis, in *Life in the Iron Mills* (1861), published in the *Atlantic Monthly*, described a "city of fires that burned hot and fiercely in the night. . . . caldrons filled with boiling fire. . . . Fire in every horrible form." It was, she wrote, "like a street in Hell. . . . like Dante's Inferno" (20, 27). Industrial Pittsburgh, just sixty miles north of Davis's Wheeling, was characterized in 1883 by a travel writer as "the great furnace of Pandemonium . . . the outer edge of the infernal regions" (Glazier 332).

Such accounts of industrial, technologically driven America corresponded to the characterization of "American Nervousness," which, in 1881, George Beard attributed to an urbanizing American environment of traction railways, industrial machinery, electrification, steam engines, factories, the very locomotive rods and pistons moving the passenger railroad cars of the Northern Pacific, the Burlington Route, and the Oregon Short Line that brought visitors to Yellowstone as of the 1880s. While Frederick Jackson Turner affirmed the westward path of civilization as "the steady growth of a complex nervous system," Beard blamed that same civilization for overtaxing the body's neural system in a world thought to engender a host of diseases, including consumption and neurasthenia, the etiology found in cities, industrial plants, fast-paced temporal pressures.

The tourists at Yellowstone came to experience awe at Old Faithful, but evidence indicates that visitors who produced travel texts on their experience at the park did so as inhabitants of an industrial, technological world. This is to say that the texts representative of their experience show a Yellowstone—and especially Old Faithful and the geyser basin—framed in experience largely of industrialism and its conditions of production and labor. As Old Faithful became an icon of industrial America, the erratic surrounding geysers, boiling springs, and mud volcanoes were read as a statement on the industrial pulse-body under mortal threat. The geyser area was a rearview-mirror image of the industrializing United States.

Muir, as active agent in the production of a Yellowstone Wonderland, worked to allay anxieties about danger there. The mansion and its grounds are entirely hospitable to visitors. Addressing a middle-class reading public, Muir framed his park description in reassurances that "most of the dangers that haunt the unseasoned citizen are imaginary," that "over-civilized people" are subject to "irrational dread," for instance, of rattlesnakes and murderous Indians ("No scalping Indians will you see" [*Our National Parks* 51]). "Fear nothing," he says, for "no town park you have been accustomed to saunter in is so free from danger as the Yellowstone" (57–58). Muir then tries to make the old hellish nicknames sound zany and fun, as though anticipating the later-twentieth-century theme park. Names like "Hell Broth Springs," the "Devil's Caldron," and "Coulter's Hell" are "so exhilarating that they set our pulses dancing" (58). Muir sets up a sympathetic pulsing of the geothermal and the arterial in the realm of rhythmic movement whose beat is emphatically more musical than mechanical. As partners, the visitors and the geysers have a ball.

Others, however, did not reproduce Muir's terpsichorean rhetorical strategy. Travelers' accounts through the 1880s–1910s continued to enforce a somber linkage between the geyser basin and the Inferno. By implication, their descriptions are shadowed by the presumed presence of demonic, monstrous bodies in hell. And their statements show the extent to which industrial-age America did not efface the old Yellowstone identity as "a place where hell bubbles up," but actually renewed it. They described "a seething caldron over a fiery furnace" emitting a "villainous smell" ("Washburn Expedition" 434). One of the mud volcanoes bears "testimony to the terrible nature of the convulsion that wrought such destruction" (Langford 354). A writer in *Scribner's Magazine* noted the "weird, uncanny, sulphurous, at times even dangerous" aspect of the geyser area (Hague, "The Yellowstone National Park" 516). Another said, "It seemed as if we were looking upon a panorama of the Inferno," and still another remarked that the air was "burdened with such sulphurous odors that at times it was rendered almost unfit for respiration" (King 597, Owen 193). A mother shepherding her seven children through a Yellowstone vacation in 1905 recalled that "like everybody else, we loved Old Faithful . . . feared Excelsior, admired the Giant and Beehive." But, she said, "the horrible rumbling as if an earthquake were imminent and the smell of brimstone made me eager to get my brood into the valley of safety beyond the Yellowstone" (Corthell 1466). Even the scientists reverted to fraught language in description of the geyser: the Excelsior is "a violently boiling cauldron . . . its waters may be seen in violent ebullition" (Jagger 324).

Absent Old Faithful, and unable to join in the spirit of Muir's injunction to "fear nothing" and dance, texts from the 1870s, including Muir's, authorially link the geyser basin with the Inferno in affirming its volcanic geophysics. In 1896, Arnold Hague of the United States Geological Survey asserted that "all geologists who have visited [Yellowstone] concur that the 'great body' of rock and mineral is 'volcanic' " (Hague, "Age of Igneous Rocks of the Yellowstone" 447). Two years later, a geologist graphically described the process: "Volcanoes developed throughout the entire Rockies. . . . Great masses of lava were intruded into the rocks. . . . Beds of volcanic ash testify to violent explosive volcanic activity" (Tarr 1407). The novelist Owen Wister's eponymous hero, the Virginian, visits the geysers and smells a "volcanaic whiff" (Sears 169). One writer compared the probable eruptive force of the Yellowstone-area volcanoes with those of the widely publicized recent eruptions of Krakatoa (1883) and of Tarawera, New Zealand (1886) (Weed, "Fossil Forests of the Yellowstone" 235).

U.S. visitors to Yellowstone were not encouraged to consider the likelihood of renewed volcanic activity. (Muir reassured them that "the fire times had passed away, and the volcanic furnaces were banked" [*Our National Parks* 64]). The "glass road" of volcanic obsidion over which they rode in wagons and stagecoaches to the geysers was considered a wonder, not a threat.

Yet readers of "The Yellowstone National Park" find even Muir drawn repeatedly to the subject of eruptive violence. Despite his assurance that destruction is creation and that the volcanic era is safely removed in the distant past, Muir's inscription of Yellowstone as a mansion with lawns, library, and artistic furnishings is repeatedly challenged—even threatened—by textual preoccupation with volcanic eruptions. Among constant reassurances that the park is wholesome, healthful, and civil, Muir's reader encounters recurrent "hot lava beds," the subterranean "fierce furnace fire," deracinating "awful subterranean thunder," "volcanic fires . . . [spewing] immense quantities of ashes, pumice and cinders . . . into the sky," the "shocks and outbursts of earthquakes, volcanoes, geysers, storms" (37, 41, 45, 61–62, 70). Readers may see in the desultory repetition an essayist reproducing the very erratic eruptions of which he writes. Apparently unable to contain the volcanic past or the eruptive present in a single passage or section of the essay, Muir obsessively returns to descriptions of geyser violence time after time throughout the text. Discursively he enacts the very erratic and dangerous actions of the region's geomorphology. It is as if the Yellowstone mansion and estate and its occupants stood liable to be destroyed, to be buried in the molten lava of an American Pompeii.

Images of the Inferno in Muir and other writers indicate anxieties not allayed by reassurances that the fires are extinct. The spewing, hissing eruptions were proving otherwise. The "Editor's Study" column in *Harper's* (January 1897) cited a "lady" who considered the geyser area of Yellowstone as "the safety-valve of the United States." These function as "vent-holes of its internal fires and explosive energies." But for their relief, "the whole country might be shaken with earthquakes and blown up in fragments" (320). The "lady" reported it "not encouraging" to feel the hot crust underfoot and identified the subterranean area as "a terrible furnace."

The imagery of safety valve and furnace, together with that of the danger, destruction, and chaos of the Inferno, tends once again to collapse boundaries between Yellowstone and the industrial East and Midwest. Public discourse indicates that apart from the pleasures of Old Faithful, the Yellowstone visitors alighted at the geyser basin only to encounter a geophysical version of the very Inferno familiar to them from fictional and journalistic accounts of the material environment of industrial Eastern and upper Midwestern cities of the United States.

Just as Old Faithful provided reassurance about the health of the industrial order, so the erratic and frightening geyser basin was read as a geophysical text on sociocultural threats to the new industrial order. There is some evidence that such threat was perceived in bodily terms referent to industrial workers who occupy "t' Devil's place," workmen who are "bad" and "desperate" enough to be condemned to hell (Davis 20, 27). The heaving, spewing, violent, and capricious geysers and volcanoes replicate an industrializing scene periodically rife with social turmoil, including strikes and riots devolving from conditions of labor and wages. In this sense, the erratic, arrhythmic geysers are a homology of the bodies necessary to keep the industrial world in mechanistic synchrony, but which, at intervals, instead subvert its clockwork rhythms. One Homestead steelworker told Hamlin Garland in 1893, "The worst part of this whole business is this. It brutalizes a man" (Serrin 62). Such brutalized bodies, perhaps versions of the swarthy, sooty, muddy industrial laborers' bodies—as Davis termed them, "filthy and ash-covered. . . . coarse and vulgar"—threaten the clockwork pulse of the industrial order. As erratic geysers, they "pulsate in rhythmic beats from the mighty heart of internal chaos" (Davis 24, Townsend 163). In *Life in the Iron Mills* they are "boisterous," but at Yellowstone "infernally roiled enough to emit 'sighs, moans, and shrieks' " (Davis 26, Sedgwick 3573).

The sulphurous, heaving mud volcanoes, hissing steam vents, and explosive eruptions—in short, the Inferno—had a textual foreground, moreover, in the dire volcanic social vision recurrent in public discourse in the United States from the early nineteenth century and deeply engaged with the social body of nonelites. Political, religious, and educational figures had recurrently exploited volcanoes as a terrifying metaphor for the collapse of social order in the United States, as Fred Somkin has shown. Back in 1789, Fisher Ames of Massachusetts warned at a political convention that "a democracy is a volcano, which conceals the fiery materials of its own destruction" (24). In 1817, the *Columbian Orator* reprinted Yale president Timothy Dwight's description in *The Conquest of Canaan* of "a fiery Judgment Day marked by quaking, fire-belching mountains" (Somkin 39). The possibility that slavery or some other issue might prompt riotous rupture of the social order led Reverend Ephraim Peabody in 1846 to say that while "all may be smooth and fair on the surface," the "fires of a volcano are moving beneath the thin crust, and . . . in a moment they may burst through and lay the labors of centuries in ruins" (7). In 1855, the Reverend Richard Storrs voiced his fear that crime, slavery, vice, and Catholicism threatened the United States, which he feared slept "on the crater's edge" as "fiery floods threaten an overflow . . . more terrible than was felt by Pompeii or Herculaneum" (21). In a Fourth of July oration of 1842, Horace Mann speculated that the nation "is an active volcano of ignorance and guilt" (29).

The eruption of strikes and riots of the later nineteenth and early twentieth centuries also prompted description in volcanic terms. The "political and industrial battles" in Colorado, 1894–1904, for instance, led to the publication of a report from the U.S. Commissioner of Labor (1905): "The reading of that report leaves one with the impression that present-day society *rests upon a volcano* [italics mine], which in favorable periods seems very harmless, but, when certain elemental forces clash, it bursts forth in a manner that threatens with destruction civilization itself" (Hunter 303). Statements of this kind produce a volcanic social body correlative with the rumored western hell-on-earth at Yellowstone, and thus the nineteenth-century United States becomes a continuum of volcanic geopolitics, one to be continued in the 1930s Depression, when a Homestead, Pennsylvania, coronor and detective-turned-burgess, John Cavanaugh, observed that "the entire lower Monongahela Valley and Pittsburgh has been resting on a [communistic] smoldering volcano, which has been ready to burst out at any moment" (qtd. in Serrin 176).

Possibilities for sociocultural "volcanic" explosion apparently intensified with the availability of the new explosives invented by Alfred B. Nobel in 1866 and developed in the United States by the Du Pont Corporation and others. Nobel's work enabled production of a stable explosive in which nitroglycerine was mixed with an inert filler, such as sawdust, then pressed into paper cylinders and set off with a detonator. Used in construction, in mining, in civil engineering, it was lightweight and portable.

And like the explosive volcano, it served to express deep anxieties about hidden dangers of social disorder. Any*body* in possession of a stick of dynamite became a potential one-person volcano. Josiah Strong's best-selling social critique, *Our Country: Its Possible Future and Its Present Crisis* (1885), described as "social dynamite" the "largely foreign" male population of "roughs . . . lawless and desperate men of all sorts" (132). Strong's "social dynamite" gained credence the following year, when some of the eight anarchists found guilty of detonating the bomb that killed a policeman in Chicago's 1886 Haymarket Riot spoke in the language of explosive social change. August Spies declared, "From Jove's head has sprung a Minerva—dynamite!" Revolutions, he added, result from certain "causes and conditions . . . like earthquakes and cyclones" (*The Accused, the Accusers* 7, 8). One may recall the Yellowstone visitor anxious about the earth hot under her feet as Spies's speech warned that laboring wage slaves would rise in revolt: "Everywhere, flames will blaze up. It is a subterranean fire. You cannot put it out" (10). Spies's fellow anarchist Albert P. Parsons, who denied using dynamite to cause the Haymarket riot, nonetheless seized the term to declare its efficacy as "a democratic instrument" and was quoted by one alarmed author as citing the "splendid opportunity . . . for some bold fellow to make the capitalists tremble by blowing up [the Chicago Board of Trade] building and all the thieves and robbers that are there" (McLean 33).

The texts celebrating a clocklike Old Faithful and deploring the infernal adjoining geysers would seem authorially hostile to the notion of dynamiting buildings or otherwise altering the social order in incendiary ways. Such texts were not produced by those laboring twelve hours daily in dangerous, debilitating, low-paying toil, but by those sufficiently affluent to buy rail and coach seats to the Rockies, to stay at hotels or to camp in the Wylie Company's system of tents, beds, and meals with campfires at the rate of five dollars per day, to take leave of a primary residence for weeks at a time. These, and not the self-described wage-slave laborers with anarchist views, were the visitors poised to applaud Old Faithful.

And these were the visitors who shuddered when, unexpectedly, one or another of the other geysers "burst forth again without warning, and even greater violence," who saw eruptions "pulsate in rhythmic beats from the mighty heart of internal chaos" (Francis 35). For civil violence had abated but not ceased in the decades following the Civil War, as verified in such events as the deadly Great Railroad Strike of 1877 over the issue of hourly wages; the Haymarket Riot of 1886, which started over the eight-hour work day; the New Orleans race riots of 1866; the Homestead Strike of 1892; the Pullman Strike of 1894; the miners' strike at Coeur d'Alene, Idaho, in 1899; and the above-mentioned Colorado strikes and riots, 1894–1904—all of which seemed to nativists dangerously explosive. Add to these the actual explosives, from the bomb thrown into Chicago's Haymarket to the carload of dynamite detonated by striking miners to blow up the mine concentrator, an area where wastes were extracted from ores, at the Coeur d'Alene mine.

It is important to recognize that Yellowstone's visitors, camped with their own "wagons, tents, and provisions," their "coffee pot, frying pan and kettle," and "a buffalo robe to spread on a pile of fir, pine, or hemlock twigs, with blankets for covering, [that] makes a bed which renders that city pest, *insomnia*, an impossibility" (Logan 160)—that these very tourists looked to Old Faithful to help them keep faith in an industrializing nation which was built, some feared, on incendiary volcanic soil. Given their class position, the American body politic and the mechanistic body of the new industrial order must have seemed tenuous, contingent, and contested. Dr. Osler's Wall Street bodily engine, driven relentlessly, would wear out with aneurysms or cardiac failure at age fifty, "fit only to be scrapped," while Old Faithful itself could break rhythm or, like other geysers, go extinct. The "immense quantities of ashes and cinders thrown into the sky" and dimming the sun in "sulphurous clouds" could signal industrial progress and prosperity or, on the contrary, indicate cataclysmic destruction (Muir, *Our National Parks* 62). In the post-1870s decades, it was not at all clear

whether the America of the pulse of Old Faithful would become an enduring industrial-age Wonderland or manifest its long-term national, geopolitical identity as "a place where hell bubbles up."

To return to the familiar tropes of environmental bodies in American
literature, to Twain's incarnated Mississippi, Thoreau's pugilist Cape Cod,
F. Scott Fitzgerald's "fresh green breast" of the New World in *The Great
Gatsby* (1925), and so on, is to recognize that such figures can and do con-
duct cultural work far beyond the bodily topographic (Fitzgerald 182).
Critical inquiry discloses just how problematic is the incarnated "nature's
nation," which was Perry Miller's coinage in "Nature and the National
Ego" (1955) (208). "If there was such a thing as an American character,"
Miller had said in his analysis of national myth, "it took shape under the
molding influence" of a salutary natural world and the "impositions of geography" (210). In such reading, American geography is the active agent
in moral and ethical suasion, and environmental embodiment logically the
expression of moral ideals.

At the turn of the twenty-first century, of course, such a viewpoint is
idolatry. Environmental incarnations, instead, enable investigation of
characteriological complexities involving special interests, class positions,
congeries of conflicting and competing social pressures. Environmentally,
then, nature's nation shifts in function from shrine to deconstructive heuristic. It is perhaps fitting, then, that in the late 1990s, Old Faithful has itself
become erratic in its eruptions, its seventy-seven-minute average intervals
exceeding the pulse clock as geologists speculate that Yellowstone-area
earthquakes may be affecting geyser activity (Brooke). In irony fitting the
major modes of critical inquiry, Old Faithful has itself become a geologic
project of self-reflexive deconstruction.

NOTE

1. A succinct account of the exploration of the Yellowstone region and its development as a national park can be found in Sears 158–63.

WORKS CITED

The Accused, the Accusers: The Famous Speeches of the Eight Chicago Anarchists in Court.
   Chicago: Socialist Publishing Society, n.d.
Alger, Horatio. *Ragged Dick* and *Struggling Upward*. 1868, 1890. New York: Pen-
   guin, 1985.
Armstrong, Katherine. "Work Indoors and Out: The Flowers of Yellowstone Park."
   Independent 50, no. 2578 (May 1898): 562.

Banta, Martha. *Taylored Lives: Narrative Productions in the Age of Taylor, Veblen, and Ford.* Chicago and London: U of Chicago P, 1993.

Barwell, Richard. *On Aneurism: Especially of the Thorax and Root of the Neck.* London: Macmillan, 1880.

Beard, George M. *American Nervousness; Its Causes and Consequences, a Supplement to Nervous Exhaustion (Neurasthenia).* New York: W. Wood & Company, 1881.

Bierley, Paul. *John Philip Sousa: American Phenomenon.* Englewood Cliffs: Prentice-Hall, 1973.

———. *The Works of John Philip Sousa.* Westerville: Integrity P, 1984.

Bodner, John. *Remaking America: Public Memory, Commemoration, and Patriotism in the Twentieth Century.* Princeton: Princeton UP, 1992.

Brooke, James. "Time Trouble for Geyser: It's No Longer Old Faithful." *New York Times* February 6, 1996, natl. ed.: A6.

Burroughs, John. *Camping and Tramping with Roosevelt.* Boston: Houghton, Mifflin, 1907.

Clendening, Logan, ed. *Source Book of Medical History.* 1942. New York: Dover, 1960.

Comstock, Theodore B. "Engineering Relations of the Yellowstone Park." *American Journal of Science* November–December 1878: 460–61.

Corthell, N. E. "A Family Trek to the Yellowstone." *Independent* 58, no. 2952 (June 29, 1905): 1460–67.

Dale, Stephen M. "Through Yellowstone on a Coach." *Ladies Home Journal* 21, no. 9 (August 1904): 5–6.

Davis, Rebecca Harding. *Life in the Iron Mills.* Ed. Tillie Olsen. 1861. New York: Feminist P, 1972.

"Editor's Study." *Harper's New Monthly Magazine* 94, no. 560 (January 1897): 320–25.

Emerson, Ralph Waldo. "The American Scholar." *Selections from Ralph Waldo Emerson.* Ed. Stephen E. Wicher. Cambridge: Houghton Mifflin, 1957. 63–80.

———. *Natural History of Intellect.* Boston and New York: Houghton Mifflin, 1904.

———. *Society and Solitude.* 1870. *The Complete Works of Ralph Waldo Emerson.* Vol. 6. Boston and London: Houghton Mifflin, 1912.

Fitzgerald, F. Scott. *The Great Gatsby.* 1925. New York: Scribner, 1953.

Francis, Fr. "The Yellowstone Geysers." *Little's Living Age* 153 (5th ser., vol. 38), no. 1972 (April 8, 1882): 31–36.

Glazier, Willard. *Peculiarities of American Cities.* Philadelphia: Hubbard Brothers, 1883.

Hague, Arnold. "Age of Igneous Rocks of the Yellowstone." *American Journal of Science* June 1896: 445–56.

———. "The Yellowstone National Park." *Scribner's Magazine* May 1904: 513–27.

Hales, Peter. *William Henry Jackson and the Transformation of the American Landscape.* Philadelphia: Temple UP, 1988.

Hayden, F. W. "The Hot Springs and Geysers of the Yellowstone and Firehole Rivers." *American Journal of Science and the Arts,* 3d ser., 3, no. 15 (March 1872): 161–76.

———. "The Yellowstone National Park." *American Journal of Science and the Arts,* 3d ser., 3, no. 16 (April 1872): 294–97.

Henderson, C. Hanford. "Through the Yellowstone on Foot." *Outing* 34, no. 2 (May 1899): 161–67.

Hunter, Robert. *Violence and the Labor Movement*. New York: Macmillan, 1922.

Jagger, T. A. "Some Conditions Affecting Geyser Eruption." *American Journal of Science*. 4th ser., 5, no. 29 (May 1898): 323–33.

Jehlen, Myra. *American Incarnation: The Individual, the Nation, the Continent*. Cambridge: Harvard UP, 1986.

King, Frank B. "In Nature's Laboratory: Driving and Fishing in Yellowstone Park." *Overland Monthly*, 2d ser., 1, no. 174 (June 1897): 594–603.

Kinsey, Joni Louise. *Thomas Moran and the Surveying of the American West*. Washington, D.C., and London: Smithsonian Institution P, 1992.

Koch, J. "Discovery of the Yellowstone National Park." *Magazine of American History* 11, no. 6 (June 1884): 497–512.

Kolodny, Annette. *The Lay of the Land: Metaphor as Experience and History in American Life and Letters*. Chapel Hill: U of North Carolina P, 1975.

Langford, Nathaniel P. "The Folsom-Cook Exploration of the Upper Yellowstone in the Year 1869." *Contributions to the Historical Society of Montana* 5 (1904): 349–69.

Lawton-Peebles, Robert. *Landscape and Written Expression in Revolutionary America*. New York: Cambridge UP, 1988.

Le Conte, Joseph. "Geysers and How They Are Explained." *Popular Science Monthly* 12, no. 6 (1878): 401–17.

Logan, Mrs. John A. *The Home Manual: Everybody's Guide in Social, Domestic, and Business Life*. Chicago: H. J. Smith, 1889.

Mackenzie, James. *The Study of the Pulse, Arterial, Venous, and Hepatic, and of the Movements of the Heart*. New York: Macmillan, 1902.

McKinsey, Elizabeth. *Niagara Falls: Icon of the American Sublime*. New York: Cambridge UP, 1985.

McLean, George N. *The Rise and Fall of Anarchy in America*. Chicago and Philadelphia: R. G. Badoux, 1888.

Mann, Horace. *An Oration, Delivered before the Authorities of the City of Boston, July 4, 1842*. Boston, 1842.

Miller, Perry. "Nature and the National Ego." *Errand into the Wilderness*. Cambridge: Harvard UP, 1956.

Mitchell, S. Weir. "Through the Yellowstone Park to Fort Custer." *Lippincott's Magazine of Popular Literature and Science* 25 (June 1880): 688–704.

Muir, John. *Our National Parks*. 1901. Madison: University of Wisconsin P, 1981.

———. "The Wild Parks and Forests of the West." *Atlantic Monthly* 81, no. 483 (January 1898): 15–28.

Osler, William. *The Principles and Practice of Medicine*. New York: D. Appleton & Co., 1895.

———. *William Osler's Collected Papers on the Cardiovascular System*. Ed. with introd. by W. Bruce Fye. Birmingham: University of Alabama P, 1985.

Owen, W. O. "The First Bicycle Tour of the Yellowstone Park." *Outing* 16, no. 3 (June 1891): 191–95.

Peabody, Ephraim. *A Sermon Delivered before the Boston Fraternity of Churches, April 2, 1846*. Boston, 1846.

Practical Guide to Yellowstone National Park, Containing Illustrations, Maps, Distances, Altitudes, and Geyser Time Tables. St. Paul: F. Jay Haynes, 1890.

Rollins, Alice Wellington. "The Three Tetons." *Harper's New Monthly Magazine* 74, no. 444 (May 1887): 869–90.

Schlereth, Thomas J. *Victorian America: Transformations in Everyday Life, 1876–1915.* New York: HarperCollins, 1991.

Schmeckebier, L. F. "Our National Parks." *National Geographic Magazine* 23, no. 6 (June 1912): 531–39.

Sears, John F. *Sacred Places: American Tourist Attractions in the Nineteenth Century.* New York: Oxford UP, 1989.

Sedgwick, Henry D. "On Horseback through the Yellowstone." *The World's Work* June 1903: 3569–76.

Seltzer, Mark. *Bodies and Machines.* New York: Routledge, 1992.

Serrin, William. *Homestead: The Glory and Tragedy of an American Steel Town.* New York: Vintage, 1993.

Sessions, Francis C. "The Yellowstone Park." *Magazine of Western History* 6, no. 5 (September 1887): 433–45.

Somkin, Fred. *Unquiet Eagle: Memory and Desire in the Idea of American Freedom, 1815–1860.* Ithaca: Cornell UP, 1967.

Sousa, John Philip. *Marching Along: Recollections of Men, Women, and Music.* Introd. by Paul Bierley. 1928. Rev. ed. Westerville: Integrity P, 1994.

Storrs, Richard. *Home Missions: As Connected with Christ's Dominion.* New York, 1855.

Strong, Josiah. *Our Country: Its Possible Future and Its Present Crisis.* New York: The American Home Missionary Society, 1885.

Tarr, Ralph S. "Geology of the Yellowstone Park," I and II *Independent* 50, nos. 2607 and 2609 (November 17 and December 1, 1898): 1406–8, 1572–76.

Thoreau, Henry David. *Thoreau.* New York: Library of America, 1985.

Townsend, Mary Trowbridge. "A Woman's Trout-Fishing in Yellowstone Park." *Outing* 30, no. 2 (May 1897): 163–65.

Trachtenberg, Alan. *Reading American Photographs: Images as History, Matthew Brady to Walker Evans.* New York: Hill and Wang, 1989.

Turner, Frederick Jackson. *The Frontier in American History.* 1920. Reprint. New York: Dover, 1996.

Turner, Victor and Edith. *Image and Pilgrimage in Christian Culture.* New York: Columbia UP, 1978.

Twain, Mark. *Life on the Mississippi.* 1883. New York: Penguin, 1984.

"The Washburn Yellowstone Expedition, Nos. 1 and 2." *Overland Monthly* 6, nos. 5 and 6 (May and June 1871): 431–37, 489–96.

Weed, Walter. "Fossil Forests of the Yellowstone." *School of Mines Quarterly* 13, no. 3 (April 1892): 230–36.

———. "Geysers." *School of Mines Quarterly* 11, no. 4 (July 1890): 289–306.

Wilkinson, Norman B. *Lammot Du Pont and the American Explosives Industry, 1850–1884.* Charlottesville: U of Virginia P, 1984.

"Yellowstone Park as a Summer Resort." *Nation* 71, no. 1839 (September 27, 1900): 248–50.

CHAPTER 4

Melville, Garibaldi, and the Medusa of Revolution

DENNIS BERTHOLD

> To rightfully appreciate this, or, in fact, any other
> statue, one must consider where they came from
> and under what circumstances they were formed.
> In other respects they reveal their own history.
> *(Herman Melville, "Statues in Rome")*

IN Washington Square, just across the park from New York University, stands an enormous statue of Giuseppe Garibaldi (1807–82), leader of the Risorgimento, Italy's 1814–71 struggle for unity and independence from foreign domination. Buried in an unpublished poem by Herman Melville, a New Yorker who lived about twenty blocks from the statue, lies a tribute to Garibaldi, a complexly allusive verbal portrait ignored by most critics and misunderstood even by specialists on Melville's late poetry. The statue was erected in 1888, three years before Melville's death; the two-part poem—"At the Hostelry" and "Naples in the Time of Bomba," which I refer to as Melville's "Neapolitan diptych"—was probably written in the mid-1870s and was certainly revised as late as 1882, for it concludes with Garibaldi's death that year. This juxtaposition of public icon and private utterance locates Melville's political views within the context of Americans' enthusiastic support for Garibaldi and the Risorgimento, a phenomenon evident in the works of William Cullen Bryant, Henry Wadsworth Long-fellow, John Greenleaf Whittier, James Russell Lowell, and Margaret Fuller, as well as many travelers to Italy, but never linked to Melville (Marraro, *American Opinion* and "American Travelers"; Peterson). Like these writers, Melville viewed Garibaldi through the popular metaphors and iconography of his time; unlike them, he saw in Garibaldi a signifier of fundamental political and philosophical paradoxes endemic to a century of revolution and civil war. For Melville, Garibaldi was more a product of his time than a shaper of it.

As iconographic construct Garibaldi grounds Melville's view of history, politics, and art in a cultural materialism that mediates one of the most vexing polarities in Melville criticism: between critics such as Wai-Chee

Dimock, James Duban, Stanton Garner, and Larry Reynolds, who stress Melville's authoritarian impulses, and those such as Marvin Fisher, Carolyn Karcher, and Nancy Fredricks, who emphasize his egalitarianism. This conflict, I suggest, was not abstract for Melville or his age; rather, it was integral to a period when Jacksonian democracy confronted civil wars at home and abroad, a time when the virtues of expanding personal freedom were being daily tested against increasing threats to social order. Like Michael Paul Rogin, who finds evidence of Melville's shift away from democratic idealism imaged in the iron dome of the Capitol, the badge of the Society of the Cincinnati, and Vere's navy buttons, I see a Melville who seeks visual analogues to represent his complex and shifting ideology. Political cartoons, magazine illustrations, and eventually civic statuary provided Melville with a popular iconography that presented Garibaldi as an image of anarchy coexisting with authority, a concrete manifestation of the ideological ambiguities that pervade Melville's fiction, undergird the Neapolitan diptych, and culminate in *Billy Budd*. But instead of polarizing debate, such iconography reifies it in images that represent the complexities, paradoxes, and outright contradictions that characterize all attempts to reduce experience and emotion to rigid political doctrines. Coming to prominence in an increasingly visually mediated age, Garibaldi became a living icon of the bewildering complexity of history, a case study of the reciprocal influence of individual purpose, political idealism, and blind historical event. Garibaldi showed how tyranny could merge with magnanimity in one person, how authority and freedom might be two sides of the same coin, how violence might be necessary to ensure peace. So while these paradoxes riddle current debates about Melville's political views, they are far from being the creation of ideologically driven scholars; rather, they were the blood and marrow of nineteenth-century debates about the Risorgimento and Garibaldi, its most charismatic figure.

THE CULT OF GARIBALDI

Garibaldi was first introduced to the American public in Margaret Fuller's dispatches to the New York *Tribune* in 1849, when he courageously but unsuccessfully defended the fledgling Roman Republic from the French. Defeated and forced into exile, he arrived in New York City on July 30, 1850, and spent the winter as a tallow chandler on Staten Island (Mack Smith 46–51), a far cry from his world-shaking role as enemy of the pope and defender of Rome. Although praised by Horace Greeley as one "known the world over as the hero of Montevideo and the defender of the Roman Republic" (qtd. in Mitgang 36), Garibaldi found no role to play in American life and soon left New York to resume his old career as a sailor. By

Fig. 4.1. Giuseppe Garibaldi. Frontispiece to *Democratic Review* 31, no. 171 (September 1852). Photographic Services, Texas A&M U.

1854 the political situation in Italy had calmed down enough for him to return home, leaving behind a secure reputation with American liberals and republican sympathizers. After Mazzini, Garibaldi was probably the best-known, most admired Italian to emerge from the revolutions of 1848. In perhaps the first portrait of him published in America, a frontispiece for the September 1852 *Democratic Review*, Garibaldi appears plainly dressed in nonmilitary garb, a simple and straightforward man of the people implicitly contrasted to the splendors of aristocracy (fig. 4.1). Although the accompanying article devoted only a page or two to Garibaldi, it presented him in terms guaranteed to appeal to the American public: "The type of his character is antique, and belongs rather to one of Plutarch's heroes as Plutarch has painted them, than to any which our own times or the Middle Ages offer" ("Second Campaign" 313). Safely cloaking Garibaldi in the garb of Roman idealism, much as the sculptor Horatio Greenough had reconceived Washington as a Roman tribune, the *Democratic Review* muted

Garibaldi's revolutionary ideology and enveloped him with the nostalgic aura of classical heroism. Melville, whose own reading of Plutarch influenced his conception of Roman history, drew on such popular associations in "At the Hostelry" when he painted Garibaldi as one of "Plutarch's men" (Sandberg, "Melville's Unfinished Book" 43). Such traditionary allusions distinguished Garibaldi from the radical intellectual Mazzini, whose continuing support of socialist revolution undermined his appeal to Americans (Rossi 101–7).

Political necessity more than individual will precipitated Garibaldi's ascent into the American consciousness and modified his ideology to make him even more appealing to a country teetering on the brink of civil war. In 1858, prime minister Count Camillo Benso di Cavour (1810–61) of Piedmont-Sardinia, a strict constitutionalist and monarchist who nevertheless advocated Italian unity, recruited Garibaldi to the banner of King Victor Emanuel II, presenting the revolutionary with a pragmatic middle way between papal conservatives and Mazzinian republicans. Garibaldi willingly subordinated his republicanism to the greater cause of unity and independence, disavowed Mazzini, and pledged his support to the king (Mack Smith 54). With the support of Napoleon III, a combined French-Piedmontese army invaded Lombardy in April 1859. Garibaldi commanded the romantic Cacciatori delle Alpi, a daring cavalry of irregulars who swooped out of the mountains to harass the Austrians from the rear while traditional warfare continued on the plains. By placing patriotism before politics, Garibaldi conformed to American ideologies and increased his stature in the United States, as an article in Melville's local weekly, the Berkshire County *Eagle*, asserted: "It is, by the way, a curious fact that this same Garibaldi, who fought so bravely against the French some ten years ago, would now be enlisted in the very cause to which they are so great a support; and it proves that Garibaldi is no ranting Red Republican, but can lay aside all personal prejudices, and really and patriotically devote himself to the great cause of Italian amelioration and liberty—a cause in behalf of which Louis Napoleon and the French seem now to be powerful instruments" ("Who is Garabaldi [*sic*]?"). Pragmatic yet principled, selfless yet individualistic, a revolutionary in the service of a monarch, Garibaldi represented the ideological paradoxes at the core of an America striving for national unity yet riven with increasing sectionalism, an America on the eve of its own civil war.

American newspapers followed the Italian war closely, and the new illustrated journals thrived on publishing engravings of battle scenes, officers in full military regalia, and charts of military movements. *Harper's Weekly*, one of Melville's favorite magazines, offered detailed analyses of the conflict every week and even printed three folio-sized maps of northern Italy so readers could better follow military maneuvers (May 28, July 9, and July 30, 1859). Melville's local newspapers, the Pittsfield *Sun* and the Berkshire

County *Eagle*, unabashedly supported the king and Garibaldi. The *Sun* of
May 12 reminded readers of "the evils under which Italy was suffering from
foreign despotism, ecclesiastical thraldom, and the tyranny of domestic
rulers," specifically Austria, the pope, and the king of Naples ("Exciting
War News"), and on June 3 the *Eagle* printed William Cullen Bryant's
attack on Austrian perfidy. Nor were Italy's French allies to be entirely
trusted. Although Napoleon III argued that he aided Sardinia only "to
restore to freedom one of the finest parts of Europe" ("Three Days Later"),
Senator Charles Sumner, who supported the revolution (Marraro, *American Opinion* 289, 302), expressed highly qualified confidence in the emperor
in the July 1 *Eagle* ("Senator Sumner"). In this highly charged political
atmosphere, Melville wrote a poem on July 6 inviting his lawyer friend
Daniel Shepherd to Arrowhead:

> Come, Daniel, come and visit me:
> I'm lost in many a quandary:
> I've dreamed, like Bab'lon's Majesty:
> Prophet, come expound for me.
> —I dreamed I saw a laurel grove,
> Claimed for his by the bird of Jove,
> Who, elate with such dominion,
> Oft cuffed the boughs with haughty pinion.
> Indignantly the trees complain,
> Accusing his afflictive reign.
> Their plaints the chivalry excite
> Of chanticleers, a plucky host:
> They battle with the bird of light.
> Beaten, he wings his Northward flight,
> No more his laurel realm to boast,
> Where now, to crow, the cocks alight,
> And—break down all the branches quite!
> Such a weight of friendship pure
> The grateful trees could not endure;
> This dream, it still disturbeth me:
> Seer, foreshows it Italy?

(Writings 14:337–38)

In their allusive precision these lines reveal Melville's detailed understanding of Italian politics. Framed as a dream-allegory, the poem questions
Napoleon III's motives and implies that French domination may follow
Italian independence. The "bird of Jove" is Austria's double eagle, the
"chanticleers" represent the French, and the laurel branches are the Italian
states.[1] As much as Italy needs rescuing, Melville wonders whether its "laurel grove" can sustain the weight of French "friendship," a burdensome
bond that contrasts sharply with the convivial relationship the poet envis-

ages with Shepherd. Melville shares Sumner's distrust of Napoleon III and asks whether Italy may simply be trading one foreign ruler for another. Prophetically, Melville wrote the poem the same day Napoleon asked Franz Joseph of Austria for a truce, an act that betrayed the Italian cause and led to the notorious Treaty of Villafranca which allowed Austria to remain in parts of northern Italy. Melville's prescience indicates a keen understanding of European politics and Louis Napoleon's strategies. He knew that expressions of friendship from the lips of a Napoleon meant little, for, unlike the enlightened rulers he later praised in "The Age of the Antonines," modern emperors will sacrifice noble ideals (the "laurel" that wreathes Italy's separate states) to political expediency—here, Napoleon's fear of republics. Constitutional authority depends on the character of its executives, and Napoleon III, as Sumner suspected, was more concerned with self-preservation than principle.

In this cynical atmosphere, Garibaldi emerged in the American press as the only man of integrity, one who refused mendacious treaties and stayed true to his vision of a united Italy. In 1860, with the king's covert support and over the objections of Cavour, Garibaldi undertook the most famous and daring military action of his career. Almost single-handedly, he carried the war into the south. Ferdinand II, "King Bomba," had died in 1859, and his son, Francis II, now sat on the unsteady throne of the Kingdom of the Two Sicilies. Boldly leading a red-shirted legion of some 1,100 men— "Garibaldi's Thousand"—and vastly outnumbered by the Neapolitan armies, Garibaldi quickly took Palermo and proclaimed himself dictator of Sicily. Within weeks he crossed the Straits of Messina and stormed up the Calabrian coast ahead of his legion into Naples, meeting little resistance and wide popular acclaim. Without firing a shot he entered the city by the new railroad to the cheers of the Neapolitan army. Francis II fled to Gaeta, a nearby coastal fortress, and Naples, for the first time in centuries, was free of Bourbon monarchy. After consolidating his triumph at Volturno Garibaldi united forces with the Piedmontese army and, in the defining act of his life, handed over his conquered territories to the king, a gesture of astonishing fealty that earned him a permanent reputation for selflessness and magnanimity. He returned to Caprera and resumed his life as a simple farmer (Mack Smith 111), coupling military fame and pastoralism in the best tradition of ancient Rome.

After the fall of Naples in 1860 Garibaldi was the best-known leader of the Risorgimento in the world. Newspapers reported his every move, periodicals embellished their pages with engravings of his colorful troops, scholars translated his memoirs, and journalists wrote fawning hagiographies. When he visited London in 1864, a half million people lined the streets to see him in an outburst of "Garibaldi-mania" (Viotti 147). His image was everywhere, on tins of Virginia tobacco and bottles of perfume, a picture of a soldier with piercing blue eyes, a gentle smile, a thick beard, long hair,

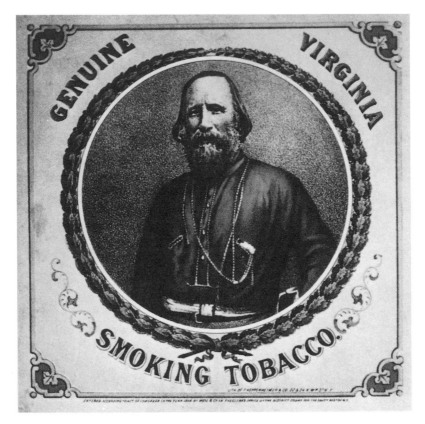

Fig. 4.2. Garibaldi's image on tin of Virginia smoking tobacco (no date). Reproduced from *American Heritage* 26, no. 6 (October 1975), back cover, by permission. Original in Library of Congress.

and square shoulders, dressed in a brilliant red shirt (fig. 4.2). As the most romantic military hero of the day, he and his exploits inspired poetry by Elizabeth Barrett Browning and Walter Savage Landor, as well as Whittier, Lowell, and Longfellow (Peterson). After 1859 his fame spread so rapidly that by early 1861 the *Christian Examiner* asked, "Garibaldi—who has not heard of him? Who does not feel interested in his success? Who but wishes to know something more about him than what is reported in newspapers?" (Torricelli 110).

The American press eagerly shaped Garibaldi's legend to fit the contours of national ideology. Theodore Dwight rushed into print his translation of Garibaldi's memoirs (1859) and argued that the Italian cause was providentially designed to fulfill "some of the most glorious prophesies and promises recorded in the Bible, especially in overturning popery" (9). Such a typol-

GARIBALDI.

Fig. 4.3. Frontispiece to Orville J. Victor, *The Life of Joseph Garibaldi, the Liberator of Italy* (1860). Author's photograph.

ogy effectively enlisted Garibaldi as a New World enemy of the Antichrist and satisfied any latent Protestant fears of unwittingly supporting a nominal Catholic. The Beadle Publishing Company initiated its "Dime Biographical Library" with Orville J. Victor's *The Life of Joseph Garibaldi, The Liberator of Italy* (1860) (frontispiece shown as fig. 4.3) and advertised the book as "Garibaldi, the Washington of Italy," a catchphrase repeated frequently in popular journals (see *Harper's Weekly*). Victor claimed that Garibaldi was of noble descent (9–10n) and compared him favorably to Roman generals (70), Napoleon Bonaparte (81), Saint Paul, Martin Luther, Cromwell, and Washington (92). Like them, he was "the representative man" who carried out "the purposes of Divinity itself" (97) in the service of a cause ordained by Providence (61). *Harper's Weekly* devoted its June 9 and November 17, 1860, covers to full-length engravings of the general, first showing him astride a white horse leading men into battle, then portraying his head only, an image of a calm and controlled man in simple military garb. Periodicals extended the Americanization of Garibaldi by describing him in Protestant and Jacksonian tropes that merged him into the American vision of historical progress. Writing for the conservative *North American Review*, Melville's friend Henry T. Tuckerman characterized Garibaldi as "one of Nature's noblemen" (35), a phrase formerly reserved for Andrew Jackson. And J. B. Torricelli, reviewing five French and Italian books on Garibaldi for the *Christian Examiner*, affirmed the millennialist strain: Garibaldi is *"predestined* to be the deliverer of Italy, the messenger of the Almighty to whom the commission was given to prepare his own countrymen for a new life" (137).

Of equal importance with his military successes was Garibaldi's return to his farm on Caprera. Such a repudiation of power, like George Washington's, recalled the legendary Roman hero Cincinnatus who was called from his fields to lead the Roman army. After defeating the foe he returned to the plow, preferring agrarian peace to military conquest. A central trope in the press, this comparison sanitized the revolutionary socialist Garibaldi for emergent American capitalism. *Littell's Living Age* reprinted a British assessment that portrayed Garibaldi as "another Cincinnatus" whose "chief glory is, that, being a ringleader of rebels, he is the servant of order" ("The Sicilian Game" 737, 736). Orville Victor considered Garibaldi's renunciation of dictatorship even greater than Washington's refusal of a crown: "George Washington, retiring from his power as commander-in-chief of the American army, to his farm at Mount Vernon, glad to return to the quiet of home, was an act [*sic*] of great moral sublimity: but that of Garibaldi far transcends it" (101). "Cincinnatus," Garry Wills has argued, "was an icon meant by the Enlightenment to *replace* churchly saints with a resolutely secular ideal" (23), an aim that targeted perfectly both Washington and Garibaldi. For Americans who fancied their own republic a second Rome, Garibaldi provided one more link in a typological chain that extended back through Washington and the Pilgrims to ancient Rome and consecrated America's rebellious spirit with the halo of providential order.

Whatever the reality of his politics, the Garibaldi represented to the American public was neither a Mazzinian social democrat nor a slavish monarchist. Such balance gave him admirers from across the American political spectrum. Longfellow covertly compared him to a volcanic Titan in the poem "Enceladus" (1859), while the more radical Whittier, long a supporter of the Risorgimento, apostrophized him as "God's prophet" in the poem "Garibaldi" (ca. 1869; Peterson 239, 235). Even the splenetic Henry Adams rushed from Rome to Palermo to witness the triumph of the Thousand and admiringly described Garibaldi as a "compound nature of patriot and pirate" who "illumined Italian history from the beginning" (95). "At that moment, in the summer of 1860," Adams continued, "Garibaldi was certainly the most serious of the doubtful energies in the world; the most essential to gauge rightly" (94). This was precisely the kind of energy that Abraham Lincoln sought to enlist when he offered Garibaldi the post of major general in the Union army in June 1861, a two-star rank equivalent to that of George B. McClellan, the highest-ranking officer of the time. Although Garibaldi finally declined the appointment, partly because he refused to fight unless Lincoln immediately emancipated the slaves, his name became indelibly associated with the Union cause. A New York regiment of enthusiastic émigrés marched to war as "The Garibaldi Guard" (*Rebellion Record* 306), and at the New York Metropolitan Fair in 1864, an enormous benefit for the Union cause, one could buy an autograph of Washington, John Hancock, Louis Kossuth—and Garibaldi (Garner 297). From Lincoln down, Garibaldi represented a force for unity and national identity that Americans in 1861 desperately needed and revered.

Melville understood this conflation of cultural values—the intersection of American and Italian history that Garibaldi represented—and as he turned to poetry during and after the Civil War, he found in these parallels a rich resource for understanding present conflicts in American society. The discourse of Risorgimento politics runs through both *Battle-Pieces* (1866) and *Clarel* (1876), connecting those works' personal meditations on art, politics, and religion with the typologies and iconography of Italian and Roman history. The poems that best depict and dissect the modern legend of Garibaldi, however, remained in manuscript until long after Melville's death in 1891.

THE NEAPOLITAN DIPTYCH

"At the Hostelry" and "Naples in the Time of Bomba" are two long poems composed as part of Melville's abortive Burgundy Club project. Although Melville never published any of this material, it has been included in the Melville canon in one form or another since 1924, and textual scholars have thoroughly, if inconclusively, debated its structure, intent, and dates of composition.[2] Melville spent at least twenty-five years creating and revising these poems. He could have begun "Naples in the Time of Bomba" as early as 1857 and certainly tinkered with it as late as 1882, for it concludes with Garibaldi's state funeral. There is good reason for viewing the poems as the product of Melville's final years, perhaps even the late 1880s, after the spate of reverential obituaries for Garibaldi and during the period when journalists began to assess Garibaldi's romantic career more judiciously. Just as America maintained its obsession with Garibaldi during these years, so Melville periodically returned to his Neapolitan poems as events unfolded, expanding and revising his art in reaction to history, letting events lead his imagination back to the question of Italy and the charismatic figure of Garibaldi.

Of the two poems' 1,428 lines, approximately 200 allude to Garibaldi, Cavour, and the Risorgimento. Garibaldi allusions occur in three places: the beginning and end of the first poem and the end of the second poem. They thus frame the entire diptych and provide a link between the two parts. A different persona narrates each poem, and the topics shift uneasily between history, politics, and art, as other voices intrude to complicate the issue of authorial presence with what Robert Sandberg calls an "adjustment of screens." Allusions to Garibaldi connect every voice, however, and offer differing perspectives on this complex hero. "At the Hostelry," narrated by the Marquis de Grandvin, begins with 100 lines recounting Garibaldi's victories in Sicily and the annexations leading up to Rome's incorporation into Italy in 1870; it concludes with a biographical reminiscence of Garibaldi's days on Staten Island. Thickly sandwiched in between is a long debate on the merits of the "picturesque," dramatized in the voices of thirty "Old Masters" such as Jan Steen, Adrian Brouwer, William Van de Velde, Tintoretto, Rubens, and Paolo Veronese. "Naples in the Time of Bomba," narrated by Major Jack Gentian, recounts the major's entry into Naples during the last years of Ferdinand II's reign and draws heavily on Melville's own experiences during his 1857 visit to Naples (Poole 71n). The poem interfuses these scenes with disturbing recollections of Neapolitan history, including some of its darkest moments. Then, in a surprising turn, it concludes with an elegy for Garibaldi. Garibaldi, as historical figure and poetic symbol, provides the strongest unifying motif in a seemingly fragmented, even discordant pair of poems.

"At the Hostelry" opens with a rush of details that authoritatively demonstrates Melville's familiarity with popular representations of Garibaldi's finest moment—the conquest of Sicily and Naples in 1860. A cartoon in the July 7, 1860, *Harper's Weekly*, published while Melville was at sea, anticipates the poem's opening metaphor by depicting Garibaldi as a "Modern Perseus" rescuing Sicily-Andromeda from "Bomba Junior," caricatured as a grotesque sea monster (fig. 4.4). "At the Hostelry" applies this iconography to Garibaldi's liberation of Naples, a city

GARIBALDI THE LIBERATOR; or, The Modern Perseus.

Fig. 4.4. *Harper's Weekly* July 7, 1860, 432. Photographic Services, Texas A&M U.

> long in chains
> Exposed dishevelled by the sea—
> Ah, so much more her beauty drew,
> Till Savoy's red-shirt Perseus flew
> And cut that fair Andromeda free.

(79; 1.10–14)

Fig. 4.5. Guido Reni, *Perseus and Andromeda* (1635–36). Galleria Pallavicini Rospigliosi, Rome, Italy. Courtesy Alinari/Art Resource, New York.

This cartoon appropriated classical iconography well known to Melville. In chapter 55 of *Moby-Dick*, Ishmael refers to two traditional depictions of Perseus rescuing Andromeda, one by Guido Reni and one by William Hogarth (*Writings* 6:261).[3] Melville's familiarity with this iconography suggests that he would have noticed the *Harper's* cartoon. But he also would have noticed the cartoon's departure from tradition, alterations in the traditional iconography that increase the ambiguity of Garibaldi's military exploits. In Guido's painting (fig. 4.5), Perseus descends astride Pegasus, brandishing a sword in a recognizable pose of military valor, like Victor's frontispiece (fig. 4.3); in contrast, Hogarth's Perseus (fig. 4.6), unquestionably supernatural and mythic, flies through the air unaided, holding the

Fig. 4.6. William Hogarth, *Perseus Rescuing Andromeda*. Engraving from Lewis Theobald's *Perseus and Andromeda: A Verse Drama* (1730). Courtesy of The Kendall Whaling Museum, Sharon, Massachusetts, USA.

head of Medusa. The cartoon changes these representations in several important ways. It eliminates Pegasus and gives his wings to Garibaldi, angelizing him and reinforcing his moral distance from the sea monster, now transformed into Francis II, the misshapen prince of hell.[4] It gives Garibaldi a spear, linking him with Saint George as well as Perseus, a common archetypal comparison that Melville used in *Moby-Dick* and one that further sanctifies Garibaldi's efforts (see *Moby-Dick* chap. 82; *Writings*

6:363). Importantly, Andromeda wears clothes, lessening her sexuality; Medusa's disappearance eliminates the chief sign of Perseus's violence; and Garibaldi wears a Roman uniform, which places him in the service of the state. The cartoon's alterations conform the story of Perseus and Andromeda to American ideology by validating accepted gender roles and obsessions with empire while eliding disruption, anarchy, and "Red Republicanism." They are iconographic euphemisms, calculated changes designed to obscure the brutality behind the Perseus myth and the radical politics of Garibaldi.

Seductive as such iconographic euphemisms are, Melville's poem resists them by leavening mythical representations with biographical details in order to subvert simpleminded notions of heroism. Immediately after the allusion to Perseus and Andromeda, the poem turns toward the facts of Garibaldi's life. Recalling popular descriptions of Garibaldi, the poem calls him "The banished Bullock from the Pampas" (79; 1.23) and a "red Taurus plunging on" (79; 1.29), metaphors that combine New World and Old, Garibaldi's life in Argentina with the ancient practice of astrology. More mundane historical facts follow, as Garibaldi arrives in Naples by rail, not on a white horse, just after his foe "King Fanny" has ignominiously packed his bags and fled to Gaeta. Garibaldi blends linear and cyclic patterns of history as an apostle of unpredictable change, a mixture of ancient myth and commonplace modern reality.[5] All his life he had been dogged by charges of rashness, impetuousness, and unnecessary risk taking, characteristics that Melville's taurine metaphor captures well. Yet these were also the source of his admired boldness, a daring comparable to the courage of classic heroes from Greece, Rome, or the Middle Ages. Meanwhile, the obscure detail of his entering Naples on a train—it was the first railway in Italy—links Garibaldi with the mechanical order that would soon dominate Europe and America and threaten the ancient ideals Garibaldi popularly represented.

Melville thus participates in "Garibaldi-mania" mainly to deconstruct it. He analyzes the process of modern image making even as he limns Garibaldi's larger significance. For example, after the liberation of Naples, Garibaldi's name shines in the "halls of history" (80; 1.36) as

> one who in no paladin age
> Was knightly—him who lends a page
> Now signal in time's recent story
> Where scarce in vogue are "Plutarch's men,"
> And jobbers deal in popular glory.
>
> (80; 1.40–44)

Even while these lines criticize newspapers' inflated rhetoric, they echo Garibaldi's obituaries. E. L. Godkin made virtually the same point as Melville, praising Garibaldi's "heroism of the antique type, the simple type which Plutarch has painted, but the reproduction of which in our time the newspapers are making less and less possible, because its largest element was its unconsciousness, and the modern hero finds it difficult to be unconscious" (477). A. V. Dicey saw knightly valor succumbing to utilitarian warfare, where mechanized armies, steel ships, and growing imperialism left no room for the "romance and generosity" of a Garibaldi (541–42). And the New York *Tribune* considered Garibaldi "the last heroic figure in Italian history" ("Necrology" xv). A revolutionary hero cloaked in classic Roman virtue, Garibaldi is one of Melville's "kingly commons," perhaps the last of his kind, a hero whose unquestioned merit reveals the shallowness of contemporary "popular glory." Yet he is also a product of the "jobbers," a simple man elevated into living legend for the entertainment of newspaper readers and commodified as "picturesque" by well-intentioned writers like Fuller, Dwight, Tuckerman, and even the percipient Adams. Whether wearing the regalia of the gaucho or that of the Roman legion, Garibaldi is one of Godkin's self-conscious modern heroes, as much a construct of his time as a force shaping it. The "popular glory" that surrounds him parallels the process Melville complained about in a late letter: "This species of 'fame' a waggish acquaintance says can be manufactured to order, and sometimes is so manufactured thro the agency of a certain house that has a correspondent in every one of the almost innumerable journals that enlighten our millions from the Lakes to the Gulf & from the Atlantic to the Pacific" (*Writings* 14:492–93; Leyda 795).

As an icon of modern heroism, Garibaldi runs the risk of being absorbed by a greedy and commercial age of increasing utilitarianism and capitalism. The Marquis de Grandvin, ever practical, realizes that some loss of heroic stature inevitably follows fame. Revolutionary idealism must give way to practical diplomacy in order to make Italy "A unit and a telling State / Participant in the world's debate" (80; 1.65–66), the Marquis says. The greater good may now be better served by a canny politician like Cavour: "Few deeds of arms, in fruitful end / The statecraft of Cavour transcend" (80; 1.67–68). With the successive incorporation of Florence, Ancona, Venice, and finally Rome into a unified republic, presided over by Turin (the capital of Piedmont), Italy's leaders must turn their attention to practical matters:

> Swart Tiber, dredged, may rich repay—
> The Pontine Marsh, too, drained away.
> And, far along the Tuscan shore
> The weird Maremma reassume
> Her ancient tilth and wheaten plume.
>
> (81; 1.94–98)

One critic, William Bysshe Stein, reads these lines as a criticism of Garibaldi, who actively supported these projects and thus betrayed his idealism with utilitarianism (228–29). But in Garibaldi's time, these projects were considered visionary attempts to recapture the glories of ancient Rome by making Italy a more industrialized and progressive nation. And because they are agricultural improvements, they link Garibaldi even more closely with Cincinnatus, a figure whose heroic stature rests on his combining the military with the agricultural. It is not so much Garibaldi whom Melville is criticizing as it is the inflated imagery and rhetoric of contemporary media.

Still, real questions about Garibaldi's fame exist. Can his reputation survive his popularity? Or will he be reduced to a mere advertising image, a picture on a tin of smoking tobacco, a product of the "jobbers" at Beadle's, the cartoonists at *Harper's Weekly*, or the columnists at the *Nation*? At the conclusion of "At the Hostelry," the Marquis wonders whether Garibaldi's fame can survive the coming age of utilitarianism. Consider his costume:

> The Cid, his net-work shirt of mail,
> And Garibaldi's woolen one:
> In higher art would each avail
> So just expression nobly grace—
> Declare the hero in the face?
>
> (94; 8.11–15)

Is Garibaldi's noble physiognomy sufficient to overcome his unheroic garb? Can he retain the heroic associations of the Cid even though he is customarily portrayed wearing ordinary clothes instead of armor? These questions, as editor Gordon Poole has noticed (xxviii–xxxi), are implicit in the long debate on the picturesque that takes up most of "At the Hostelry." In this debate, painters like Jan Steen, Adrian Brouwer, and Tintoretto discuss the meaning and value of the picturesque in painting. Although the debate is finally inconclusive, Jan Steen's pragmatic response to the issue suggests the dilemma Garibaldi faces as he becomes a more and more legendary figure:

> Utility reigns—Ah, well-a-way!—
> And bustles along in Bentham's shoes.
> For the Picturesque—suffice, suffice
> The picture that fetches a picturesque price!
>
> (82; 2.17–20)

Garibaldi, typically referred to as "picturesque" in the media, becomes little more than an advertising gimmick, a cheap means of increasing magazine sales or selling tobacco. The Garibaldi of history fades before the

Garibaldi created by the media, an artificial and "picturesque" figure that serves the interests of publishers, not the ideals of revolution. This more ambiguous vision of Garibaldi informs the view of him at the end of "At the Hostelry":

> There's Garibaldi, off-hand hero,
> A very Cid Campeadór,
> Lion-Nemesis of Naples' Nero—
> But, tut, why tell that story o'er!
> A natural knight-errant, truly,
> Nor priding him in parrying fence,
> But charging at the helm-piece—hence
> By statesmen deemed a lord unruly.
>
> (95; Sequel 17–24)

These lines capture the debate between coolheaded politicians like Cavour and King Victor Emanuel over Garibaldi's long-term value. The king respected Garibaldi's military genius and encouraged him when it served his ends, but when Garibaldi recklessly set off on a buccaneering expedition against Rome, the king placed him under house arrest on Caprera. With the revolution over, "the dragons penned or slain, / What for St. George would then remain!" (95–96; Sequel 39–40), asks the Marquis. It is a question Garibaldi, imprisoned by the king he had so selflessly supported, must have asked himself.

The final lines of "At the Hostelry" confirm Garibaldi's paradoxical nature: he resists both the historical typologies that seem to explain him and the picturesque aura conferred by the popular press. "A don of rich erratic tone," evidently a conservative member of the Burgundy Club, reminds the audience of Garibaldi's days on Staten Island. Were he born today, the don asserts, the "Red Shirt Champion" would never

> "quit his trading trips,
> Perchance, would fag in trade at desk,
> Or, slopped in slimy slippery sludge,
> Lifelong on Staten Island drudge,
> Melting his tallow, Sir, dipping his dips,
> Scarce savoring much of the Picturesque!"
>
> (96; Sequel 56–61)[6]

The don's linear view of history as progressively more common and ignoble presages Adams's pessimism, where primal "forces" such as Garibaldi suffer from increasing entropy. To this bleak outlook a "cultured wight / Lucid with transcendental light" (96; Sequel 62–63) responds with a cyclical view of history:

"Pardon, but tallow none nor trade
When, thro' this Iron Age's reign
The Golden one comes in again;
That's on the card."

(96; Sequel 64–67)

While it is always tempting to find caricatures of Emerson in Melville's writings, this "transcendental" view is decidedly non-Emersonian. "All history resolves itself very easily into the biography of a few stout and earnest persons," Emerson wrote in "Self-Reliance" (267), privileging the individual above cyclical events. Both the cynical don and the "cultured wight" disagree with Emerson's view and see men as products of their historical situation, whether it extends into an infinite and unpredictable future or returns to a familiar past. The puzzle of Garibaldi is that he seems to be all three: one of Adams's primal energies exhausting itself in supreme effort, a picturesque Roman hero returned to usher in a golden age of Italian prosperity and independence, and a "representative man" who incorporates the spirit of the age so completely that it seems to have flowed from his veins. Garibaldi illustrates the impossibility of deciding whether man makes history or history makes man. Instead of an Emersonian motto, Melville presents a multivoiced, necessarily inconclusive debate on fundamental issues. The eloquent Marquis de Grandvin ends this "rhyming race" with a moderate position on the relationship between history and the self:

Angel O' the Age! Advance, God speed.
Harvest us all good grain in seed;
But sprinkle, do, some drops of grace
Nor polish us into commonplace.

(96; Sequel 74–77)

Drawing upon his famous reserve of geniality, the Marquis appeals for a middle way that sustains the mystique of Garibaldi ("the drops of grace") even while acknowledging the inevitable leveling of the advancing age of utilitarianism.

The second poem, "Naples in the Time of Bomba," counterpoints "At the Hostelry" by suggesting the limits of individuality as a moderating force on history. Whereas "At the Hostelry" focuses on Garibaldi's life and major accomplishments, "Naples" mentions him only once—at his death. The genial perspective of the poem's narrator, Civil War hero and "Dean of the Burgundy Club" Major Jack Gentian, foregrounds the stereotypically carefree world of "sunny Italy," focusing, like Melville's own travel journals, on the sensuous pleasures of Neapolitan life. This is Naples in 1857, before either the Italian or the American civil war, and its gaiety seems eternal. Yet Jack recites his tale much later, after his years in the

Union Army, after losing an arm in the Civil War and experiencing first-hand the dark forces of historical necessity that complicate our appreciation of individual valor and turn yesterday's hero into today's geriatric amputee. If Jack voices the final lines describing Garibaldi's funeral, a plausible conjecture, his recitation to the Burgundy Club occurs sometime after 1882, making the poem a retrospective account of events some twenty-five years earlier. Jack's auditors would know of Garibaldi's quixotic forays on Rome, his house arrest on Caprera, and his failed plans to reverse the Tiber. The postbellum "Iron Age" of utilitarianism is well under way, and Garibaldi's reputation is undergoing reassessment and historical critique, a theme cautiously advanced in some of the obituaries and overtly presented in William Roscoe Thayer's 1888 *Atlantic Monthly* pieces.

Melville struggled with his portrait of Jack Gentian, an autobiographical figure in some ways, but one rather concretely historicized in others. Jack shares many of Garibaldi's contradictory qualities. Of Southern stock, he grew up in the North and fought for the Union. Impulsive, straightforward, rash, he startles genteel society by swearing like a "Roman consul exhorting his infantry" (Sandberg, "Melville's Unfinished Book" 98). No one, however, mistakes his natural merit, his noble bearing that inspires respect even in a New York "cabby" (98). On the surface democratic, Jack is in fact a natural aristocrat, that rare American who maintains the dignity of tradition yet, as Jack did, in the Union Army, fights on the side of a leveling utilitarianism. Like Garibaldi, Jack symbolizes the contradictory values of authority and individualism, violence and peace, aristocracy and democracy, all of them the inevitable consequences of modern war.

Melville historicizes Jack by making him a member of the Society of the Cincinnati, the same order conferred on Melville's maternal grandfather, General Peter Gansevoort, for his service in the American Revolution. Composed of Revolutionary War officers, their direct descendants, and French allies, the Cincinnati was America's only hereditary association, a sort of republican knighthood memorializing American-French cooperation. From its beginning in 1783, the society was steeped in controversy stemming from its aristocratic tendencies and foreign connections. Although Washington agreed to serve as its first president, on the advice of the anti-Federalist Jefferson he accepted only on condition that the society refrain from politics and moderate its elitism. Wills concludes that "Washington retained his membership in the Society only to check it" (145), and notes that after 1786 Washington never wore the Cincinnati's distinctive badge (142). When the France of Lafayette metamorphosed into the France of Robespierre, the society came under suspicion from conservative Federalists, for it now seemed allied with anarchy and rampant republicanism. Caught in the ongoing debate between authority and individualism, the Society of the Cincinnati served as a lightning rod for American uncertainty about the nature of republican ideology.

These tensions explain Melville's obsessive rewriting of Jack's biography, the different points of view he provides on the Cincinnati, and Jack's own insistence on wearing the order's badge rather than the Grand Old Army medallion. For his service in the American Revolution, Jack's grandfather, a South Carolinian, earned "the eagle-wings in gold of the Cincinnati, a venerable order whereof he who still reigns 'first in the hearts of his countrymen' was the original head" (99). Since membership passed to the oldest son, Jack, like Melville's cousin Guert Gansevoort (Rogin 291), now wears the badge of the Cincinnati, an American eagle attached to a blue ribbon bordered with white in honor of the French Bourbon flag. The eagle's breast bears an emblem of three Roman senators presenting Cincinnatus with a sword. Some of the major's friends believe the badge betrays an aristocratic tendency, even "a weakness for certain gewgaws that savor of the monarchical"; but the narrator responds, "an inherited badge of the Cincinnati, every American however ultra in his democracy, must allow to be something of which no other American need be ashamed" (99). "The Cincinnati," a superseded sketch by one of the most conservative Burgundians, defends "the guillotined victim" Louis XVI and recalls "the violent democratic crusade" that began shortly after his death and briefly discredited the society (140). In another version of Jack's biography, one "Colonel Josiah Bunkum," an unreflecting voice of Radical Republicanism, the cash nexus, and utilitarianism, attacks the Cincinnati as archaic, impractical, antidemocratic, and monarchical. Yet "[j]ustly proud art thou of thy decoration of the Cincinnati" (143) asserts a subsequent fragment, while another calls Jack "a democrat, though less than of the stump than of the heart" (135). From every political position—conservative, liberal, radical—Jack remains a puzzle. He embodies the political paradoxes of Revolutionary America allied with monarchical France, Union officers of Southern heritage, modern military heroes with ancient Roman virtues, and Jacksonian Americans claiming inherited nobility.

Like Garibaldi, Jack extends the typology of Cincinnatus-Washington into the present, an ambiguous iconography of military valor combined with pastoral humility that justifies force by moderating ambition. The inability of Jack's friends to understand these contradictions reveals their shortcomings, not Jack's. Outdated though he may seem to a "Bunkum," Jack, with his missing arm, dignity, geniality, and magnanimity, is a picturesque reminder of genuine heroism and patriotism. Encompassing contradictory ideologies, he surpasses any single ideology save that of the "representative man," the Emersonian ethos popularly applied to Garibaldi. Yet as a man enmeshed in history he complicates even that transcendental lure, that sop to individualism which mitigates the forces of historical necessity so obviously formative in Jack's life. Rogin, following Hershel Parker, suggests that Melville's custom-house badge—which he wore daily when he was writing these poems—reminded him of the Cincinnati badge and what Rogin terms his "moral right" to wear it (291). One need not accept this psychological speculation to recognize that the Cincinnati motif symbolizes Melville's recognition that history alternately demands aristocratic authoritarianism and democratic individualism, demands only rarely satisfied by a Cincinnatus, Washington, Garibaldi, or Jack Gentian.

Such historical alternations riddle Jack's meditation in "Naples in the Time of Bomba." In 1857, Bomba reigns, frivolity dominates, and the Roman Republic of 1849 has faded from memory. Although Jack enjoys the gaiety and thoughtlessness of the Neapolitan mob, he knows the "shocking stories bruited wide, / In England which I left but late, / Touching dire tyranny in Naples" (111; 2.4–6), an allusion to Gladstone's famous letters of 1851 describing the Two Sicilies as a land where "[t]he negation of God was erected into a system of government" (qtd. in Marraro, *American Opinion* 102). Seeing through the gay facade into the darkness of Bomba's tyranny, Jack notices cannons turned toward the populace instead of the sea, troops mustered in a daily show of force, political prisoners in the Castel dell'Ovo, spies masquerading as blind beggars, and sycophantic Jesuits ready to rationalize Bomba's "lawless power" (124; 8.69). He also knows Neapolitan history, and recalls such abuses of authority as Queen Joanna I's murder of her husband and Tiberius's exile of Agrippina, Germanicus's noble wife. As twinned perversions of patriotism and filial loyalty, these events paint tyranny as the Janus face of anarchy, perhaps the fundamental paradox in Neapolitan history, culminating in the present reign of "A braggadocio Bourbon-Draco!" (127; 9.87). Underneath a smiling face, Naples is bubbling with Vesuvian fire, as Jack sees emblems of revolution everywhere: Vesuvius itself, of course, "a Power even more nitrous and menacing than the Bomb-King himself" (116); "Mariners in red Phrygian caps" (124; 8.48), the cap of proletarian revolt; and allusions to "Parthenope" (125; 9.12; 147, 148), both the ancient name of Naples and the short-lived republic established by French Jacobins in 1799.

When Garibaldi reenters the diptych at the end, he seems to bring order to chaos:

> She [Naples as Andromeda] sobbed, she laughed, she rattled her chain;
> Till the Red Shirt proved signal apt
> Of danger ahead to Bomba's son,
> And presently freedom's thunder clapt,
> And lo, he fell from toppling throne—
> Fell down, like Dagon on his face,
> And ah, the unfeeling populace!

But Garibaldi:—Naples' host
Uncovers to her deliverer's ghost,
While down time's aisle, mid clarions clear
"Pale glory walks by valor's bier."

(130–31; 12.50–60)

The final image of Garibaldi presents him in all his contradictory power, as a live hero toppling monarchy yet initiating anarchic terror ("the unfeeling populace" that might revenge itself on its oppressors) and as a dead hero monumentalized in the language of the popular press. Now liberated, Naples must learn to use its freedom wisely and take its place in a unified Italian nation. Its turbulent history suggests difficulties, however, and for both the United States and Italy the unity that follows civil war will prove elusive.

THE MEDUSA OF REVOLUTION

I have argued that Melville understood the modern process of image making we are so familiar with today, the process that apparels white, middle-class American youth in T-shirts emblazoned with portraits of Che Guevara and Malcolm X. In his Burgundy Club poems and sketches, Melville created multivocal, dialogical dramas that are less important as statements of his actual political beliefs than as hermeneutical texts that expose this process of transforming people into icons, politics into art, and events into history. As Henry James showed in "The Real Thing" (1892) and as Jean Baudrillard argues today, our thickly mediated culture produces "simulacra" that stand in place of and even oust actual people and events from observation and history. But rather than simplifying the underlying ideologies of historical creation, these icons complicate it immensely. As a combination of biography, art, politics, history, and myth in one pictorial representation, Garibaldi—or any complex iconic figure—resists ideological reductionism and opens unsuspected paths of connection between distant cultures. To understand this process better, I want to unravel Melville's allusion to Medusa, one of the most densely knit references in the poem, and reweave it into an interlinked web of associations that captures Garibaldi's paradoxical significance and suggests how iconographic representations do their cultural work.

When "At the Hostelry" introduces Garibaldi as a "Red-shirt Perseus" rescuing Andromeda, it implicates him in the slaying of Medusa, one of the most powerful emblems of revolution and emergent feminism in the nineteenth century. Historicizing Freud's equation "to decapitate = to castrate" (qtd. in Hertz 165), Neil Hertz finds conservative male fears of revolution conflated with misogyny in the iconography surrounding the French revolutions of 1789, 1848, and 1870. Female figures frequently represented rebellion, as in Eugène Delacroix's famous painting of liberty scaling the barricades, while decapitation connoted the Red Terror. A beheaded woman, then, simultaneously suppresses political and sexual revolutions and points to "a theory of representation—bound up with a still more explicit linking of what is politically dangerous to feelings of sexual horror and fascination" (Hertz 168). Garibaldi-as-Perseus participates in this linkage, liberating one woman only at the expense of beheading another. Nor is Naples-as-Andromeda truly liberated. According to Adrienne Munich, Victorian painters appropriated the entire Andromeda myth as a "cipher for gender politics, useful for reinscribing traditional authority" (84). Domestic Andromeda replaces feminist Medusa as Persean "liberation" maintains patriarchal oppression.

Melville understood these contemporary connotations well, as Ishmael's comparison of Guido and Hogarth shows (figs. 4.5 and 4.6). Guido's Perseus is a comparatively naturalistic military hero, like Garibaldi astride his white horse; Hogarth's Perseus hovers supernaturally in the air, holding before him the gruesome head of Medusa. Which Perseus is Garibaldi? For Melville, the answer is both—the man on the winged white horse and the self-sufficient beheader of women. Both are romantic figures of liberation, but only the second implicates liberators in the violence their goals require.[7] As a "Red-Shirt Perscus," Melville's Garibaldi images the "Red Republicanism" Americans feared and evaded, as in the *Harper's Weekly* cartoon, yet he also recalls a decapitating misogyny that, as I have argued elsewhere (see Berthold), underlies part of "At the Hostelry." Garibaldi is thus both revolutionary and conservative, an apostle of both individual liberation and patriarchal authority who reminds Americans—or at least Melville—that revolution is acceptable when its violence is turned against an obvious Other, in this case women.

The best-known representation of Perseus, Benvenuto Cellini's famous statue (1554; fig. 4.7), reifies these ambiguous values in a work Melville called an "astonishing conception" ("Statues in Rome," 1857–58; *Writings* 9:406). Cellini's Perseus thrusts Medusa's head forward, bringing the spectator under its awful gaze while the demigod looks down and away with one foot resting on his victim's contorted, naked body. Blood flows freely from head and torso, suggesting a frozen moment of life-in-death commonly associated with the Laocoön group in the Vatican. As in Hogarth's picture, the Medusa head is what makes the iconography so paradoxical: before Perseus can rescue one woman, he must behead another. Charles Anthon, the Columbia professor who wrote a standard dictionary on myths that Melville consulted, interpreted both Perseus and Hercules as "just murderers" who "purify the stains of evil by force and by the shedding of

Fig. 4.7. Benvenuto Cellini, *Perseus with the Head of Medusa* (1549). Loggia dei Lanzi, Florence, Italy. Courtesy Alinari/Art Resource, New York.

blood," combining virtue and violence as two "Mithraic" figures of intertwined goodness and evil (1007). Since, in some myths, Hercules was the founder of Naples, Neapolitan history bears the taint of blood and violence from its beginning. Garibaldi extends this heritage of justified violence into the present. Wrapped in the contradictions of Ahabian leadership and revolt, Garibaldi shares the iconographic paradoxes of the *Pequod*'s captain,

Fig. 4.8. Flemish School, *Head of Medusa* (ca. 1620–30?). Uffizi, Florence, Italy. Courtesy Alinari/Art Resource, New York.

whose first appearance on the quarterdeck reminds Ishmael of "Cellini's cast Perseus" (*Writings* 6:123).

Even more than the authors and painters Hertz and Munich study, Melville consciously exploits the interfusion of politics and aesthetics contained within Medusan iconography, recognizing in it the mixed allure and repulsion of revolution figured as female. In the painters' debate on the picturesque in "At the Hostelry," the key issue is whether subjects repulsive in reality—a tortured saint, a squalid ghetto, a filthy inn—are fit subjects for painting. Herman Swanevelt, a realistic Dutch painter, tries to mediate the debate with the example of Leonardo da Vinci's *Head of Medusa*:

> Like beauty strange with horror allied,—
> As shown in great Leonardo's head
> Of snaky Medusa,—so as well
> Grace and the Picturesque may dwell
> With Terror. Vain here to divide—
> The Picturesque has many a side."

(83; 2.65–70)

Art conjoins opposites and offers spectators the frisson of Medusa's gaze yet protects them from the consequences of actual experience: they gaze unpetrified. The *Head of Medusa* (fig. 4.8)—falsely attributed to Leonardo in 1783, an attribution uncorrected until 1907—was the nineteenth century's standard referent for finding both beauty and horror in Medusa, a tradition that began with Goethe and ran through Shelley, Hawthorne, Pater, Swinburne, and William Morris.[8] Such an aesthetic explains the power Melville found in Cellini's Perseus and links Melville with Shelley, whose poem "On the Medusa of Leonardo Da Vinci in the Florentine Gallery" is the probable source for Swanevelt's definition of the picturesque: "Its horror and its beauty are divine" (582), Shelley wrote, "Yet it is less the horror than the grace / Which turns the gazer's spirit into stone" (582), as "the tempestuous loveliness of terror" (583) mirrors "all the beauty and the terror there" (583).[9]

By mediating the aesthetic object through the poetry of Shelley, perhaps the most outspoken English supporter of the Italian revolution, Melville offers a covert intertextual recognition of art's political dimensions. Like the *Head of Medusa*, revolution has its own "beauty strange with horror allied," a combination imaged in Garibaldi, revolution's current dominant icon. As Perseus holding the Medusa head, Garibaldi is a revolutionary decapitator, inextricably bound up with the iconography of beheading that, as Larry Reynolds has shown, represented for Americans the Red Terror of the guillotine and the anarchy of the French Revolution (81–83). Unmediated by myth, decapitation horrifies, like Babo's staring head on a pike at the end of "Benito Cereno" (1856) or the sinking whale head that almost kills Tashtego in *Moby-Dick*. But filtered through the legend of Perseus or the modern representations of Garibaldi, decapitation becomes acceptable as a metaphor for revolutionary violence, a necessary means to a noble end. And this of course was the great distinction Americans drew between the French and the Italian revolutions: the Risorgimento, despite its history of political assassinations and terrorist attacks, avoided the anarchy of regicide and the sheer horror of the guillotine, the symbol of revolt gone mad, and thus fell within territory susceptible to the meliorizing ideology of American politics. Like the American Revolution, the Risorgimento was supported by the middle and upper classes and sought to overthrow foreign rule, not to institute universal suffrage or state socialism. Furthermore, it challenged papal authority, thereby appealing to American anti-Catholicism and extending Enlightenment secularism into the stronghold of the Antichrist. Garibaldi's elevated classicism sanitized revolutionary excess and allowed him to function as an American hero, a rebel with a cause cloaked in Roman idealism.

One final allusion locates Medusan ambiguity in Neapolitan history itself and transgresses gender roles by applying it to a male. In "Naples in the Time of Bomba," Jack Gentian cannot stop his mind from wandering between present beauties and past horrors, as in the legends of Queen Joanna and Agrippina, both strong women who challenged male hegemony. When Jack hears the lilting song of a fruit girl selling blood oranges, a fruit whose very name blends horror and beauty, he recalls the story of Tommaso Anniello, a twenty-five-year-old Amalfi fisherman known to history as Masaniello, who in 1647 galvanized Neapolitans into a tax rebellion with eloquent speeches demanding economic justice. Realizing his power over the mob, the authorities removed the taxes and granted Masaniello amnesty, but too late. Three days after the treaty, the mob killed him: as the *Penny Cyclopedia* records, "his head was cut off, fixed on a pole, and carried to the viceroy" (1:32), a startling analogy to Babo's fate. For Jack, Masaniello is a leader of "riff-raff," "Brigands and outlaws," a specter of "incensed Revolt / With whose return Wrath threatens still / Bomba engirt with guards" (122; 7.142–43). He is the dark anarchic side of Garibaldi. Yet Jack admits that Masaniello faced an unjust and oppressive foreign authority "Whose iron heel evoked the spark / That fired the populace into flame" (122; 7.154–55). Jack senses, however dimly, the moral ambiguities of revolt.

As a historical figure exalted into legend by contemporary writers—Daniel Auber's opera *Masaniello* or *La Muette de Portici* (1828) played repeatedly in New York—Masaniello adumbrates the literary glorification that engulfed Garibaldi. Furthermore, he too combines revolutionary ardor and decapitating violence in the paradoxical conjunctions of Medusan iconography. Although the conservative Jack questions whether Masaniello is any better than the "foreign lords" he opposes (122; 7.153), as a figure of romantic Neapolitan history he, like Medusa, is both a victim and an oppressor whose deeds testify to the situational ethics of history.[10] And as a character in Melville's poem, he is a prototype of Billy Budd, an ambiguous figure of youthful innocence and murderous violence that makes moral judgments impossible:

> And, see, dark eyes and sunny locks
> Of Masaniello, bridegroom young,
> Tanned marigold-cheek and tasseled cap;
> The darling of the mob; nine days
> Their great Apollo; then, in pomp
> Of Pandemonium's red parade,
> His curled head Gorgoned on the pike,
> And jerked aloft for God to see.
> A portent."
>
> (122; 7.156–64)

Masaniello, like Billy, is at once apotheosized and punished; like "weird John Brown" in the introductory poem to *Battle-Pieces*, he is "a portent" of revolution and war to come (11); and like Babo, his severed head is displayed to enforce a moral, however ambiguous and unfathomable. Masaniello's abortive revolution, uninspired as it was by any higher aim than lowering taxes, reminds Jack of the French Revolution,

> When Freedom linkt with Furies raved
> In Carmagnole [a peasant dance] and cannibal hymn,
> Mad song and dance before the ark
> From France imported with *The Terror*!"

(7.166–69)

Yet Masaniello's beauty makes him as affecting as Billy Budd, the Billy of nautical folklore whose legend soothes generations of sailors. Both are, to use terms Melville applies to Billy Budd, "Handsome Sailors," "nautical Murats," "Apollos," and martyrs to "the Rights of Man," uneasy symbols of beauty joined with terror, simultaneously appealing and appalling, unpredictable, volatile, and violent, gyrating from one extreme to another: Melville's masculinized Medusas of revolution.

Garibaldi, as Perseus, is the one figure of all these revolutionary archetypes who exercises some control over anarchic excess even while partaking of it, one who, like Vere, accepts the mysteries of "just murderers" and dictatorial liberators even though he cannot rationally resolve them. Although he remains a beheading Perseus, Garibaldi is no guillotiner of kings. Like Jack, whose Cincinnati medal blends both revolution and monarchy and Roman imperialism and American democracy, Garibaldi retains a personal integrity that justifies his simultaneous exhortations to the mob and submission to the king. Unlike a Robespierre or Napoleon, Garibaldi is magnanimous to his enemies, constrains the mob, and retires when his aims are fulfilled. Medusan iconography images the violence of rebellion and the sexual exclusiveness of revolutions fought mainly to liberate white men; but, as wielded by Perseus-Garibaldi and artistically rendered by Melville-Cellini-da Vinci-Shelley, the Medusa myth restrains revolutionary excess by giving the victims power even in death and justifying their murder with the overriding need for order. Unabated revolutionary activity kills Masaniello, Babo, and Robespierre—the beheaders beheaded. Garibaldi, a "knight-errant" with the common touch, both a "Perseus" and a "candle-dipper," offers a secure icon to represent violent historical change, one approved by Americans and, I believe, Melville as well.

Melville ruminated on this process in all of his work after 1860, as my references to *Battle-Pieces*, *Clarel*, and *Billy Budd* are intended to suggest. Their political ambiguities, variously seen by critics as reactionary, revolutionary, meliorist, naturalistic, and so forth, mirror the historical paradoxes that surrounded Garibaldi and Risorgimento ideology.[11] They are incapable of final resolution because they incorporate contradictions Melville found in the politics of his own century even as we continue to find them in ours. Idealists might scoff at hypocritical oxymorons like "waging peace" or "Peacemaker" missiles, but they are no more contradictory than the "just murders" of Perseus or Garibaldi. The continuing presence of revolution, whether in Kosovo or Sri Lanka, the Middle East or Mexico, makes ideological consistency impossible. Order and justice make uneasy partners, as Melville realized in *Billy Budd*. Both Vere and Billy, "two of great Nature's nobler order" (115), are natural noblemen like Garibaldi who share in the virtues and flaws that nature contains. In the figure of Garibaldi, Melville found a contemporary icon of that uneasy partnership, an icon that problematized ideology and complicated his search for consistent political principles.

NOTES

1. This poem first appeared in Willard Thorp's *Herman Melville: Representative Selections* (1938). Thorp inferred these glosses from the political context (425n). My own reading in the period suggests that Melville was using generally understood metaphors but nothing so precise that we can read much out of them.

2. These problems have engaged numerous scholars since Merton M. Sealts, Jr., undertook a serious study of the manuscripts in the 1940s. Sealts's basic findings are still unchallenged and are readily available in *Pursuing Melville*. A definitive analysis is expected in the last projected volume of the Northwestern-Newberry edition of Melville, the forthcoming *Poems* edited by Robert Ryan. The documentary completeness of Robert Sandberg's edition of the poems and sketches is invaluable. Since it is expected to be the basis of the forthcoming Northwestern-Newberry edition of this material, I cite it as my primary text. The poems are most readily available in Poole or Kramer, and the sketches in Berthoff.

3. The figures reproduced here follow Stuart Frank's identifications in *Herman Melville's Picture-Gallery: Sources and Types of the "Pictorial Chapters" of Moby-Dick* (Fairhaven: Edward J. Lefkowicz, 1986), 8–11.

4. A poem published on the front page of *Harper's Weekly* a few months later clothed Garibaldi's triumph in the rhetoric of millennialism, explicitly comparing him to "an angel from the skies" and "Heaven's own chosen king" (October 13, 1860). Such metaphors almost transform Garibaldi into an evangelical Protestant.

5. William Bysshe Stein interprets Garibaldi as a figure of cyclic history, a Dionysian reformer of the failed linear history of Christianity (229). Such a reading, while valuable, emphasizes anarchy to the exclusion of authoritarianism, a common bias of critics who prefer to view Melville as disruptive and iconoclastic.

6. Both Stein (245) and William H. Shurr (216), in the only extended studies of Melville's poetry, read these lines autobiographically, taking them as references to Melville's own dreary career in the custom house, a suggestion that Poole, in the best published edition of the poem, repeats (39n). Yet Melville worked on Manhattan, not Staten, Island and seldom drudged at a desk, instead walking the docks in the open air as, in his own words, an "outdoor Custom House officer" (Leyda 818). Of course, the lines allude directly to Garibaldi's 1850–51 exile on Staten Island, a

fact well known at the time and mentioned in all standard biographical dictionaries today. Melville's poem is trying to enter history, not evade it, to engage experience, not retreat into autobiography.

7. Ishmael mentions the Guido only briefly, but the specificity of the Hogarth description suggests that Melville had access to a copy of the engraving, either in a book or in his own art collection. The Berkshire Athenaeum holds Melville's personal collection of prints, an extensive and diverse group of nearly three hundred illustrations (see Wallace). Melville also had access to numerous illustrations in books, periodicals, and even newspapers, as Christopher Sten abundantly demonstrates. Although we are unsure about when he began collecting art, we know from his journals that he purchased both books and prints on his 1849 visit to London and Paris. By the time he wrote his Neapolitan diptych, he owned numerous prints and art history books.

8. Goethe ushered in the romantic phase of appreciation for Medusa's paradoxical qualities in 1788 when he expressed extravagant praise for the Rondanini mask in Rome: "[t]he Medusa Rondanini—a marvelous, mysterious and fascinating work, which represents a state between death and life, pain and pleasure" (489). Even in the simplified mythology of *A Wonder Book*, Hawthorne granted aesthetic ambiguity to Medusa's face: "It was the fiercest and most horrible face that ever was seen or imagined, and yet with a strange, fearful, and savage kind of beauty in it" (29). Melville employed Medusan iconography throughout his career, as Gail H. Coffler's compendium of Melville's classical allusions indicates. For a conspectus of Romantic and Victorian appropriations of the myth, see McGann.

9. Although Melville could have seen Leonardo's painting at the Uffizi in 1857, he acquired a volume of Shelley in 1861 and obtained others in 1868 and 1873 (Leyda 640, 694, 735, 950). Other Shelley poems, such as "Lines Written among the Euganean Hills" and "Ode to Naples," bear marked similarities to the opening section of "At the Hostelry" and subtly add Shelley's Risorgimento sympathies to the political framework of Melville's Italian poems.

10. Facts on Masaniello follow those in Melville's usual reference work, the *Penny Cyclopedia*, whose two-page article suggests the reader's interest in this figure. Masaniello is a fixture in the travel literature on Italy, a well-known symbol of male beauty conjoined with revolutionary ardor. Henry W. Bellows compared a picturesque beggar to Masaniello (61), while Joel Tyler Headley quoted a peasant who said, "We want another Massaniello [*sic*] to lead us," and then made a beheading gesture (105). Headley considered Masaniello "the People's Washington" (105). In "Specimen Days" Walt Whitman recalled seeing Auber's opera during the 1840s (704).

11. For a thorough overview of the ongoing critical debate on *Billy Budd*, see Efron. Arthur Efron's synopses (and his own analysis) reveal that most interpretations of the story are driven by critics' ideological needs and presuppositions, their demands for a moral reading of one sort or another. I have tried to historicize the deconstructionist approach of Barbara Johnson, suggesting that the story's resistance to polarized interpretations is not only part of its linguistic apparatus but also its historical situation.

WORKS CITED

Adams, Henry. *The Education of Henry Adams.* 1918. Ed. Ernest Samuels. Boston, Houghton Mifflin Company, 1973.

Anthon, Charles. *A Classical Dictionary.* . . . New York, 1841.

Baudrillard, Jean. "Simulacra and Simulations" (1981). *Jean Baudrillard: Selected Writings.* Ed. Mark Poster. Stanford: Stanford UP, 1988. 166–84.

Bellows, Henry W. *The Old World in its New Face: Impressions of Europe in 1867–1868.* Vol. 2. New York, 1869.

Berthoff, Warner. *Great Short Works of Herman Melville.* New York: Harper, 1966.

Berthold, Dennis. "Dürer 'At the Hostelry': Melville's Misogynist Iconography." *Melville Society Extracts* 95 (1993): 1–8.

Bryant, William Cullen. "Italy and Austria." Berkshire County *Eagle* June 3, 1859: 1.

Coffler, Gail H. *Melville's Classical Allusions: A Comprehensive Index and Glossary.* Westport: Greenwood P, 1985.

Dicey, A. V. "Garibaldi and the Movement of 1848." *Nation* June 29, 1882: 540–42.

Dimock, Wai-Chee. *Empire for Liberty: Melville and the Poetics of Individualism.* Princeton: Princeton UP, 1989.

Duban, James. *Melville's Major Fiction: Politics, Theology, and Imagination.* De Kalb: Northern Illinois UP, 1983.

Dwight, Theodore, trans. *The Life of General Garibaldi: Written by Himself.* . . . New York, 1859.

Efron, Arthur. "Melville's Conjectures into Innocence." Chap. 22 of *Billy Budd, Sailor (An Inside Narrative). REAL: Yearbook of Research in English and American Literature.* Vol. 9. Ed. Herbert Grabes, Winfried Fluck, Jürgen Schlaeger. Tübingen: Narr, 1993.

Emerson, Ralph Waldo. "Self-Reliance." *Essays and Lectures.* Ed. Joel Porte. New York: Library of America, 1983. 257–82.

"Exciting War News." Pittsfield *Sun* May 12, 1859: 1.

Fisher, Marvin. *Going Under: Melville's Short Fiction and the American 1850s.* Baton Rouge: Louisiana State UP, 1977.

Fredricks, Nancy. *Melville's Art of Democracy.* Athens: U of Georgia P, 1995.

Fuller, Margaret. *"These Sad But Glorious Days": Dispatches from Europe, 1846–1850.* Ed. Larry J. Reynolds and Susan Belasco Smith. New Haven: Yale UP, 1991.

Garner, Stanton. *The Civil War World of Herman Melville.* Lawrence: UP of Kansas, 1993.

Godkin, E. L. "Garibaldi." *Nation* June 8, 1882: 477.

Goethe, Johann Wolfgang von. *Italian Journey.* Trans. W. H. Auden. New York: Pantheon, 1962.

Harper's Weekly. November 17, 1860: 722.

Hawthorne, Nathaniel. "The Gorgon's Head." *A Wonder Book and* Tanglewood *Tales.* Vol. 7 of *The Centenary Edition of the Works of Nathaniel Hawthorne.* Ed. William Charvat et al. Columbus: Ohio State UP, 1972. 10–34. 20 vols. 1962–.

Headley, J[oel] T[yler]. *Letters From Italy.* Rev. ed. New York, 1851.

Hertz, Neil. "Medusa's Head: Male Hysteria under Political Pressure." *Representations* 4 (1983). Rptd. in *The End of the Line: Essays on Psychoanalysis and the Sublime.* New York: Columbia UP, 1985. 161–92.

Johnson, Barbara. "Melville's Fist: The Execution of Billy Budd." *The Critical Difference: Essays in the Contemporary Rhetoric of Reading.* Baltimore: Johns Hopkins UP, 1980. 79–109.

Karcher, Carolyn. *Shadow over the Promised Land: Slavery, Race, and Violence in Melville's America.* Baton Rouge: Louisiana State UP, 1980.

Kramer, Aaron. *Melville's Poetry: Toward the Enlarged Heart. A Thematic Study of Three Ignored Major Poems.* Rutherford: Fairleigh Dickinson UP, 1972.

Leyda, Jay. *The Melville Log: A Documentary Life of Herman Melville, 1819–1891.* 2 vols. New York: Gordian, 1969.

McGann, Jerome J. "The Beauty of the Medusa: A Study in Romantic Literary Iconology." *Studies in Romanticism* 11 (1972): 3–25.

Mack Smith, Denis. *Garibaldi: A Great Life in Brief.* Great Lives in Brief 13. New York: Borzoi-Knopf, 1956.

Marraro, Howard R. *American Opinion on the Unification of Italy, 1846–1861.* New York: Columbia UP, 1932.

———. "American Travelers in Rome, 1848–50." *Catholic Historical Review* 29 (1944): 470–509.

Melville, Herman. *Battle-Pieces and Aspects of the War.* 1866. Gainesville: Scholars' Facsimiles and Reprints, 1960.

———. *Billy Budd, Sailor (An Inside Narrative).* Ed. Harrison Hayford and Merton M. Sealts, Jr. Chicago: U of Chicago P, 1962.

———. *The Writings of Herman Melville.* Ed. Harrison Hayford et al. 15 vols. to date. Evanston: Northwestern UP and Newberry Library, 1968–.

Mitgang, Herbert. "Garibaldi and Lincoln." *American Heritage* October 1975: 34+.

Munich, Adrienne Auslander. *Andromeda's Chains: Gender and Interpretation in Victorian Literature and Art.* New York: Columbia UP, 1989.

"Necrology." *New York Tribune Index* 1882: xv.

The Penny Cyclopedia of the Society for the Diffusion of Useful Knowledge. 14 vols. London, 1833–43.

Peterson, Roy M. "Echoes of the Italian Risorgimento in Contemporaneous American Writers." *PMLA* 47 (1932): 220–40.

Poole, Gordon, ed. *"At the Hostelry" and "Naples in the Time of Bomba."* Naples: Istituto Universitario Orientale, 1989.

The Rebellion Record: A Diary of American Events. Ed. Frank Moore. Vol. 1. New York, 1862.

Reynolds, David S. *Beneath the American Renaissance: The Subversive Imagination in the Age of Emerson and Melville.* Cambridge: Harvard UP, 1989.

Reynolds, Larry J. *European Revolutions and the American Literary Renaissance.* New Haven: Yale UP, 1988.

Rogin, Michael Paul. *Subversive Genealogy: The Politics and Art of Herman Melville.* New York: Knopf, 1983.

Rossi, Joseph. *The Image of America in Mazzini's Writings.* Madison: U of Wisconsin P, 1954.

Sandberg, Robert Allen. " 'The Adjustment of Screens': Putative Narrators, Authors, and Editors in Melville's Unfinished *Burgundy Club* Book." *Texas Studies in Literature and Language* 31 (1989): 426–50.

———. "Melville's Unfinished 'Burgundy Club' Book: A Reading Edition Edited from the Manuscripts with Introduction and Notes." Diss. Northwestern U, 1989.

Sealts, Merton M., Jr. *Pursuing Melville 1940–1980: Chapters and Essays.* Madison: U of Wisconsin P, 1982.

"Second Campaign of Charles Albert." *Democratic Review* October 1852: 305–25.

"Senator Sumner on the Italian War." Berkshire County *Eagle* July 1, 1859: 1.

Shelley, Percy Bysshe. *The Complete Poetical Works of Percy Bysshe Shelley.* Ed. Thomas Hutchison. 1905. London: Oxford UP, 1948.

Shurr, William H. *The Mystery of Iniquity: Melville as Poet, 1857–1891.* Lexington: UP of Kentucky, 1972.

"The Sicilian Game." *Littell's Living Age* December 27, 1860: 734–48.

Stein, William Bysshe. *The Poetry of Melville's Later Years: Time, History, Myth, and Religion.* Albany: State U of New York P, 1970.

Sten, Christopher, ed. *Savage Eye: Melville and the Visual Arts.* Kent: Kent State UP, 1991.

Thayer, William Roscoe. "The Close of Garibaldi's Career." *Atlantic Monthly* December 1888: 758–65.

———. "The Makers of New Italy." *Atlantic Monthly* November 1888: 656–67.

Thorp, Willard. *Herman Melville: Representative Selections.* New York: American Book, 1938.

"Three Days Later From Europe." Pittsfield *Sun* June 30, 1859: 1.

[Torricelli, J. B.] "Garibaldi." *Christian Examiner* January 1861: 108–37.

[Tuckerman, Henry T.] Rev. of *Italy in Transition; or Public Events and Private Scenes in the Spring of 1860* by William Arthur. *North American Review* 92 (1861): 15–56.

Victor, O[rville] J. *The Life of Joseph Garibaldi, The Liberator of Italy.* New York, 1860.

Viotti, Andrea. *Garibaldi: The Revolutionary and His Men.* Poole, Eng.: Blandford, 1979.

Wallace, Robert K. "Melville's Prints and Engravings at the Berkshire Athenaeum." *Essays in Arts and Sciences* 15 (1986): 59–90.

Whitman, Walt. "Specimen Days." *Complete Poetry and Collected Prose.* New York: Library of America, 1982. 689–925.

"Who is Garabaldi [*sic*]?" Berkshire County *Eagle* 24 June 1859: 1.

Wills, Garry. *Cincinnatus: George Washington and the Enlightenment.* Garden City: Doubleday, 1984.

Part Two

REPRESENTATIONAL FRAMEWORKS AND
THEIR OTHERS: THE POLITICS OF
RACIALIZED GENDER AND SEXUALITY

CHAPTER 5

Miscegenated America: The Civil War

SHIRLEY SAMUELS

1

This essay enacts the stresses of what it tries to explicate: competing identities for the American nation between the revolution and the Civil War. Such competitions draw on racial and sexual embodiments even when the text or institution under discussion—such as the Declaration of Independence or the Bank of the United States—appears removed from race or sex or body. Such an occlusion may be illustrated by Mark Twain's description of pulling *Those Extraordinary Twins* from *Pudd'nhead Wilson*, an act he calls a "literary Caesarean" (Clemens 119). Haunted by Twain's image, I want to trace the competing identities within the composite body of America as it moves toward an uncertain gestation.

In his novel of a Civil War within, Twain's fantasy of a literary Caesarean both reveals and covers the centrality of monstrous birth in his project of imagining race. That is, it reveals—literally opens—a woman's body and yet covers that body in its deflection onto the emergent text. The uncertainty about whether a woman is even visible in the imagination of birth might invoke Roxy's near invisibility in *Pudd'nhead Wilson*. This is a familiar deflection: in the period of the earlier republic that Twain's later projects so uncomfortably recapitulate, the figuring of Columbia as a maternal emblem of the republic paradoxically suggests the invisibility of domesticity and housekeeping to conceptions of the republic as a house. To ask who shall have access to the national home and to ask who shall have access to this woman's body become two sides of determining a relation to the image of Columbia as a national mother.

The further appropriateness of Twain's problematic imagining of birth is its application to a work in which the legally mandated separation of Siamese twins means death. To pull one body from another in birth is to produce two bodies from one. To find two amalgamated bodies in one and then to pull them apart here means death for both. The twinned bodies that supplant those extraordinary twins in *Pudd'nhead Wilson* are two boys with juridically distinct racial identities who are switched after birth by Roxy, the mother of one and the nursing mother of the other. The defining moment for Pudd'nhead Wilson, the lawyer who will eventually pull them apart, is his ironic announcement when annoyed by a town dog that if he owned "half that dog," he would kill his half (3). Here I want to pursue the stunning sense that in many representations miscegenation produces a fatal desire to pull apart one body from another, a desire that produces bodily instantiations of the house divided.

Such unsteadiness infuses Civil War political representations that focus on maternal monitoring over who will occupy the national home, especially as a house divided along racial lines. Through a close look at two pictorial representations of this national house, I want to begin to discuss how such imaginings of a home cast into sharp relief the constitution (in the racial and the federal sense) of the families imagined to live in this home and nation. Beginning with these pictures, I will proceed through the biography of Stephen Girard, the Philadelphia philanthropist par excellence, and will turn finally to *Uncle Tom's Cabin* to ask what determinations of the boundaries of families, homes, and nations are posited there.

Both pictures, "South Carolina Topsey in a Fix" (1861) and "Abraham's Dream!" (1864), have a political purpose; they seek to describe a historical situation as well as to motivate political action, motivations perhaps clearer for their contemporary viewers than for us. Baldly put, that purpose might be described as blaming the victim, though what they produce along the path of that blame is what concerns me here. The action in both cartoons is dominated by the powerful form of Columbia. As the national monitor, she regulates, she disposes, and she kills. Notably, bodies are refused or killed at the point of their insertion into or removal from an emblematic national space—that of the flag of the United States in the first, of the White House, in the second.

In the first cartoon, allusions to *Uncle Tom's Cabin* specifically locate the plantation home as the appropriate site of national values. "South Carolina Topsey in a Fix" shows a white matron who rebukes "Topsey" for "picking stars out" of the nation's flag, an allusion to her sleight-of-hand disruptions of housekeeping in Stowe's novel. Abject before the violation of national cloth, Topsey is blamed for disunion: she is found "at the bottom" of this "piece of work," work that runs against the housekeeping values of her white accuser. Echoing Harriet Beecher Stowe's infamous object of pity and dread in *Uncle Tom's Cabin*, this Topsey can answer only, "[C]ause I's so wicked," about a scenario in which she has no opportunity to have a national voice. She stands forlornly as a resonant example of a continuing political strategy to reverse categories of blame and responsibility.[1]

Images of Columbia as the republic thus show her to be the republican mother as a national housekeeper who assists with domesticity and racial violence. In both cartoons, the woman guards the entrance to the national home, protecting and debarring. *Inside* the republic in "South Carolina

Fig. 5.1. "South Carolina Topsey in a Fix." Bernard F. Reilly, Jr., *American Political Prints, 1766–1876: A Catalog of the Collections in the Library of Congress* (1991), 463.

Topsey in a Fix" is the viewer—who watches apparently from the front door and looks onto the veranda. Positioned inside the home guarded by the national mother, the viewer is both infantilized and implicated in the transparently specious form of blaming in which she engages: "So, Topsey, you're at the bottom of this piece of wicked work—picking stars out of this sacred Flag! What would your forefathers say, do you think? I'll just hand you over to the new overseer, Uncle Abe. He'll fix you!" (Reilly 463). But why Topsy, the misbehaving orphan of *Uncle Tom's Cabin* whose domestic pilfering prompts the northern Aunt Ophelia to try various ineffectual punishments? Topsy, who "never had no mother nor father, nor nothin' " (Stowe 356), has been raised by speculators, her family origins obscured as she is produced as property. Hence at the bottom of this piece of work, property attacks property, picking out stars or states from the national fabric. Slavery is held responsible for secession; the loss of property in the nation or the change in the boundaries of the nation finds tangible form in the texture of the material Columbia holds on her lap.

Holding the American flag on her lap, the accusing matron has her face in shadow and her arm and her lap in the light. The shading across her face, cast by the roof of the plantation house, peculiarly suggests that her whiteness is already compromised. Further, it suggests the scarcely-to-be-named possibility that Columbia herself is the offspring of a miscegenated union, having inherited more than whiteness from the forefathers of whom she reminds Topsey. Presented as without mother or father, Topsey is imagined with white *fore*fathers (and an overseer who will "fix" her, uncomfortably suggesting an assault on her own reproductive future). That, raised by speculators and reproved by a symbolic mother, she should understand herself to be answerable to forefathers seems odd; that is, why should she feel loyalty to men from whom she is not biologically descended and whose legislative determinations concerning her status have left her as property, not person?

The shadow cast across the face of this matron also produces an effect whereby her dark head and light body are mirrored by the light head and dark body of the eagle incongruously perched at her left. This national symbol further suggests the shadows Topsey's putative forefathers cast across the founding document of the republic. That is, the allusion to forefathers raises another point of national origins—the moment when a new nation was, as Abraham Lincoln recapitulated it, "conceived in liberty," during what might be called the first Civil War, the American Revolution. In this conception story, male generativeness was implicitly addressed as the authors who began debates about liberty found themselves assessing it through property. More specifically, when, after ratifying the Declaration of Independence in 1776, the assembled delegates addressed the Articles of Confederation, their first debates concerned the relation of war to taxation and citizenship to representation. What counted as property and what counted as a person preoccupied the delegates the most, according to Thomas Jefferson's *Autobiography* (1821, published in *Writings*). When the delegates tried to determine what sort of nation they were bringing into being, they began by counting inhabitants and assessing property. Slavery was the exacerbating factor in that accounting. As they debated the prosperity of a state and determined the relation between inhabitants and property, they asserted that "negroes are property . . . that negroes should not be considered as members of the state more than cattle and that they have no more interest in it" (Jefferson 25).[2]

The infamous subtraction of agency that slavery performs in conflating cattle with chattel led the delegates to further qualify their positions. According to Jefferson, "Mr. John Adams observed that . . . in some countries the laboring poor were called freemen, in others they were called slaves; but that the difference as to the states was imaginary only" (25). Adams tried to recuperate this "imaginary" distinction by asserting "that the condition of the laboring poor in most countries is as abject as that of slaves" (26). While such a contrast foreshadows the proslavery justifications of antebellum America, these debates also establish a hierarchy of national values that has persistently embedded capitalist determinations about labor within democracy. The delegates' attention seems limited to what to "call" slaves as though, whatever the nomenclature, their subject positions could not be altered. The Federalist concern with relating agency to property, with John Adams as a notable spokesperson, is an understood inheritance of the early national period. Nonetheless these narratives are haunted by the implication of so rendering property and persons together and its effect on the national imagining of racial and gendered identifications.

Jefferson's original wording displays the destructive ambivalence expressed by a Declaration of Independence that retained slavery. His *Autobiography* famously restores the passage that was excised from the final document. At first, the delegates' decision to remove this paragraph seems to tone down inflammatory accusations. This effect is clearly generated by other excisions from the declared production of two political entities where there had been only one. According to the removed passage, the king of England has, among other abuses already enumerated,

> waged cruel war against human nature itself, violating it's [*sic*] most sacred rights of life and liberty in the persons of a distant people who never offended him, captivating and carrying them into slavery in another hemisphere, or to incur miserable death in their transportation thither. . . . Determined to keep open a market where MEN should be bought & sold, he has prostituted his negative for suppressing every legislative attempt to prohibit or to restrain this execrable commerce. And that this assemblage of horrors might want no fact of distinguished die, he is now exciting those very people to rise in arms among us, and to purchase that liberty of which he has deprived them by murdering the people on whom he also obtruded them: thus paying off former crimes committed against the LIBERTIES of one people, with crimes which he urges them to commit against the LIVES of another. (22)

This passage locates the "sacred rights" of life and liberty in "persons" who are held as slaves. As such, a challenge to slaveholding practices in the colonies that are declaring themselves free, its very removal calls attention to an untenable contradiction. These colonies, themselves determined to keep open markets to buy and sell "MEN," are filled with the "very people" who might "rise in arms among us," suggesting a repetition of the seizure of liberty that the delegates are in the act of endorsing.

That Jefferson is further disturbed by a "market where MEN should be bought & sold" and does not mention women not only suggests the invisibility of women's labor in "this execrable commerce" but also occludes a different form of repetition. What is not surprising is that this economic and gender conflation at once removes sexuality and reproduction and retains the threat. That sexual reproduction will supplant the overseas traffic in human bodies and that these very forefathers are notoriously implicated in both reproductive and marketing practices with people held as slaves further align national economic, racial, and sexual practices. Beyond their uneasy position in the market lies the danger that these "MEN," like the men who meet to debate this document, might "rise in arms among us." The fear of such a repetition combined with the attention to (or, paradoxically, the invisibility of) the threat of reproduction fuels much political rhetoric of the early republic.

2

The white woman as emblem of America confronts the racial Other as she takes over admonition and housekeeping in the national house. In the second, anti-Lincoln cartoon, the national home is the White House. "Abraham's Dream!" shows a prostrate Lincoln in the foreground. Beyond the blanket of stars that covers his body and beneath the arch of a labeled White House, an irate Columbia kicks at a smaller disguised Lincoln while she holds aloft a severed head. Driven off by the decapitating force of the national female, he can say only, "This don't remind me of any joke!!" (Reilly 545). Clutching a severed head with the caricatured features of a male slave, this American Medusa freezes onlookers in a vision of national horror displaced onto female embodiment.[3]

A woman stands at the door to the "White House" and warns away the man who wants to enter (only tangentially the president of the United States). She invites another suitor. To frighten away the white man who wants to enter her house, she uses the severed head of an African-American man with caricatured features, who presumably has already entered the house with her for her to have had the opportunity—à la Judith and Holofernes—to decapitate him. By means of this white woman's body we see the massively compromised republic. And she is represented as the "dream" of a recumbent man snuggled under a blanket with stars on it—domesticity and national eroticism snuggle together in a dream about a white woman and an African-American man in the White House. Both images depict reprimand and shame, and the force of this shame persists to the present where we can scarcely, for the sake of our own embarrassment about the indecorousness of such comments on or about the body of the president of the United States, note that his upraised and foreshortened knee resembles an erection beneath the blanket of stars that covers his limbs.[4] The stars that have been picked out of the national flag in the first image have returned to be incorporated in the bedclothing of the dreamer, the president whose purported relation to miscegenation

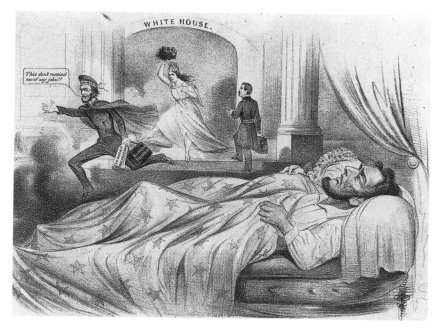

Fig. 5.2. "Abraham's Dream!" Bernard F. Reilly, Jr., *American Political Prints, 1766–1876: A Catalog of the Collections in the Library of Congress* (1991), 545.

may figure symbolically as a kind of national castration. He dreams of castration but finds it no "joke."

In thus interpreting the woman who guards the national home, I find content that for its primary audience may not have been even latent. This image may have been presented as a proleptic celebration of the triumph of the trim masculine figure of George McClellan over the faintly feminized disguise of Lincoln, who races clumsily away from the outstretched foot of Columbia.[5] The allusion to Judith and Holofernes, that is, that Judith's sexual complicity made it possible for her to decapitate the enemy general, would have been available to its audience. For the slave to be identified as the enemy is a deflection yet also a conflation of Lincoln's position with that of the slave. These images thus mobilize cognitive energies that they cannot presume to control. The citation, quotation, and allusion of the text buttress or call into question the citation, quotation, or allusion of the image. Such a relation between word and image complicates, extends, and shifts our sense of what we respond to: that we cannot read and "see" at once might mean that to choose either at least momentarily dislodges the force and effect of the other. Hence, in the oscillation between one and the other, the stasis of allegory is nudged by language that alludes to or insists on a connection to other images and texts.[6]

As broadsides sold for display in city streets, these images were intended for reproduction and mass circulation. They were packaged and sold as public art to influence a public that viewed them in the context of literary and political events.[7] To imagine how that viewing operates may be helped by a concept that has been called the suture, which not only unites the spectator with the viewed object but also describes how the spectator's identity may be affected by the viewing. In the case of these political cartoons, suturing takes on a still more problematic valence. The subject who faces this version of Medusa's head may be frozen, but these images are not to be contemplated in immobility, not to be understood as private, but rather in their public display they are to mobilize to action. Taken off the street, these images appear at once iconographically (as visual codifications of ideology) and as multivalently referential (as situated within a framework of literary and political texts).

It is not surprising that the presidential campaigns during the American Civil War used caricatures of the president and a female embodiment of the American nation. Nor should it be surprising that some chastising be depicted. But what appear quite stunning here are the particular shame and humiliation and the rather unusual establishment of these scenes on the threshold of an imagined national home. Homi Bhabha has argued that it is through the "syntax of forgetting" that "the problematic identification of a national people becomes visible"—"[b]eing obliged to forget becomes the basis for remembering the nation, peopling it anew, imagining the possibility of other contending and liberating forms of cultural identification" (160, 161). While these cartoons remind us of powerful and disturbing omissions and insist on certain forms of forgetting, what peopling the nation anew might mean without reproduction is arguably as problematic in Bhabha as in these imaginings of the nation. They provide a "liberating" form of cultural and national identification insofar as to identify with this white woman's body as a repository of national beliefs is "to forget" that she can literally people the nation anew.

Looking at a dream of race in the nation means looking at sexualized racial difference; these stereotypes and clichés powerfully negotiate national imaginings about race and sexuality (see, e.g., Wiegman 43–62). In Michel de Certeau's account, *"intelligibility is established through a relation with the other"* (3). Hence history is a "practice of meaning" that " 'legitimizes' the force that power exerts; it provides this force with a familial, political, or moral genealogy" (7). Such a legitimizing practice of meaning emerges in fictional narratives as well: "fiction can be found at the end of the process, in the product of the manipulation and the analysis" (9). A literary history of such nation-home imagining has always implied the presence of sexual misconduct with an alien or alienated population, from the homes with secret closets of Charles Brockden Brown's *Wieland* (1798) to the secret abortion of Caroline Kirkland's *A New Home—Who'll Follow?* (1839), from the map of Indian territory in the hidden space behind the patriarchal portrait of Nathaniel Hawthorne's *The House of the Seven Gables* (1851) to the intimate space of *Uncle Tom's Cabin*, a home whose enshrined portrait of George Washington makes the national father unrecognizable. As Cassy and Emmeline make themselves into ghosts in the attic at the end of *Uncle Tom's Cabin*, they reveal the horror of what bodies can occupy these homes or in which nations these homes can be inhabited.[8] For Stowe, the answer is emigration to Liberia and not assimilation in the United States, and like so many of these narratives the attempt to imagine a home in the nation and a nation in the home results in the *unheimlich* business of dispossession—of removal to a new territory. *A New Home—Who'll Follow?* can be told only by someone who has retreated from the landscape of mud-holes back to the urban territory of her readers. Stowe's readers are already in the North toward which her subjects journey, and yet, for all her appeals to the home, her characters do not find a home in the nation of her readers.

3

To lay claim to a home in the nation is to lay claim to an inheritance, to property transmitted through generations. Obsessions with genealogy and with the hereditary transmission of identity compete in the narratives of the early republic with a concept of identity transmitted through writing or print culture.[9] Documents such as the Declaration of Independence or Benjamin Franklin's *Autobiography* equivalently display extraordinary faith in the effect of written declarations of identity that supersede biology or nation. The anxiety about how to manage an inheritance of identity as well as property informs the context of another surprise best-seller in nineteenth-century America, the last will and testament of Stephen Girard. Among other feats, Girard single-handedly purchased the Bank of the United States and bailed out the nation by underwriting the War of 1812. Some similar conjunctions of money and race emerge among the stranger details of the posthumous biography written by Girard's employee Stephen Simpson, obviously to cash in on the excitement generated by the death of the richest man in America, but also because Girard, a sort of alternative Franklin, refused to write any account of himself other than his will— leaving his will to represent him in dispersals of cash, since he left no offspring. With no son to inherit it, his wealth took on a different character: "To *money*,—to millions only could he look, as the medium between him and after times" (Simpson 45).

According to his 1832 biographer, Girard's extraordinary fortune had an unlikely origin in the San Domingo uprising. Along with the French Revolution, the San Domingo insurrection posed the greatest challenge to an identity born from revolution since slaves did become free, "rise in arms among us," and "purchase" liberty through murder. Since Girard was heavily engaged in shipping, his ships were in the harbor when the planters who "rushed" to them "to deposit their most valuable property" returned to meet "an unexpected doom from the hands of their slaves. In this manner the most precious valuables were deposited in his vessels, whose proprietors and heirs were cut off, by the ruthless sword of massacre." When the ships hurried out to sea, "much of the unclaimed and *heirless* property, justly fell to the lot of the owners. Girard received a large accession to his wealth by this terrific scourge of the hapless planters of St. Domingo. All heirship was swept away, in the total extinguishment of entire families, and the most extensive advertising failed to produce a legal claimant to the property thus poured into his lap" (Simpson 41–42).[10] This origin story about Girard's wealth may be combined with the salacious detail provided by his biographer, who notes that the walls of his bedroom "were ornamented with coloured prints, representing the female negroes of *St. Domingo*" (Simpson 187). Both the presumed sexual availability of such women and the erotics of property poured into his lap.

In seeking to connect with posterity through his money, Girard wished historical immortality: "that the name of *Girard* should be lisped by infant tongues, and extolled by ancient wisdom, when that of *Penn* should be almost forgotten, and that of *Franklin* was only to be found in *books*" (Simpson 64). The romance of the republic for him was to run "the institution of a bank, destined to control millions, and to rescue a sinking country from impending ruin; whose operations were to become blended with the currency of the nation" (Simpson 96). Speculating in the stock of the old "Bank of the United States . . . an institution founded by GEORGE WASHINGTON" led him to it. He bought the Bank of the United States for $120,000 and supported the United States after the War of 1812 broke out. In saving the Bank of the United States he acted to maintain the civil and economic order of the government. "Money is the sinew of war. A nation that becomes belligerent, without having previously amassed wealth, must necessarily become more or less a slave to the *capitalist*" (128). The slavery exacted by this capitalist included the conversion of all objects and persons under his control as part of a particular passion for production.

A typical physiocrat economics emerges, for example, in the details of Girard's exemplary utilitarian relation to men and plants. Like his contemporary J. Hector St. John de Crevecoeur, Girard understood men and plants as producers and had little patience with or interest in other claims for his sympathy: "The great object of his life was to *produce*." "So powerful was this passion for production," says his biographer, "that he often declared it was ridiculous to plant a tree that would not bear fruit" (Simpson 151). The conversion of persons into categories of economic interest may be seen as already coextensive with such conversions or reductions in slavery and also as displaced sexual production. Girard's affection for gardening, for example, had extreme results: "[H]is passion for pruning was excessive; and often found no end but in the total extermination of the tree; especially when he found it obstinate in growth, or slow in bearing fruit" (Simpson 150–51).

Girard's last illness kept all of Philadelphia in suspense, perhaps because he had loaned out four million dollars. Rumors "followed one another in quick succession, till the excitement of the public mind grew to a pitch equal to that which would have attended the illness of the first public character of the republic" (Simpson 210). After the first great American financier finally died, his will was published: "Thousands of copies were disposed of in a few days; and being quickly copied into the public journals throughout the Union, it was more extensively diffused than any document of a similar character, not excepting the will of *George Washington*" (Simpson 213). The provisions he made for canals, public building, and Girard College were debated, but there was also prurient curiosity about his personal bequests, and moral judgments were passed on other decisions. In particular, his biographer declared that the "part of his Will respecting the *slaves* on his *Louisiana Estate* has been justly and warmly condemned, as at total variance with the character of philanthropy that has been so lavishly ascribed to him." He "left them in perpetual bondage" when he could have "provided the fiscal means to transport these *miserables* to their native country; and have provided them with the means of independent subsistence for a limited number of years. . . . The *colony of Liberia* would have been the proper destination of these unfortunate beings" (267). Girard's capitalist construction of the nation becomes inseparable from origin stories through slavery and revolution or dissemination stories that work through slavery and exile.

The manner in which the erotics of slavery haunts the nation becomes visible, for instance, through repeated references to the uprisings in San Domingo. In what Stowe's novel calls "the San Domingo hour," she imagines that "sons of white fathers . . . will rise, and raise with them their mother's race" (392). Her already compromised solution or evasion of such domestic and national violence is relocation to a new nation based on race. Colonization to Liberia was a suspect and challenged project twenty years before the publication of *Uncle Tom's Cabin*—that Stowe cannot imagine a nation *not* based on race informs her colonialism from the inside out. According to a recent study of their origins, " 'race' and 'nation' derive from the same concept of 'lineage' or 'stock' yet it was 'race' that ultimately became the major term of ethnographic scholarship while 'nation' was reserved to describe the political and social divisions of Europe. . . . In our century, the close relation of 'race' and 'nation' has proved to be an especially volatile source of political passions and conflict" (Hudson 248). In the late eighteenth century, race became separated from nation according to the same binary logic that opposed biology to custom or nature to habits and beliefs. In the mid–nineteenth century, there was a "violent reunion" (Hudson 258).

The violence of this reunion—of putting nation and race back together—is most emphatic in the racial and sexual violence of miscegenation. What do we see when we see race? The matter of skin might be inconsequential to this seeing. The matter of sexuality might be central to it. To "rescue" *Uncle Tom's Cabin* as a woman's novel is not yet to address the imbrications of sexuality with racial identification (see Tompkins chap. 5). If to see race in *Uncle Tom's Cabin* means to see miscegenation, what image of miscegenation is presented? What we see when we see race in these representations is sexual—that is to say, both sexual availability and the promise/threat of miscegenation.

In "Mama's Baby, Papa's Maybe: An American Grammar Book," Hortense Spillers calls attention to the crisis caused by "laws of inheritance" that "need to know which son of the Father's is the legitimate heir and which one the imposter. For that reason, property seems wholly the business of the male" (65; see also Spillers, "Changing the Letter"). As property and inheritance are so bound up with legitimacy, so property becomes bound up with subjectivity:

> 1) the captive body becomes the source of an irresistible, destructive sensuality; 2) at the same time—in stunning contradiction—the captive body reduces to a thing, becoming *being for* the captor; 3) in this absence *from* a subject position, the captured sexualities provide a physical and biological expression of "otherness"; 4) as a category of "otherness," the captive body translates into a potential for pornotroping and embodies sheer physical powerlessness that slides into a more general "powerlessness," resonating through various centers of human and social meaning. (Spillers, "Mama's Baby" 67)

To rework this model of the gendering of race for the purposes of imagining the relations of families and nations, we might look at how "captured sexualities [that] provide a physical and biological expression of 'otherness' " extend into the matter of miscegenation. Racism in many respects depends on keeping otherness in view, and the visible changes that result from miscegenation make that, at the least, difficult.

The loss of subjectivity translates not just into being a "thing"—as, for example in the original subtitle of *Uncle Tom's Cabin*, "The Man Who Was a Thing"—but crucially into "*being for* the captor." In "being for," the possibility of being becomes always connected to a primary subject who owns. Yet if the captor's being has been incorporated in "being for the captor," then the places of both captor and captive seem vividly threatened. Such destabilized positions may explain abolitionist interest in promoting the figure of the tragic mulatta. To contemplate this figure arouses at once the sexuality and the implicated identity of the onlooker if not the possessor-father.

To imagine eradicating that connection is also to question the possibility of ownership. It is necessary not only to promote the ownership of yourself ("being for" yourself) but also to evade the loss of ownership experienced in the moments when the self-owned becomes the other-owned, when being for yourself becomes being for anyone else who might claim you.[11] But the relations of families and nations incorporate property in the matter of reproduction. To quote Spillers again: "Certainly if 'kinship' were possible, the property relations would be undermined, since the offspring would then 'belong' to a mother and a father." The matter of belonging means in effect that "genetic reproduction" appears as "an extension of the boundaries of proliferating properties." Finally, "the captive female body locates precisely a moment of converging political and social vectors that mark the flesh as a prime commodity of exchange" ("Mama's Baby" 74, 75). To note how flesh is marked as a commodity for exchange moves the matter of desire in the direction of reproduction. That both desire and reproduction are political emerges in the political cartoons that, among other things, unite the imagined sexuality and/or violence of an African-American identity with the body of the president of the United States, Abraham Lincoln.

Now Lincoln famously did (or did not) say upon meeting Harriet Beecher Stowe that she had started this "big war." That act of naming, placing credit and blame for the bloodiest conflict in the history of the United States on the shoulders of a small New England housewife, also condenses (or places in strange perspective) the attitude that fiction permeates national politics. In considering the interrelation of political and artistic acts of representation, we discover in their shared images and anxieties an engaging paradigm for how national identities are produced.[12]

4

The convergence of racial and sexual matters leads me to consider again the extraordinary twins of *Uncle Tom's Cabin*. Augustine St. Clare explains, halfway through the novel, "My brother and I were twins . . . but we were in all points a contrast. He had black, fiery eyes, coal-black hair, a Roman profile, and a rich brown complexion. I had blue eyes, golden hair, a Grecian profile, and a fair complexion" (333–34). In so describing the contrast of their appearances with racial codes, Augustine implies that his brother passes for white. They also claim different parents, a prelude to the amazing statement that sons of white fathers will rise, and that in rising they will take with them their mother's race. Since the sons of white fathers must emerge from the same body as the sons of their presumed not-white mothers, the separation of twinned racial identities in the ideological claims of these brothers seems all the stranger. In debating the San Domingo uprising, the darker brother Alfred says, "The Haytiens were not Anglo-Saxons; if they had been, there would have been another story. The Anglo-Saxon is the dominant race of the world, and *is to be so*" (392). Such certainty eerily echoes the portion of the Declaration of Independence which posits that these united colonies are and of right ought to be free and independent states. Augustine seizes on one implication of the possible contradiction that lurks beneath Alfred's prophetic utterance of "is to be so":

> "Well, there is a pretty fair infusion of Anglo-Saxon blood among our slaves, now," said Augustine. "There are plenty among them who have only enough of the African to give a sort of tropical warmth and fervor to our calculating firmness and foresight. If ever the St. Domingo hour comes, Anglo-Saxon blood will lead on the day. Sons of white fathers, with all our haughty feelings burning in their veins, will not always be bought and sold and traded. They will rise, and raise with them their mother's race." (392)

How to imagine racial separation within one body is the project not only of these twins but of Twain's twinning of *Pudd'nhead Wilson* with *Those Extraordinary Twins*. Myra Jehlen, among others, has noted how the attempt to imagine the nature/nurture debate through race becomes as painful and inextricable as the separation of Siamese twins—which is guilty?[13] To separate out the body that commits the crime from the body that is innocent radically unsettles how to understand this question racially, but also how to understand it sexually—how did the sons of white fathers become engendered?

Pregnancy is already two bodies in one, but the birth of twins literalizes the split. Two bodies emerge from one, and racializing the two bodies is at the core of the problem of reproduction. An unnerving detail about women in this account is that bodies emerge from them bearing the blood of the fathers. Bodily impressibility—bodily inscription—is the crime and the punishment at once. And the bodily inscription can be lethal: slavery kills little Eva as, echoing Frederick Douglass's narrative, she announces that "these things sink into my heart" (237).[14]

Dramatizations of Stowe's novel further explore the possibility of revenge. Even more people than the extraordinary number who read the novel saw these dramatizations through a proliferation of stage companies who specialized in "Tomming."[15] What kinds of revenge are acted out in scenes where Cassy gets to shoot Haley or where Haley is revealed as the villain who stabbed St. Clare—or where Eva and Uncle Tom are reunited in Heaven? These scenes collapse property and will: property willed ethereally where it cannot be left materially. In the concluding scene, staged for many audiences, was a "safe" version of their worst nightmare: the body of a white female entwined with the body of an African-American male. In the novel, Eva kisses Uncle Tom, drapes him with flowers, and gives him a lock of her hair. In the dramatization, she waits for him in heaven with her arms outstretched, and they are joined in the afterlife in transubstantial miscegenation.[16]

George Aiken's *Uncle Tom's Cabin* brings the drama to a close when Marks shows up as a comical lawyer who presents a warrant for the arrest of Legree for murdering Augustine St. Clare just as "Cassy produces a knife and stabs Legree who falls dead" (83). In another version by Aiken, Legree is shot by Marks. In still another version, by the British playwright Thomas Hailes Lacey, he is shot by Cassy, who says, "[N]ow we are quits, and if they burn me alive, I shall die rejoicing in the deed that has avenged the martyrdom of so many hapless victims" (29). George Harris enters with George Shelby, and the last lines of the play, from Uncle Tom, are "bless you, George Harris!—bless you, dear—little—mas'r George!" (Lacey 30).

This last dramatization emphasizes another form of implicit twinning in Stowe's novel: the case of the two "Georges"—George Shelby and George Harris—twinned Georges who may be understood as the alternative sons of the father, George Washington. While this dramatization finds them together at the end, blessed by Uncle Tom, the novel places them very far apart. After his doomed journey to the South, George Shelby returns to Kentucky. After his successful escape to the North, passing as a white man despite the brand left on his hand, George Harris heads to Liberia.

Stowe's novel explicitly aligns race and nation when George Harris writes of his choice of nation. Where his earlier declaration of independence has him declare himself ready to die for freedom, he now proclaims himself ready to "work till I die" (298, 611). He says, "My sympathies are not for my father's race but for my mother's" (608). These sympathies, however, appear not as racial but as national: "I have no wish to pass for an American. . . . The desire and yearning of my soul is for an African *nationality*" (608). Still nationality is read as a racial inheritance that, he laments, cannot be found in the uprisings of San Domingo: "[T]he race that formed the character of the Haytiens was a worn-out effeminate one" (608–9). He proclaims that "[a] nation has a right to argue . . . the cause of its race,—which an individual has not" (610).[17] Seeking to find a nation which can make such an argument, he claims that, "[i]n these days, a nation is born in a day" (609). The day of this imagined nation's birth, like the "birth" of the United States, shows a nationalism inseparable from sexuality and race. If a nation that has the "right" to argue the cause of its race can be born in a day, the engendering makes race and sexuality inseparable.

NOTES

1. I have in mind the stereotyping of the welfare mother as the blame figure for the crisis of family values in an election year.

2. The etymological relation between the origins of cattle and chattel arguably influences their conjunction in slavery discussions. John Adams further asserts, according to Jefferson, that "[r]eason, justice, and equity never had weight enough on the face of the earth to govern the councils of men. It is interest alone which does it, and it is interest alone which can be trusted" (29).

3. For a complementary discussion of the trope of the Medusa, see Samuels 3–14.

4. Only after looking at this image many times did I notice that the president has his arm around the shoulders of a body whose frilled cap is all that signals an identity, presumably that of Mary Todd, the irrelevance of whose presence may be noted in what he dreams about.

5. Lincoln was ridiculed for a rumored attempt to enter Washington, D.C., disguised as a Scotchman after an assassination threat.

6. W.J.T. Mitchell approaches the "image-text conjunction" in cartoons through the concept of "suture." Extending this position to include "*reader* and *listener*" (91–92n15), he further asserts that the cartoon page involves "the clear subordination and suturing of one medium to the other" in which "word is to image as speech (or thought) is to action and bodies" (91–92). The incitement to action is a way of separating propaganda from art, though it is not my intent here to address that distinction.

7. Some of the images carry at their borders details on how to purchase them. The racist anti-Lincoln print of "Miscegenation, or the Millennium of Abolitionism" (1864), for example, could be bought in bulk from Currier and Ives, otherwise famous as purveyors of pastoral landscape images. This purchasing of political art further extends the implications of the work of art in the age of mechanical reproduction. For reproduction of this print (542), as well as others in the collection of the Library of Congress, and for helpful commentary, see Reilly.

8. I am also drawing on the forms of gothic imaginings about women threatened at home, and in particular on the account Karen Halttunen gives of *Uncle Tom's Cabin* as a gothic narrative informed by the temperance agitation rhetoric of Henry Ward Beecher.

9. See the variant accounts of transmitting identity through language in this period, one emphasizing performance and the other publication, by Jay Fliegelman (*Declaring Independence: Jefferson's Natural Language and the Culture of Performance* [1993]) and Michael Warner (*Letters of the Republic: Publication and the Public Sphere in Eighteenth-Century America* [1990]).

10. I also have in mind the contrast here between two monolithic, extraordinary, willfully dynastic figures, Toussaint L'Ouverture and Stephen Girard. Each tried

to imagine himself within the context of a nation-building enterprise that transforms him from his origins.

11. Hence the attention to possessive individualism and sentimental fetishism in Gillian Brown's accounts of Stowe in *Domestic Individualism: Imagining Self in Nineteenth-Century America* (1990).

12. A number of abstract categories here could use unpacking: "race," "nation," and "identity" are mutually constitutive, hardly, and only with violence, to be separated into the components that fracture the surfaces of these fictions and cartoons.

13. Harriet Beecher Stowe's first children were twins: daughters born when her husband was off in Europe buying books for Lane Seminary. She named the first-born after her husband's first (deceased) wife Eliza, and the second she named Isabella. When her husband returned and found out the names, he wrote her very excitedly to insist that the second be renamed: "Eliza and Harriet! *Eliza and Harriet!* ELIZA AND HARRIET!" He wanted to give these twins the twinned identities of his two wives. That Stowe then gives the name of Eliza to the heroine of her most famous episode establishes her own identity as a shadow twin to this protagonist (qtd. in Hedrick 112). Stowe later wrote that one child was "hers" and the other "his"—an early instance of the strange sense of separate gestations that pervades her account of Alfred and Augustine St. Clare. For another intriguing account of essentialist identity, see Jehlen.

14. "These words sank deep into my heart" (Douglass 48). The novel does allow something that Cassy threatens: the annihilation of a child. The understood agony of her retelling of this story is that her loss of children has driven her to this mode of "protection."

15. The first stage version was presented three months before the serialization in the *National Era* was completed and, of course, did not contain the ending. By the fall of 1853, five versions were playing simultaneously in New York City, including one at P. T. Barnum's American Museum that had a happy ending. During the Civil War the drama fell into disuse. In the 1870s it was revived with a vengeance. Within twenty years there were close to five hundred traveling companies of "Tommers."

16. "Gorgeous clouds, tinted with sunlight. Eva, robed in white, is discovered on the back of a milk-white dove, with expanded wings, as if just soaring upward. Her hands are extended in benediction over St. Clare and Uncle Tom, who are kneeling and gazing up to her. Impressive music. Slow curtain" (Aiken 396).

17. Frederick Douglass may be seen responding to this in his plea for individual as opposed to national rights—"Oceans no longer divide, but link nations together"—in "What to the Slave is the Fourth of July" (1852) (*Reader* 108–30).

WORKS CITED

Aiken, George, adapt. *Uncle Tom's Cabin*. 1852. New York: Garland, 1994.

Bhabha, Homi K. *The Location of Culture*. London: Routledge, 1994.

Brown, Gillian. *Domestic Individualism: Imagining Self in Nineteenth-Century America*. Berkeley: U of California P, 1990.

Clemens, Samuel Langhorne [Mark Twain]. Pudd'nhead Wilson *and* Those Extraordinary Twins: *Authoritative Texts, Textual Introduction, and Tables of Variants, Criticism.* Ed. Sidney E. Berger. New York: Norton, 1980.

de Certeau, Michel. *The Writing of History.* Trans. Tom Conley. New York: Columbia UP, 1988.

Douglass, Frederick. *The Oxford Frederick Douglass Reader.* Ed. William L. Andrews. New York: Oxford UP, 1996.

Fliegelman, Jay. *Declaring Independence: Jefferson's Natural Language and the Culture of Performance.* Stanford: Stanford UP, 1993.

Halttunen, Karen. "Gothic Imagination and Social Reform: The Haunted Houses of Lyman Beecher, Henry Ward Beecher, and Harriet Beecher Stowe." *New Essays on* Uncle Tom's Cabin. Ed. Eric J. Sundquist. The American Novel 6. Cambridge: Cambridge UP, 1986. 107–34.

Hedrick, Joan D. *Harriet Beecher Stowe: A Life.* New York: Oxford UP, 1994.

Hudson, Nicholas. "From 'Nation' to 'Race': The Origin of Racial Classification in Eighteenth-Century Thought." *Eighteenth-Century Studies* 29 (1996): 247–64.

Jefferson, Thomas. *Writings.* New York: Library of America, 1984.

Jehlen, Myra. "The Ties That Bind: Race and Sex in *Pudd'nhead Wilson.*" *American Literary History* 2 (1990): 39–55.

Lacey, Thomas Hailes, adapt. *Uncle Tom's Cabin.* London: Thomas Scott, 1853.

Mitchell, W.J.T. *Picture Theory: Essays on Verbal and Visual Representation.* Chicago: U of Chicago P, 1994.

Reilly, Bernard F., Jr. *American Political Prints, 1766–1876: A Catalog of the Collections in the Library of Congress.* Boston: Hall, 1991.

Samuels, Shirley. *Romances of the Republic: Women, the Family, and Violence in the Literature of the Early American Nation.* New York: Oxford UP, 1996.

Simpson, Stephen. *Biography of Stephen Girard, with His Will Affixed. . . .* 2d ed. Philadelphia, 1832.

Spillers, Hortense. "Changing the Letter: The Yokes, the Jokes of Discourse, or Mrs. Stowe, Mrs. Reed." *Slavery and the Literary Imagination: Selected Papers from the English Institute 1987.* Ed. Deborah McDowell and Arnold Rampersad. Baltimore: Johns Hopkins UP, 1989. 25–65.

———. "Mama's Baby, Papa's Maybe: An American Grammar Book." *Diacritics* (1987): 65–81.

Stowe, Harriet Beecher. *Uncle Tom's Cabin: Or, Life among the Lowly.* 1852. New York: Penguin, 1981.

Tompkins, Jane: *Sensational Designs: The Cultural Work of American Fiction 1790–1860.* New York: Oxford UP, 1986.

Warner, Michael. *Letters of the Republic: Publication and the Public Sphere in Eighteenth-Century America.* Cambridge: Harvard UP, 1990.

Wiegman, Robyn. *American Anatomies: Theorizing Race and Gender.* Durham: Duke UP, 1995.

CHAPTER 6

The Whiteness of Film Noir

ERIC LOTT

In the final moments of Edward Dmytryk's *Murder, My Sweet* (1944), the police offer private dick Philip Marlowe (Dick Powell) the priceless jade necklace Marlowe has at last recovered for his wealthy client. The chief object of mercenary desire in the film and therefore a figure for the corruption and deceit of its dramatis personae, the necklace also suggests an Oriental(ist) languor whose fruits could now be all Marlowe's. Marlowe declines: "No thanks," he says; "it's wrong for my complexion." We are given to understand "complexion" first and foremost in the moral sense; Marlowe has beaten the forces of greed and graft that threaten to swamp him no less than the roués, quacks, idle rich, and petty mobsters who surround him. In another and equally pressing sense, though, Marlowe has remained true to a racial physiognomy, that of whiteness, which indexes his pristine soul.

Film noir—"black film" as French critics first dubbed it in 1946—has long fascinated observers with its interest in darkened frames and darkened lives. But the specifically racial means of noir's obsession with the dark side of 1940s American life has been remarkably ignored. Perhaps this should come as no surprise: raced metaphors in popular life are as indispensable, and rendered as invisible, as the colored bodies who give rise to and move in the shadows of those usages. Yet not to call attention to film noir's fairly insistent thematizing of spiritual and cinematic darkness by way of bodies beyond the pale is to persist in a commonsense exploitation enacted by films (running from roughly the early 1940s to the mid 1950s) that stress the unwholesome predicaments of whites and have been accepted by a rich history of commentary. I would enlarge the frame of recent work by Toni Morrison, Kenneth Warren (10–11), William Boelhower (109), and others on the ways in which racial tropes and the presence of African Americans have shaped the sense and structure of American cultural products that on their face have nothing to do with race.[1] The informing presence of racial difference in the American imaginary, which amounts to little less than a constitutive condition of cultural articulation, not surprisingly suffuses a cinematic mode known to traffic in black hearts and minds. At a moment when bold new forms of black, Chicano, and Asian activism and visibility confronted resurgent white revanchism and vigilantism, film noir's relentless cinematography of chiaroscuro and moral focus on the rotten souls of white folks, I will argue, constantly though obliquely invoked the racial dimension of this figural play of light against dark.

Criticism of film noir since the 1940s has variously sensed the form's uses of otherness. In the French critical notice that brought "film noir" into our vocabulary, that otherness is chiefly moral or psychosocial—a preponderance of crime, violence, obsession, and guilt— the "dark" side of the white Western self (see Frank; Chartrier; Borde and Chaumeton). Nicholas Ray's *In a Lonely Place* (1950), for one, associates its protagonist Dixon Steele (Humphrey Bogart) with all of these, though his actual culpability is left in some doubt. The Stateside burst of critical activity on noir in the late 1960s and early 1970s, which brought the form firmly into the orbit of American critical allure, took for granted this emphasis and began to expand on its innovative stylistic expressions (see, for example, Higham and Greenberg 19–36; Place and Peterson). Paul Schrader went so far as to claim that noir was characterized primarily by its emphasis on visual style. First noting the hardened sociopolitical mood of the 1970s that precipitated an embrace of noir's thematic affinities (8), Schrader acutely observes the peculiar cinematic attack 1940s films made on their own political moment: "[*Film noir*] tried to make America accept a moral vision of life based on style. . . . *Film noir* attacked and interpreted its sociological conditions, and, by the close of the *noir* period, created a new artistic world which went beyond a simple sociological reflection, a nightmarish world of American mannerism which was by far more a creation than a reflection" (13). In Schrader's account, the stylistic recurrence in noir of night scenes, shadows, oppressively composed frames, odd angles of light, actors dwarfed by overly prominent surroundings, complex chronologies, and the like (11) is itself a negation of the corrupt society responsible for producing this corrosive cinematic response. Given a social prod, in other words, noir comes back with style. Although the world of noir is bleak, stylistically it is (as Richard Poirier once called American literature) a world elsewhere; we confront it in forms that transcend its perils. What Schrader calls film noir's "shades of black" (9) are in fact strategies of artistic othering meant to surmount the cynicism, meaninglessness, and psychosis that they nonetheless portray.

If the blackness of style is seen here as a kind of clear-eyed, panicky refuge—which only extends earlier critics' celebration of noir's bringing the dark to light in what Mike Davis calls noir's "Marxist *cinema manqué*" (41)—many recent critics have on the contrary seen the frightening "other" side of American life portrayed in film noir as crucially reliant upon the villainous and villainized women to be found there. E. Ann Kaplan's collection *Women in Film Noir* (1978) first established that the faithless, ruthless women in noir exemplify and perform the dark deeds that signify the underside of the self which upstanding men must refuse in the interest of self-preservation. Female power is the quite apparent crime these women represent, and films noir typically require that power to be renounced, compromised, or destroyed. Noir men like Walter Neff (Fred MacMurray) in Billy Wilder's *Double Indemnity* (1944) often fall prey to them, of course, thereby succumbing to the "darkness" noir firmly associates with feminine wiles. The feminist critique of noir constitutes the most far-reaching account of the self's partitioning (into good/masculine and evil/feminine) in this run of American films, and without it our understanding of noir would be impoverished indeed. My own essay follows in its tracks, and since the processes of identification and disavowal that I will explore here usually involve an overlapping series of gender and racial feelings, this work on noir has already begun to ask the sorts of questions whose answers, I believe, require a racial component. My purpose is to ask why, as yet, no one has challenged the association in these films of the self's and society's darkness with a racial dimension, and why that dimension in the form of striking black appearances on film has seemed merely marginal, local, and insubstantial. Even Joan Copjec's recent collection *Shades of Noir*, which explicitly attempts to place noir within more specific urban and political topographies, does not trouble the racial unconscious of noir possibly at work in her very title. The opening pages of Manthia Diawara's contribution to the Copjec anthology—on the way noirs by current black directors work classic noir codes to their own purposes—have a clear sense of the racial metaphorics of noir's "shades" (261–63), but this sort of analysis is not undertaken between the volume's covers.[2]

Diawara rightly remarks the interanimation of noir's stylistic, moral, and implicitly racial concerns. "[A] film is *noir* if it puts into play light and dark in order to exhibit a people who become 'black' because of their 'shady' moral behaviour" (262). The slippage in Diawara's own exact epigram ("black" racially or morally?) clues us into the ease with which racial tropes are both literalized and dissipated; or rather, since both racial and moral senses here are metaphorical, it shows us how elusive yet coherent is the metaphorical character of racial definition. Such slippages indicate, then, the ready use-value and real centrality of racial tropes despite their emanation from the margins of white texts and Caucasian lives. In this the figurations of race work like most important features of the psychosymbolic domain. As Peter Stallybrass and Allon White write, the "most powerful *symbolic* repertoires" of bourgeois societies are situated at their "borders, margins and edges, rather than at the accepted centres" (20); they reprocess, displace and condense, perform the labor of the signifier on the social formation's boundary-defining events, materials, and relationships, and thrust them to the center of its socially symbolic narrative acts: there are no simple correspondences or one-to-one relations here. Indeed, the apparent marginality of racial Others in the postwar U.S. social formation (whatever their absolute centrality to its labor and culture) might encourage us to dismiss any seemingly racial associations in film noir as merely coincidental, tricks of demography, or the ruses of metaphor; when in fact such metaphorical ruses and the presence of black, Asian, or Mexican bodies confirm the central symbolic significance of color to the black-and-white world of many noirs, which revolve upon a racial axis that exerts great force at more key moments in more films than can easily be written off as exceptions.

Whether it is the racialized dramas of interiority in such films as Wilder's *Double Indemnity*, Delmer Daves's *Dark Passage* (1947), Robert Rossen's *Body and Soul* (1947), George Cukor's *A Double Life* (1947), Orson Welles's *The Lady from Shanghai* (1948), Max Ophuls's *The Reckless Moment* (1949), or Ray's *In a Lonely Place*; the black, Asian, and Mexican urbanscapes and underworlds of Dmytryk's *Murder, My Sweet*, *The Lady from Shanghai*, *The Reckless Moment*, Rudolph Mate's *D.O.A.* (1950), or Welles's *Touch of Evil* (1958) (the self-conscious endpoint of noir and its racial tropes, as we shall see); the hysterically racialized family romances of Michael Curtiz's *Mildred Pierce* (1945), Charles Vidor's *Gilda* (1946), *The Reckless Moment*, Otto Preminger's *Angel Face* (1953), Fritz Lang's *The Big Heat* (1953), and others; or any of a number of minor reliances and major subtexts, the troping of white darkness in noir has a racial source that is all the more insistent for seeming off to the side. Film noir is replete with characters of color who populate and signify the shadows of white American life in the 1940s. Noir may have pioneered Hollywood's unprecedentedly merciless exposure of white pathology, but by relying on race to convey that pathology, it in effect erected a cordon sanitaire around the circle of corruption it sought to penetrate. Film noir rescues with racial idioms the whites whose moral and social boundaries seem so much in doubt. "Black film" is the refuge of whiteness.

DOUBLE INDEMNITY

"No visible scars—till a while ago, that is": Walter Neff's account of himself at the start of *Double Indemnity* refers us not only to the gunshot wound administered by femme fatale Phyllis Dietrichson (Barbara Stanwyck) but again to the "complexion" of a man so scarred by his own deceit, violence, and cunning and so fully immersed in blackened cinematic compositions that his darkness threatens to manifest itself on his very skin. Indeed, in a very stylish conceptual move Neff's shoulder wound bleeds through his suit jacket little by little throughout his voiceover flashback so that the stain, which of course appears black on screen, grows larger with Neff's deepening involvement in passion and crime. Secluded after hours in the darkened Pacific All-Risk Insurance Company office building tended almost wholly by black janitors and custodians, Neff now inhabits the racial space *Double Indemnity* constantly links with his dark deeds.

Neff's adulterous partnership with Phyllis Dietrichson has from the beginning taken the form of a passage out of whiteness. Phyllis lives in a "California Spanish house" built, Neff surmises, in the mid-1920s, a moment of racial exoticism and primitivism perfectly appropriate to Phyllis's darkling designs. When Neff first sees her, she has been sunbathing, and this historically relatively new white interest in fashionable self-othering, together with the redoubtable signifier of Phyllis's anklet or "slave bracelet," makes even more necessary the cosmetic masquerade of Phyllis's attempt to get her "face on straight." Already the open visage of Los Angeles is consigned to the realm of mere appearances and masks, which hide the unwhite portents of no good. This diagnosis is clinched by the cut from this scene to the office of Pacific All-Risk's claims manager Barton Keyes (Edward G. Robinson), who is in the act of sniffing out Greek American Sam Garlopis's fraudulent insurance claim (he has torched his own truck—a foretaste of the "blacker" attempts at fraud to come). Garlopis's Greekness suggests his potential for moral lapse as his duplicity defines his excessive ethnicity; showing him the door, Keyes gives Garlopis a mock naturalization lesson in how to turn the handle and open it. Moral rot is quite unself-consciously aligned with nonnormative Americanness in *Double Indemnity*, giving rise to a seemingly uncontrollable profusion in the film of ethnic, national, and racial signifiers, from English soap to Chinese checkers. By the time Neff says of his voiceover confession to Keyes, "I am not trying to whitewash myself," we know exactly what he means.

Perhaps he knows the attempt would be futile. Has Keyes not described Neff's job of salesman, by contrast to his own managerial brain work, as a species of lowbrow "monkey talk"? And after Neff strangles Mr. Dietrichson from the backseat of Phyllis's car, does he not find himself under a great (literally blackening) shadow of vulnerability, the one that hobbles on crutches into the opening frames of the film? Is this not compounded by his ultimate failure to put up a convincing "impersonation" (as Keyes calls it) of Dietrichson's Stanford-educated whiteness in faking the latter's accident? When Dietrichson's daughter Lola—herself a paragon of whiteness carrying on a dangerous, proscribed relationship with one Nino Zachetti, whom Lola meets clandestinely at the superbly patriotic (and parodic) corner of Vermont and Franklin Streets—begins to suspect Phyllis and her own erstwhile paramour (ethnicity will out) of plotting her father's (not to mention her mother's) death, Neff takes her, by now not surprisingly, to a Mexican restaurant to literally seduce her into silence. Such a figural crossing of the border perfectly conveys *Double Indemnity*'s sense of the iniquity to which Neff has sunk. Neff himself is now a moral resident of Phyllis's Spanish house.

There is no greater index of this fate than Neff's two alibis for the murder of Dietrichson. The first is the black garage attendant, Charlie, whom Neff visits in the parking garage to establish his whereabouts before exiting (by the service stairs Charlie himself presumably uses) to execute his plot. The second is the Westwood Jew Lou Schwartz, whose name not only derives from the Yiddish word for "black" but whose status as another of the film's resident Others helps secure Neff's uncriminal whiteness while suggesting Neff's moral fall. Indeed, what interests me about Neff's alibis is that they throw a critical light on the way white selfhood makes exploitative use of boundary-defining nonwhites even as they register the dark depths of Neff's spiritual condition. The character and color of Neff's excuses precisely indicate his moral otherness, his guilt. The same is true at the very end, when a black janitor calls Keyes over to the insurance company to finger Neff in his office, the black presence here an embodiment of the outer darkness to which Neff has traveled and perhaps the visible sign of his guilt returning midconfession to indict him. It is no accident that Neff at the end wants to escape across the Mexican border.

Film noir is a cinematic mode defined by its border crossings. In it people fall from (g)race into the deep shadows new film technologies had recently made possible. With the help of technical innovations such as the Norwood exposure meter (which for the first time could take a weighted average of light from all directions rather than a single direction), faster film stock, photoflood bulbs that permitted better location filming, antireflective lens coatings, and the like, film noir found a world in the dark (see Salt 287–308; Place and Peterson). The moral and visual passage into "shadiness," conjoining as it does states of psychological and social definition with the actual look of white skin on screen, almost by definition has a racial analogue in the American context; and it is for this reason that any understanding of the postwar U.S. cinematic apparatus—which, as Stephen Heath puts it, "hold[s] together the instrumental and the symbolic, the technological and the ideological" (7)—must involve its racial economy. Racial borders are invoked and implicated in social and representational ones, analogizing easily with and even providing a conceptual framework for Americans gone afoul of actual and cinematic laws. Hollywood lighting conventions demonstrate this multiplex drama of transgression. Richard Dyer has suggested that the lighting of white big-screen icons (such as Lillian Gish) has given their ethical purity a racially particular form. Associations of worth and whiteness are by now of course so naturalized as to pass beneath conscious notice, and Hollywood has always exploited them. Commenting on the racial import of the brightly lit star, Dyer writes: "[S]he is more visible, she is aesthetically and morally superior, she looks on from a position of knowledge, of enlightenment—in short, if she is so much lit, she also appears to be the source of light" (2). Filmic translucence—the people on screen literally have light shining through them—is aligned with spiritual hygiene, provided that the people on screen are white. It certainly helps if they are men too, given the always available equation of radiant femininity (Rita Hayworth in *Gilda*), or at least a blonde wig (Barbara Stanwyck in *Double Indemnity*), with the entrapments of desire. But with the advent of noir even the women were mostly cast into blackness, living like the men, in shadows that suggested their racial fall from Hollywood lighting conventions no less than they mimicked the moral transgressions on screen. Notably, the exception to this rule in *Double Indemnity* is the innocent Lola, whose glowing white face at one moment evidently enchants Walter Neff in his condition of moral disrepair. More typically, the intensely shadowy scenes featuring Phyllis and Walter that plot and punctuate the film, from the drinks Walter makes in the gloom of his kitchen, to their postmurder kiss in a shadow that bisects their heads, to their final meeting in the near-total darkness of Phyllis's house, confirm their departure from social as well as stylistic norms.

Noir's crossings from light to dark, the indulgence of actions and visual codes ordinarily renounced in white bourgeois culture and thereby raced in the white imaginary, throw its protagonists into the predicament of abjection. Noir characters threaten to lose themselves in qualities that formerly marked all the self was not, and that unsettle its stable definition. Antisocial acts of lawlessness and passion, deceit and recklessness signify the state that, according to Julia Kristeva, makes borders irrelevant, repression inoperative, and the ego an Other (7–10). With stable demarcation (moral, visual, racial) replaced by fluidity, straying, "going all the way to the end of the line" (as *Double Indemnity* has it), noir's abject selves meet the world without boundaries—no mere moral failing, since it involves disturbances around the disavowal of the mother in the formation of (principally masculine) gender definition and of the racial Other in the formation of white self-identity. The two converge in the opening shadow of Walter on crutches: his wounded manhood the result of Phyllis's duping control and finally the bullet she puts in his shoulder; his "blackening" the outcome of actions he is willing to perform for thrills, passion, and cold hard cash. Thus, Neff says of his abject state after the murder, "my nerves were pulling me to pieces." Likewise, Phyllis's "black" widow role in several respects represents the film's worst white male nightmare: formerly the nurse of Dietrichson's first wife—an occupation resembling other service occupations in the picture, from the black office custodians to Charlie the garage attendant to the "colored woman" Walter says cleans his apartment—she mothers her charge badly enough to "accidentally on purpose" kill her before becoming Lola's evil stepmother and Dietrichson's scheming wife. It must indeed be said that Phyllis is so typical of 1940s Hollywood women that her loss of boundaries, endangering poor Walter's own, is hard to perceive as abjection. And yet the illicit pleasures, fantasies of omnipotence, and thoroughgoing "rottenness" she inspires are those attributes most imagined to have a black as well as female source. As Slavoj Žižek has observed, the formation of selfhood in white Western societies requires the remanding of the unspeakable powers of enjoyment—pleasure is by definition illicit and rotten—which are imagined to be the special privilege or province of racial Others and whose experience or return, therefore, threatens the white self girded by specifically racial negations (200–216). *Double Indemnity*'s attempted escape from the iron cage of respectable morality that is the prime benefit and lure of whiteness reckons the racial component of its unrespectable pleasures. Villainizing the desires that drive the narrative, utilizing racial codes implied in moral terminologies and visual devices, it preserves the idea of whiteness its own characters do not uphold.

Why, other than the pathological social formation of white interiority, might this contradiction have been present in films of the 1940s? As many historians have observed, the decade's civil rights activism presaged the better-remembered struggles of the 1960s. A. Philip Randolph's massive March on Washington Movement against discrimination in the wartime defense plants, begun in 1940, motivated Franklin Roosevelt to issue an executive order outlawing discriminatory hiring practices by defense contractors and to establish the (ineffectual) Fair Employment Practices Committee (Jones 233–34, 236). In 1941 black Ford workers at River Rouge threw their weight behind the United Auto Workers, forcing the company for the first time to sign a union contract (Meier and Rudwick 242–44, 246–48). The ranks of the NAACP began to grow in tandem with rising black political and economic desires—over half a million blacks migrated out of the South between the opening up of defense hiring and the end of the war—and in 1943 the Congress of Racial Equality was founded (Drake and Cayton 89–91). The "double V" campaign endorsed by many black newspapers and civil-rights organizations sent up the cry for a double victory over racism at home as well as fascism abroad (Parker; Himes, "Now"). Hollywood itself felt the heat in 1942 when its major studio heads met with the NAACP's Walter White and agreed to reshape black movie roles in accord with the new times; this was the period of *Cabin in the Sky, Stormy Weather, The Negro Soldier, Crash Dive, Sahara,* and *Bataan* (all 1943) (Cripps 374–83). Lest we underestimate the white hostility toward this surge of activity, however, it is well to note, for instance, that at the same moment, black noir writer Chester Himes was race-baited from the studios (Jack Warner proclaimed, "I don't want no niggers on this lot" [qtd. in Davis 43]) and spent the war years working in defense plants, writing in *If*

He Hollers Let Him Go (1945) and *The Lonely Crusade* (1947) of what he later termed the "mental corrosion of race prejudice in Los Angeles" (Himes, *Quality* 75).

In the long hot summer of 1943, such militant disgust with unbending American racism took to the streets. Urban insurrections erupted in Harlem, Detroit, and twenty-five other U.S. cities (Drake and Cayton 91–94). These were often labeled "zoot suit riots" because the black and Mexican youths so attired (in defiance, it might be added, of the War Production Board's rationing of cloth) were convenient targets of attack for the white servicemen and police servicemen and police whose violence often sparked such street combat. Pathologizing accounts of zoot subcultures were embraced as a means of defining the civilized self, as in Kenneth Clark and James Barker's 1945 study of what they called the "zoot effect in personality" (published in the *Journal of Abnormal and Social Psychology*). Writers from Ralph Ellison to Chester Himes ("Zoot Riots") to C.L.R. James and others grasped the political urgency of apparently trivial squabbles over sharkskin; meanwhile the Los Angeles City Council voted to make wearing zoot suits a misdemeanor, facilitating the easy arrest of Mexicans and blacks (Blake and Breitman; Kelley; Lott). The concurrent ordeal of the Sleepy Lagoon trial, in which seventeen pachuco zoot-suiters were convicted of and imprisoned for murder under extremely questionable legal circumstances (they were later released and the charges dismissed after the protests of the Sleepy Lagoon Defense Committee, with whom Orson Welles was allied), secured the image of the Mexican juvenile delinquent; sparked fears of internal subversion by a foreign conspiracy (the prosecution insisted on the "Oriental," pre-Columbian source of the Mexicans' "utter disregard for the value of life" [qtd. in Mazón 221]); gave rise to "Lil' Abner" creator Al Capp's widely read and virulent "Zoot-Suit Yokum" comic strip in which a zoot-suit manufacturers' conspiracy is happily thwarted (perhaps inspiring a *Los Angeles Times* caricature of Japanese premier Tojo in a zoot); and symbolized the beginning of the Chicano movement in America. Meanwhile, as is well known, hysteria about the "yellow peril" and the internment of the Japanese in California completed this picture of panicked whites in dubious battle (Tagg and Sanchez-Tranquilino; Polan 1–3, 122–24).

As one key contribution to our understanding of this period has put it, race displaced class as "the great, unsolved problem in American life" (Fraser and Gerstle xix; see also Katznelson 187). Noir responded to this problem not by presenting it outright but by taking the social energy associated with its social threat and subsuming it into the untoward aspects of white selves. The "dark" energy of many of these films is villainized precisely through the associations with race that generated some of that energy in the first place. Film noir is in this sense a sort of whiteface dream-work of social anxieties with explicitly racial sources, condensed on film into the criminal undertakings of abjected whites. This may explain two otherwise random or unremarkable matters in *Double Indemnity*. The first is Nino Zachetti's portrayal as a juvenile delinquent, a UCLA dropout dallying with both Phyllis and Lola and liable at any moment to boil over with hotheaded anger (as he does when he finds that Neff has given Lola a ride to meet him downtown—Zachetti's natural setting). He might as well be wearing a zoot; what we have instead is his ethnically marked name. Zachetti may be a mask for fairly legible social anxieties afoot in the United States of 1943. The Los Angeles zoot riots occurred in June; *Double Indemnity* started filming there in September. The second matter is the site of Neff and Phyllis's faking of her husband's death, the Southern Railroad observation car. The train, not least because of the active leadership by A. Philip Randolph of the Brotherhood of Sleeping Car Porters, was in the popular imagination associated with its black caretakers, the redcaps, Pullman porters, and cooks who serviced railroad lines across America. Randolph, recall, had used his power to desegregate the defense plants in 1941. Now *Double Indemnity* only follows James M. Cain's novel in placing the train at the center of Phyllis and Walter's plot; but the scene in which Walter mimics Dietrichson's death prominently features several black railroad workers, both sentinels and servants of the racially marked space of the coach, and not one of these workers, interestingly, casts an identifying look at Neff's face as he boards the train. *Double Indemnity* seems to suggest again the importance of black help in marking off the white self—hence their aid in this alibi—even as the black attendants betray Walter Neff's criminality by their very presence. Neff has chosen the perfect place to evince his "black" heart.[3]

DOUBLE LIVES

Rarely are the raced double lives of noir protagonists made as plain as in George Cukor's *A Double Life*. Actor Tony John (Ronald Colman), who has great difficulty leaving his stage roles in the theater, takes on the part of none other than Othello. He is reluctant at first because he knows he will as usual get too involved in the character, but the shadowy glimpses he catches of himself in mirrors and dark plate glass (which make casual use, by the way, of noir's links between dark lighting and blackness) convince him there is an Othello somewhere inside him. In fact this is perhaps intimated early on when Tony says that becoming ambitious as an actor means "tearing myself apart, and putting myself together again, and again," papering over who knows what inner life and unself-conscious rages. These come out as the play's run continues. Tony falls into a romantic intrigue with a waitress, Pat Kroll (Shelley Winters), whom he chokes to death Othello-style when he becomes jealous of the affair he suspects between his former wife Brita (Signe Hasso) and the play's publicity agent. (The racial underpinnings of this crime are stressed, if unconsciously, when Pat, in response to Tony's raving about all the assumed nationalities he carries within him, says, "I got mixed blood too.") The publicity agent's decision to link the unsolved murder to their production of *Othello* presses on the substantial interpenetration in *A Double Life* not only of art and reality but of black rage and white crime, particularly given that it is Tony's violent rage when he hears of this scheme that helps reveal his crime. Carrying the theatrical metaphor fully into the world, the police arrange to have a waitress disguised as Pat confront Tony, his horrified response to which confirms his guilt. Wandering the black streets in his blackened state, Othello is exposed: Tony impales himself on a knife during his character's final speech and dies, like Othello, of the uncontrollable rage released by his alter ego.

Usually the presentation is a bit more oblique. Delmer Daves's *Dark Passage*, for instance, plays cosmetic changes on *A Double Life*'s conceit. Vincent Parry (Humphrey Bogart) has been wrongly imprisoned for murdering his wife and escapes from San Quentin. Although the film is interested in exonerating Parry, it nonetheless saddles him with a complexion he must leave behind because it is recognizable. In fact, we do not see Parry/Bogart's face for over an hour into the film because its pivot is the cosmetic surgery that results in Bogart's face and the chance at a redemptive new life. The suspicious, as-good-as-guilty "true" face is invisible to us, either not shown within the frame or (of course) heavily shadowed; the key taxi ride that will lead Parry to the plastic surgeon who transforms his face offers indeed a striking instance of "blackening," as Bogart sits in a deep, localized shadow. For all intents and purposes, that is, Parry is guilty, and, moreover, his new face does nothing to keep blackmailers and conniving snitches off his back. Parry's "true" complexion only goes underground, first submerged under the emphatically white bandages that help heal his postoperative face and then under the face so naturalized as Bogart's. Against the film's wishes, perhaps, and despite our glimpse in a newspaper photograph of Parry's old face, we cannot help feeling that there is something *under* there, waiting to manifest itself or continuing to cause the ongoing difficulties from which Parry has so much trouble extricating himself. When Parry and his newfound sweetheart Irene Jansen (Lauren Bacall) escape to Peru, one gets the idea that this exigency was quite necessary and, given the locale and its racial associations in noir—the Mexico of Robert Mitchum and Jane Greer's illicit love in Jacques Tourneur's *Out of the*

Past (1947), for instance, or the implicit Latinizing of Glenn Ford through his close association with Uncle Pio (Steven Geray) in *Gilda*'s Argentina— quite fitting.

The racialized interiors of whites in extremis erupt most tellingly in such key texts in the noir series as Max Ophuls's *The Reckless Moment*, Nicholas Ray's *In a Lonely Place*, Rudolph Mate's *D.O.A.*, and Robert Aldrich's *Kiss Me Deadly* (1955). *D.O.A.*'s Frank Bigelow (Edmond O'Brien) has only a few days of life left to discover who it was that poisoned him with iridium. His search leads him back to a jazz dive featuring heaving, sweating black musicians—the bar where a masked unidentified stranger had dropped the lethal dose in his drink. Cast into the roles of both detective and victim, Bigelow is animated as well as, eventually, suffocated by a substance whose source is thematically proximate to blackness. *Kiss Me Deadly* is perhaps the most typical in its casual exploitation of racial tropes: the inner states and plot predicaments of detective Mike Hammer (Ralph Meeker) are conveyed at crucial moments through black characters and counterparts. The film opens with Nat King Cole on Hammer's car radio singing, "I'd rather have the blues than what I got"—a lyric that will later reappear in a low moment of Hammer's trajectory. The song portends the depths to which Hammer (and for that matter the postatomic world of the film) will be plunged, and it is amusing that Hammer feels he has to flick it off as he approaches a police roadblock, the law beyond whose barricades he will cross as a man of the "jungle," in the film's phrase. Hammer's whiteness may contrast with the Greekness of his yammering friend Nick, who runs around hysterically, salivating over nice sports cars and shouting "va-va-voom" like the automobiles with which the so-called grease monkey is literally identified before being murdered by having one lowered, crushingly, onto his chest. Despite these intermittent differentiations that confirm Hammer's racial stature—not to mention one in which a seductive mob moll named Friday tempts Crusoe Hammer—Hammer is figured as black at significant moments in the narrative. At a time of crisis Hammer drowns his sorrows so much he has to be carried in all his abjection out of the club. What is more, the climactic scene where Hammer fights the mobsters who have drugged and caged him in a bedroom plays out against the radio broadcast of a boxing match we can only guess is the one involving black boxers whose venal promoter, Eddie, Hammer had earlier visited in search of information. With some wit, but with little sense of the racial stakes, Aldrich stages Hammer's big fight as a black one, occurring on the other side of the barricade to which Hammer routinely travels but whence he can always somehow return. Something of this dynamic is at work in Robert Rossen's far richer boxing noir *Body and Soul* (1947), which, for all its sympathetic interest in the interracial relationship of Charley Davis (John Garfield) and Ben Chaplin (Canada Lee), makes Charley's success dependent upon his difference from Ben—or as Michael Rogin puts it, "Charley tries on, to free himself from, Ben's role" (220).

In a Lonely Place is far richer and deeper in its racialized suggestiveness. The cranky, hard-drinking, and, it is rumored, disturbed and violent Hollywood screenwriter Dixon Steele (Humphrey Bogart) invites a warm and quick-witted hatcheck girl back to his place so she can narrate to him a best-selling novel from which he is supposed to craft a script. She is apparently open to romance but Steele sends her away in a taxi, whereupon she is murdered and Steele is presumed the murderer. His alibi comes in the form of Laurel Gray (Gloria Grahame), with whom he quickly becomes involved and with whose aid and comfort his writing recovers its power. His jealousy and temper, however, make her uneasy, and she begins to suspect his involvement in the murder; Steele's volatility increases as he senses her doubts. Laurel tries to leave on the day of their wedding, when Steele finds her and nearly chokes her to death. At this moment the police call with the news that the hatcheck girl's killer has been discovered, but all that has transpired between Steele and Laurel has doomed their relationship. Two crucial moments in this drama, both seemingly en passant and innocuous, go straight to the heart of Steele's situation. The first occurs when Steele, upon hearing of the hatcheck girl's death, decides to send flowers but does not want to take them himself to her funeral. So he asks a black man spraying down the sidewalk in front of a florist if he will send two dozen white roses. This would appear not only to alleviate Steele's feelings of guilt (with white roses) but to implicate by association the black man in a crime Steele may sense he is perfectly capable of committing. The anonymous black figure signifies Steele's dark past relationships with women, whom we are told he has beaten and otherwise abused; Steele atones by sending his black double with white (and whitening) flowers. The second such moment is when Steele and Laurel go to a club where they are serenaded by a black chanteuse (Hadda Brooks), who mediates white heterosexual desire *Casablanca*-style—with Laurel and a black woman forming an equal and opposite homosocial bond from that of Bogart and Sam in the film of eight years earlier. The unnamed singer expresses Laurel's love for a man whose volatility may well kill it. While guilt and the capacity for violence are figured through Steele's deal with the black man, the fond hopes raised and then dashed by Steele's obsessive love are intimated in a black woman's song. I would argue that Steele's love for Laurel is indeed a failed search for his own innocence; she is after all his alibi as well as his lover, and when she espies his dark underside, Steele loses everything he originally sought in her. It is interesting to learn, then, that the working title of the film was *Behind This Mask* (Kirgo and Silver 144).

There is also, incidentally, an odd moment of Hollywood self-consciousness located in a quip by Steele's agent, Mel Lippman (Art Smith), who softens the blow in telling Steele he does not like the latter's filmscript by saying, "But then I'm the one who told Selznick to drop *Gone with the Wind!*" Here the Jew references his good racial taste—no plantation tradition for Lippman—while acknowledging what Michael Rogin has read in *Blackface, White Noise: Jewish Immigrants in the Hollywood Melting Pot* (1996) as the Jewish role in black exploitation on screen from *The Jazz Singer* (1927) to the present day, including *Gone with the Wind* (1939). In also equating Steele's script with *Gone with the Wind*, Lippman inadvertently highlights Steele's racial usages in *In a Lonely Place* itself.

The Reckless Moment departs in an important sense from these films because it uses a black figure to present the forbidden aspects of a white woman's life and thus complicates its implicit racial exploitation. The film tells the story of well-positioned Lucia Harper (Joan Bennett), who, in an attempt during her husband's absence to keep her daughter Bea from being implicated in the accidental death of a suitor (Bea hits him with a flashlight to stave off an attempted sexual assault and he pitches over a railing), hides the body she has discovered on a nearby beach. Soon, however, blackmailers inform Lucia that they possess love letters from Bea to the suitor, Darby, that they are sure the police would want to see. Martin Donnelly (James Mason), one of the blackmailers, falls in love with Lucia and tries to protect her, ultimately killing his partner in blackmail, though he is wounded in the fight. He leaves with his partner's body before Lucia can stop him, and at this point Lucia and her black maid Sybil (Frances Williams), whom we have seen several times around the house, follow Donnelly with Sybil at the wheel. They find Donnelly at the scene of his wrecked car, dying, but not before he can confess to both of the killings and exculpate Lucia's daughter. The role of Lucia's maid Sybil is another fine illustration of a marginal black character brought on to do major thematic work. Lucia's "recklessness"—her independence and incipient adulterous desire for Donnelly as well as her self-sacrifice in the effort to protect her daughter—is figured succinctly by her maid. The black woman whose very name calls up clichéd notions of penetrating wisdom not only divines the desire for Donnelly from which Lucia shrinks and expresses it for her ("I always liked him," she says); she also stands as a black double for Lucia's descent into reckless self-sacrifice, the only role we see Sybil play in all her table setting and assiduous caretaking. Sybil's commanding the wheel at the picture's climactic moment (Lucia curses her failure of autonomy earlier, saying "I should've driven my car")—the fullest expression of Lucia's agency in love and trouble—completes that agency, rounds it out, and makes it plainer than it is respectable for a white woman to do. That is, the maid here is not a figure of aversive lampoon but of sympathetic identification, and the sympathy encompasses the interracial friendship as well as the female power and mobility for which Sybil finally stands as much as Lucia does. For all that, however, Sybil's gifts of knowing and action, which manifest Lucia's own plot and cement white and black female solidarity, exile the black woman from the womanhood so brightly depicted at the film's end, when white suburban law—the law-abiding, harmonious family telephoning long-awaited Daddy on Christmas—has been, however ironically, restored.

What such films appear to dread is the infiltration into the white home or self of unsanctioned behaviors reminiscent of the dark figures exemplified in the 1940s and early 1950s imaginary by zoot-suiters, pachucos, and Asian conspirators. In this, they firmly support Elaine Tyler May's thesis that the postwar family was invented as a bulwark against this sort of dread. Though the films constituted a corollary invention, what they apparently cannot do is completely shove these figures out of the picture, though noir may stave off their most fearsome shapes or place them in a safely removed elsewhere. Many films, *The Reckless Moment* included, imagine a dark underworld that is out of sight and (usually) downtown—thus, when Lucia is scheduled to meet the blackmailer Donnelly in a bus station, one shocking frame has their conversing faces suddenly obscured by a working-class Chinese man's face in the very close foreground, as though to suggest what is out there and what, too bad for both of them, has crept *in here*. Or there is the Chinatown to which Elsa Bannister (Rita Hayworth) tries to escape in the last section of Welles's *The Lady from Shanghai*, a film that, for all its interest in narrating ethnicity (from Welles's "Black Irish" O'Hara to the various national and ethnic descents of his sailor associates to the abused black maid Bessie to Arthur Bannister's "Manchester Greek" mother to Elsa's own sojourn in China), is not above playing stereotypes for a laugh: during the trial scene two Chinese women in the courtroom, speaking sotto voce in their native tongue, break it off with one saying, "you ain't kiddin!" Chinatown and Elsa's Chinese gang herald the darkness of Los Angeles's would-be El Dorado and summon as well the ghastly nature of Elsa's fatal plotting—though the final scene in the Chinese funhouse asserts how easy it is for such racialized corruption to gnaw at the hearts of whites split (by the famous funhouse mirrors) into dissociated parts and, as O'Hara puts it, "chewing away at their own selves." For his part, Marlowe in Dmytryk's *Murder, My Sweet* refuses the temptations of this encroaching underworld of Asian erotic enchantments (the Asian dancer in the Coconut Beach Club at whom thug Moose Malloy takes a long look) and Asian styles of adornment (the jade necklace and Ann Grayle's subtly Orientalist makeup). But they have certainly laid claim to the gruesome crew that surrounds him. From Peter Lorre's feminized Far Easterner Joel Cairo in John Huston's *Maltese Falcon* (1941) to Jack Palance's diseased and ratlike Blackie in Elia Kazan's *Panic in the Streets* (1950), noirs populate a sinister subterranean milieu with roving racialized phantoms.

The great problem, indeed, is that racial Others, far from residing comfortably downtown, keep coming back into white lives in film noir. Untoward behavior and its seemingly inevitable racial echoes indelibly mark the white homes—and films—for which race typically exists somewhere else.

DOMESTICS AND DOMESTICITY

This return of the oppressed is clear enough from the foregoing examples, but it is on spectacular display in films anxious to narrate the fate of the white family. *Murder, My Sweet*, like several important noirs, depicts with varying degrees of self-consciousness a specifically racial deviance at the center of the domestic sphere. The film opens with the appearance of a dark phantom in Marlowe's office window; turning around, Marlowe discovers the reflection's source in (still fairly dark) Moose Malloy, who speaks with what sounds like a Mexican accent and whose suit looks suspiciously zootlike. Moose is in search of the similarly ethnically resonant Velma Valento and takes Marlowe to locate her to a bar called Florians, which, because of some burned-out neon, has become, appropriately, "Forins."[4] This plot crosscuts the one in which Marlowe tries to recover a lost jade necklace for some wealthy clients, Mr. and Mrs. Grayle. The circle of people revolving around Mrs. Grayle is rotten in ways already suggested by their lust for jade; but a quack psychoanalyst, Amthor, delves deep into Mrs. Grayle's past and predictably finds much with which to blackmail her. As Mrs. Grayle admits, "I haven't been good, not halfway good." Finally, since, as Marlowe says, "I had to know how the jade figured," he convenes all the parties in the Grayles' beach house only to discover, in a furiously doubled racial whammy, that Mrs. Grayle is Velma Valento. And to think Marlowe nearly succumbed to her seductive come-ons! In the storm of bullets that ensues, Marlowe escapes with scorched eyes that come too close to a firing gun, this near-castrating close call externalized in the eye patches he wears during his movie-long voiceover flashback and the implicitly mixed-race predicament of the Grayle family implicated in its demise.

Mothers, wives, and lovers are typically abjected in noir, of course, but their symbolic racialization clinches noir's sense of immanent familial dysfunction. Otto Preminger's *Angel Face* works an interesting twist on this scheme, since it literally places a bickering Japanese couple within the home they serve and whose topsy-turvy gender relations they evoke. The Japanese wife who, it is alleged, has become "too American" and so no longer obeys her husband is the counterpart of the daughter of the house,

Diane Tremayne (Jean Simmons), who takes too much power into her hands and finally kills her father and stepmother by—significantly—tampering (like a mechanic) with their car. *Angel Face* laments a putative postwar loss of innocence; Diane's real mother was killed during the war (there goes the nuclear family), and Diane's villainized discontent, which finally eventuates in the auto-death (in both senses) of Frank Jessup (Robert Mitchum) and herself, signifies an America mired in Orientalized triviality, female usurpation, and domestic war—for all of which the rancorous Japanese couple stands as a perfect figure. The Japanese wife has not become too American; the Americans are turning Japanese.

Michael Curtiz's *Mildred Pierce* perceives this sort of threat most compellingly. Mildred (Joan Crawford) determines to win her daughter Veda's love by affording her all the available luxuries, and when this desire is stymied by her husband Bert, she leaves him. Her departure, for which alone (as Pam Cook has rightly argued) she is demonized, sends her into a dizzying narrative space of female autonomy and ultimate defeat and punishment. Mildred takes a job as a waitress to provide financially, but when Veda finds out about it, she is scornful and wounding, which goads Mildred into plans to open her own restaurant. The restaurant is wildly successful—former boss Ida (Eve Arden) now comes to work for her, and Mildred's initial investment blossoms into a whole chain of restaurants—though the success depends on the help of Monte Beragon (Zachary Scott), a mysterious roué whom Mildred marries. Unthrifty Monte ultimately bankrupts the chain of restaurants and seduces Mildred's daughter to boot. Mildred catches them together and Monte disavows his interest in Veda, whereupon Veda kills him; Mildred attempts unsuccessfully to take the rap. What interests me about this rise and fall of an independent woman is that her trajectory is shadowed at every step by her black maid Lottie (Butterfly McQueen), who figures the proletarian fate Mildred is driven to beat and whose disabling likeness suggests Mildred's darkest dread. Lottie is the kitchen worker who always lurks somewhere inside Mildred, less the representative of the hard labor Mildred is perfectly willing to perform for her own interest than of the "nigger work" this labor echoes. Hence Veda's joke when she discovers her mother's waitressing: she has Lottie don Mildred's work uniform to wear about the house. The two women are versions of each other. At one key moment their parallel lives are suggested by Lottie's remark that the opening night of Mildred's restaurant feels like her own wedding night, which overlays as it distinguishes the two women's trajectories. Not surprisingly, then, Mildred increasingly uses Lottie for the differentiating purposes of household adornment, as a sort of failed mistress of the house who puts on ridiculous airs. Even in this device, however, one sees the parodic likeness between the women amid the instituted difference.

This ambiguity in the meaning of Lottie (all that Mildred has left behind or her hidden unfitness?) is overdetermined by the resonance of "gypsy fortune teller" Beragon (on one occasion, when Ida speaks of Beragon's "big brown eyes," Lottie, in one of the film's many racist cracks, says, "Beg pardon?"). He is a strange sort of raced creature—his lineage, which he says includes Spanish and Italian blood, is made the subject of fascination and discussion—now close within the family circle as Mildred's husband. His counterpart is Mildred's other daughter, Kay, whose memorable little "gypsy dance" perhaps indicates her threat to the family and therefore presages her death. Beragon's racial aura is in some sense aligned with his profligacy, and it is joltingly played on in the striking scene where we see him kiss Veda. This kiss, which is of course a near-incestuous one, is yet portrayed as its opposite, as a kind of interracial seduction—with Beragon hovering in full shadow over the virginal Veda, the metaphorics of interracial sex are hardly submerged at all in the lighting of the scene. It is an extraordinary moment, and it raises the question of just what the racial crime is here. Is it mere miscegenation, or is the racial Other living much closer to home, within it in fact, part and parcel of the incestuous act that might seem diametrically opposed to the racial threat from outside but in fact only accesses it? There's an Other in the house. Thus when Monte is killed, Mildred is not automatically restored; on the contrary, the brilliant final scene, in which Mildred and her first husband walk out into the light of day past two washerwomen scrubbing the floor on their knees, suggests that the hard labor and its racial dimension she seems to have left behind are not in fact distant at all but are, as it were, part of the frame.

The question arises as to why a Marxist cinema manqué at a time of left-liberal high tide in Hollywood would fall so readily into dubious racial devices. To be sure, good racial intentions abounded. Edward Dmytryk and Adrian Scott conceived of their picture against antisemitism, *Crossfire* (1947), as a frankly "heroic" measure (as Scott put it in a memo to RKO) to stop "anti-semitism and anti-negrism," a casual linkage that is interesting in itself (Scott references the lingering antisemitism after the war as well as antiblack rioting) (Ceplair and Englund 454). The Sleepy Lagoon Defense Committee, which featured a variety of screenwriters, directors, and actors (I have mentioned Welles, who was joined by Rita Hayworth, Canada Lee, Ring Lardner, Jr., and others), was perhaps the most intense organized antiracist initiative of the time, but there were also projects such as the UAW-sponsored antiracist cartoon film *The Brotherhood of Man* (1947) and the occasional civil-rights noir (Robert Wise's politically interesting but cinematically dull *Odds against Tomorrow* [1959]) (Allen and Denning 111–15). However, not only did the House Un-American Activities Committee's hearings on Hollywood cut into leftist enthusiasm after 1947, the studios began to retreat from liberal race pictures such as *Gentleman's*

Agreement (1947), *Pinky* (1949), and *Home of the Brave* (1949); RKO, for example, backed out of a plan to allow Scott and Dmytryk to make a movie about black life. And needless to say, racial stereotypes and foolish bit parts persisted undisturbed both out of noir (for example, *Song of the South* [1943]) and within it (Anthony Mann's otherwise honorable *Border Incident* [1949] contains a pair of thuggish Mexican goofs), and would probably have done so without either the blacklist or studio complacency. As Larry Ceplair and Steven Englund write:

> The radical screenwriters were like so many Penelopes: in the daytime, at the office, they unravelled the efforts of their evenings and weekends as political activists, for the movies they wrote reinforced the reigning cultural ethos and political-social order. No Communist (or, for that matter, liberal) screenwriter, of course, would have agreed to write an obviously anti-black, anti-Semitic, or anti-brotherhood script, but then Hollywood turned out very few movies which were so blatantly racist that they offended accepted social definitions and values. Racial and ethnic stereotypes abounded in every writer's scripts, however, as did the myths of democracy, justice, material success, etc., which were intricately interwoven into the film genres which dominated in Hollywood. (49–50)

This latter point, it seems to me, is the key one, not only for the Hollywood left but for all of noir's creators. Racial dominance was so built into Hollywood industrial and generic norms that a new cinematic mode built on human corruption and darkened compositions created, as an almost inevitable by-product, a new intensity of racialized imaging—an intensity undoubtedly overdetermined by a climate of felt social decline, cultural degradation, moral brutality, and spiritual defeat: what Joseph Losey, one of noir's leftist directors, called "the complete unreality of the American dream" (qtd. in Andersen 187). In this sense, left-liberal perceptions of decline harmonized with center-right ones in imagining white selves cast into a nightmarish world of otherness and racial aliens.

US AS THEM

The oft-stated consensus on Orson Welles's *Touch of Evil* (1958) as film noir's epitaph makes sense also because of its brilliant playing with the notion of white border crossings. Welles demonstrates an awareness in *Touch of Evil* of everything I have tried to argue about film noir's sense of the intimate proximity of racial Others to American national identity and its hysterical (if unconscious) attempts both to use and to exile them in portraits of white corruption. In Welles's counternarrative the Law comes in the form of Mexican Mike Vargas, whose nemesis is the bloated, criminal, white police detective Hank Quinlan (Welles). That Vargas is played by none other than a brown-faced Charlton Heston—or Charlton Moses, as Edward Said once called him in reference to his part in the blockbusting film of two years earlier, *The Ten Commandments* (1956)—wittily communicates (to use Homi Bhabha's terms) his not-white and yet not-quite-Mexican status with which Welles teases our perception of justice's racial tropes. Vargas's brownness curiously (and, I think, purposely) oscillates in and out of focus as we forget and remember that this is after all Charlton Heston, undermining fairly definitively the simple demarcation of whiteness. The film in fact takes internal and external border construction as its very theme; Vargas is married to a white woman (Janet Leigh), and the two are seen crossing the Mexican border into the United States at the film's start. Does America's designation of "us" and "them" adequately parse moral distinctions between right and wrong? the film asks us, and then it mixes up the racial clues we might use to answer the question. Quinlan's attempted framing of Vargas and other Mexicans only cements our sense of Vargas's moral purity and exposes the processes of projection and abjection that would pin white criminal activities on dark bodies and deploy them as racial metaphors for white crimes. When, after crossing the border, Vargas and his wife Susan kiss for the first time in, as Susan says, "my country," the bomb explosion that tellingly interrupts their forbidden kiss is a self-conscious turn away from black films of racial marking and disavowal.

NOTES

1. Cf. Hirsch: "In the flickering images of a movie screen, film noir seizes and penetrates a universal heart of darkness" (209).

2. Dean MacCannell intermittently broaches the problem of noir's racial troping, but his primary interests lie elsewhere. Copjec's introduction faults certain historicized accounts of noir for referencing "external sources" (World War II, crime, the threat of working women, etc.) rather than locating the films' "generative principle"—"the genre's 'absent cause,' . . . a principle that does not appear in the field of its effects" (xi–xii)—a fault the present study might seem to repeat. As I will argue, noir's racial reliances, while present in the field of its effects, are far more motivating in the films than is suggested by their apparent paucity, marginality, or, as in the case of Copjec's "The Phenomenal Nonphenomenal," willed absence: in the course of a fascinating reading, she symptomatically renders Walter Neff's office building in *Double Indemnity* "vacant" and "uninhabited" (189), when in fact it is humming, not with white business people, to be sure, but with black custodial workers, whose presence, as I will show, bears significantly on Neff's predicament.

3. This connection is made again in Richard Fleischer's *The Narrow Margin* (1952), in which a black waiter's confusion explicitly figures the confusion of identities at the heart of the plot.

4. In the novel from which *Murder, My Sweet* was adapted, Raymond Chandler's *Farewell, My Lovely* (1940), there is an elaborated narrative of ethnic succession and racial troping—the visit by Marlowe and Malloy to Florians reveals the club to have become a "dinge joint" (Chandler 144), that is, a black bar. This not only suggests the changes at work in Los Angeles during Malloy's eight years in jail (while affording the characters—and perhaps the author—the opportunity to evince some casual racism); it twins the fortunes of the book's underworld characters and black people, emphasizing Velma Valento's dark aspect as well as the functional accuracy of Florians' broken neon sign.

WORKS CITED

Aldrich, Robert, dir. *Kiss Me Deadly*. United Artists, 1955.

Allen, Holly, and Michael Denning. "The Cartoonists' Front." *South Atlantic Quarterly* 92 (1993): 89–117.

Andersen, Thom. "Red Hollywood." *Literature and the Visual Arts in Contemporary Society*. Ed. Suzanne Ferguson and Barbara Groseclose. Columbus: Ohio State UP, 1985. 141–96.

Blake, Philip, and George Breitman. "Zoot Suit Riots in Los Angeles." *Militant* June 19, 1943. Rpt. in Stanton 254–55.

Boelhower, William. *Through a Glass Darkly: Ethnic Semiosis in American Literature*. Venice: Helvetia, 1984.

Borde, Raymonde, and Etienne Chaumeton. *Panorama du Filme Noir Americain*. Paris: Editions de Minuit, 1955.

Ceplair, Larry, and Stephen Englund. *The Inquisition in Hollywood: Politics in the Film Community, 1930–1960*. Berkeley: U of California P, 1983.

Chandler, Raymond. *Farewell, My Lovely*. 1940. New York: Random, 1975.

Chartrier, Jean-Pierre. "Les Americains aussi font des films noirs." *Revue du cinema* 2 (1946): 66–70.

Clark, Kenneth B., and James Barker. "The Zoot Effect in Personality: A Race Riot Participant." *Journal of Abnormal and Social Psychology* 40 (1945): 143–48.

Cook, Pam. "Duplicity in *Mildred Pierce*." *Women in Film Noir*. Ed. E. Ann Kaplan. London: British Film Institute, 1978. 68–82.

Copjec, Joan. Introduction. Copjec, *Shades of Noir*. vii–xii.

———. "The Phenomenal Nonphenomenal: Private Space in *Film Noir*." Copjec, *Shades of Noir*. 167–97.

———, ed. *Shades of Noir: A Reader*. London: Verso, 1993.

Cosgrove, Stuart. "The Zoot Suit and Style Warfare." *History Workshop Journal* 18 (1984): 77–91.

Cripps, Thomas. *Slow Fade to Black: The Negro in American Film, 1900–1942*. New York: Oxford UP, 1977.

Cukor, George, dir. *A Double Life*. Universal, 1947.

Curtiz, Michael, dir. *Mildred Pierce*. Warner Brothers, 1945.

Daves, Delmer, dir. *Dark Passage*. Warner Brothers, 1947.

Davis, Mike. *City of Quartz: Excavating the Future in Los Angeles*. London: Vintage, 1990.

Diawara, Manthia. "*Noir* by *Noirs*: Toward a New Realism in Black Cinema." Copjec, *Shades of Noir* 261–78.

Dmytryk, Edward, dir. *Crossfire*. RKO, 1947.

———. *Murder, My Sweet*. RKO, 1944.

Drake, St. Clair, and Horace R. Cayton. *Black Metropolis: A Study of Negro Life in a Northern City*. New York: Harcourt, 1945.

Dyer, Richard. "The Colour of Virtue: Lillian Gish, Whiteness, and Femininity." *Sight and Sound* August 1993. Rpt. in *Women and Film: A* Sight and Sound *Reader*. Ed. Pam Cook and Philip Dodd. Culture and the Moving Image. Philadelphia: Temple UP, 1993. 1–9.

Fleischer, Richard, dir. *The Narrow Margin*. RKO, 1952.

Frank, Nino. "Un nouveau genre 'policier': l'aventure criminelle." *L'écran français* 61 (1946): 8+.

Fraser, Steve, and Gary Gerstle. Introduction. *The Rise and Fall of the New Deal Order, 1930–1980*. Ed. Fraser and Gerstle. Princeton: Princeton UP, 1989. ix–xxv.

Heath, Stephen. "The Cinematic Apparatus: Technology as Historical and Cultural Form." *The Cinematic Apparatus*. Ed. Teresa de Lauretis and Stephen Heath. New York: St. Martin's, 1980. 1–13.

Higham, Charles, and Joel Greenberg. *Hollywood in the Forties*. New York: Barnes, 1968.

Himes, Chester. "Now is the Time! Here is the Place!" *Opportunity* March 1943. Rpt. in *Black on Black:* Baby Sister *and Selected Writings*. Garden City: Doubleday, 1973. 213–19.

———. *The Quality of Hurt*. Vol. 1 of *The Autobiography of Chester Himes*. Garden City: Doubleday, 1972.

———. "Zoot Riots Are Race Riots." *Crisis* July 1943. Rpt. in *Black on Black:* Baby Sister *and Selected Writings*. Garden City: Doubleday, 1973. 220–25.

Hirsch, Foster. *The Dark Side of the Screen: Film Noir*. San Diego: Barnes, 1981.

Huston, John, dir. *The Maltese Falcon*. Warner Brothers, 1941.

Jones, Jaqueline. *Labor of Love, Labor of Sorrow: Black Women, Work, and the Family from Slavery to the Present*. New York: Basic, 1985.

Kaplan, E. Ann. *Women in Film Noir*. London: British Film Institute, 1978.

Katznelson, Ira. "Was the Great Society a Lost Opportunity?" Fraser and Gerstle 185–211.

Kazan, Elia, dir. *Panic in the Streets*. Twentieth Century–Fox, 1950.

Kelley, Robin D. G. *Race Rebels: Culture, Politics, and the Black Working Class*. New York: Free P, 1994.

Kirgo, Julie, and Alain Silver. "*In a Lonely Place* (1950)." *Film Noir: An Encyclopedic Reference to the American Style*. Ed. Silver and Elizabeth Ward. Rev. and exp. ed. Woodstock: Overlook, 1992.

Kristeva, Julia. *Powers of Horror: An Essay on Abjection*. Trans. Leon S. Roudiez. New York: Columbia UP, 1982.

Lang, Fritz, dir. *The Big Heat*. Columbia, 1953.

Lott, Eric. "Double V. Double-Time: Bebop's Politics of Style." *Callaloo* 11 (1988): 597–605.

MacCannell, Dean. "Democracy's Turn: On Homeless *Noir.*" Copjec, *Shades of Noir* 279–97.

Mann, Anthony, dir. *Border Incident.* MGM, 1949.

Maté, Rudolph, dir. *D.O.A.* United Artists, 1950.

May, Elaine Tyler. "Cold War—Warm Hearth: Politics and the Family in Postwar America." Fraser and Gerstle 153–81.

Mazón, Mauricio. *The Zoot Suit Riots: The Psychology of Symbolic Annihilation.* Mexican American Monograph 8. Austin: U of Texas P, 1984.

Meier, August, and Elliot Rudwick. *From Plantation to Ghetto.* Rev. ed. New York: Hill, 1970.

Morrison, Toni. *Playing in the Dark: Whiteness and the Literary Imagination.* Cambridge: Harvard UP, 1992.

Ophuls, Max, dir. *The Reckless Moment.* Columbia, 1949.

Parker, Albert. "Why Communist Party Attacks 'Double V.' " *Militant* April 4, 1942. Rpt. in Stanton 157–58.

Place, J. A., and L. S. Peterson. "Some Visual Motifs of Film Noir." *Film Comment* January–February 1974: 30–35.

Polan, Dana. *Power and Paranoia: History, Narrative, and the American Cinema, 1940–1950.* New York: Columbia UP, 1986.

Preminger, Otto, dir. *Angel Face.* RKO, 1953.

Ray, Nicholas, dir. *In a Lonely Place.* Columbia, 1950.

Rogin, Michael. *Blackface, White Noise: Jewish Immigrants in the Hollywood Melting Pot.* Berkeley: U of California P, 1996.

Rossen, Robert, dir. *Body and Soul.* United Artists, 1947.

Salt, Barry. *Film Style and Technology: History and Analysis.* London: Starword, 1983.

Schrader, Paul. "Notes on Film Noir." *Film Comment* 8 (Spring 1972): 8–13.

Stallybrass, Peter, and Allon White. *The Politics and Poetics of Transgression.* London: Methuen, 1986.

Stanton, Fred, ed. *Fighting Racism in World War II.* New York: Monad, 1980.

Tagg, John, and Marcos Sanchez-Tranquilino. "The Pachuco's Flayed Hide: Mobility, Identity and *Buenas Garras.*" *Grounds of Dispute: Art History, Cultural Politics and the Discursive Field.* By John Tagg. Minneapolis: U of Minnesota P, 1992. 183–202.

Tourneur, Jaques, dir. *Out of the Past.* RKO, 1947.

Vidor, Charles, dir. *Gilda.* Columbia, 1946.

Warren, Kenneth W. *Black and White Strangers: Race and American Literary Realism.* Chicago: U of Chicago P, 1993.

Welles, Orson, dir. *The Lady from Shanghai.* Columbia, 1948.

———. *Touch of Evil.* Universal, 1958.

Wilder, Billy, dir. *Double Indemnity.* Paramount, 1944.

Wise, Robert, dir. *Odds against Tomorrow.* United Artists, 1959.

Žižek, Slavoj. *Tarrying with the Negative: Kant, Hegel, and the Critique of Ideology.* Durham: Duke UP, 1993.

CHAPTER 7

"Are We Men?": Prince Hall, Martin Delany, and the Masculine Ideal in Black Freemasonry, 1775–1865

MAURICE WALLACE

Are we MEN!!—I ask you, O my brethren!
are we MEN?
*(David Walker, "Appeal to the Coloured Citizens
of the World")*

We profess to be both men and Masons; and
challenge the world to try us, prove us, and
disprove us, if they can.
(Martin Delany, The Origin and Objects
of Ancient Freemasonry*)*

THERE is hardly a more original experiment in the social (re)production of the black masculine ideal than in the ritual formalizations of identity and ideality in African-American Freemasonry. Probably no other cultural movement before the civil rights campaigns of the twentieth century has been more emblematic of the social and psychic drama of black masculinity in the American cultural context. And yet so little about the historical and cultural impact of black Freemasonry has caught the scholar's attention. Even though black Freemasonry offered the African-American male "his first opportunity to find himself," in the words of one early historian, academic neglect of this historical and cultural phenomenon has gone altogether unchallenged. This, in spite of the fact that scores of notable black men, including distinguished eighteenth- and nineteenth-century figures like David Walker, William Wells Brown, Josiah Henson, John Marrant, Richard Allen, and Booker T. Washington, have traveled the Masonic "road to self-hood" for over two centuries (Crawford 18).[1] In this essay, therefore, I seek to map the course along which the African-American male discovered the "road to self-hood" in freemasonry in 1775. More specifically, I delineate how black Freemasonry in the colonial and Victorian eras helped invent the black masculine ideal philosophically and, what is perhaps more important to this book's design, pictorially. Two elegant full-body portraits of Prince Hall and Martin R. Delany, both eminent Masons, offered African-American men at last, in 1903 and 1865 respectively, visual models of the sort of "disciplinary individualism" (Seltzer 5) and black masculine perfectibility that the earliest Masons purposed to preserve ritualistically, if they could not, in 1775, do so by the more mechanical means of reproduction realized in the pictures of Hall and Delany. Inasmuch as these two portraits, particularly, represented Hall and Delany as *models* of black exceptionalism to be emulated by other black Masons and respectable African-American men, Hall and Delany were to be taken as "typical [African] American" men. By "typical," though, I do not mean "so much the idea of the typical [African] American," as I do, following Mark Seltzer, "the idea of the [African] American *as* the typical—of [African-American men] as typical, general and reproducible" (Seltzer 55). As representative men, Hall and Delany owe no modest debt to the culturally reproductive forms and functions of masculine identity institutionally prescribed within black American Freemasonry.

THE ORIGINS OF BLACK FREEMASONRY IN AMERICA

The history of black Freemasonry in the United States is an uncommon one. Few studies of white American fraternalism even note its tradition. The number of books and articles devoted exclusively to the history of black American fraternalism is correspondingly meager. According to the most reliable of those accounts which have been published, however, the black Freemasonry movement in America was born on March 6, 1775. On that important date, Prince Hall, a free black artisan of Boston, and fourteen other free men of color entered a British encampment at Massachusetts's Bunker Hill, only weeks in advance of the first skirmishes of the War for Independence, where an outfit of Irish Freemasons attached to a British regiment there received them into Army Lodge No. 441.[2] For the price of twenty-five guineas each, Hall and his fellow Masonic aspirants were dutifully initiated into the Ancient and Accepted Order of Freemasons, a legendary fraternal order (allegedly) several centuries old. Almost immediately, Hall and his new fraters organized a "coloured" lodge of their own, Provisional African Lodge No. 1 (later African Lodge No. 459). This first lodge of black Freemasons in the United States made frater Hall its first Grand Master.

Eager to secure a permanent charter legitimizing their Masonic membership, Hall's group, according to one account, "repeatedly attempted to obtain a warrant from the white Masons of Massachusetts" (Muraskin 32), without success. African Lodge No. 1, incapable of overcoming white Ma-

sonic racism, therefore, stood as merely a provisional unit for nearly a decade, restricted by their provisional status to only some of the privileged
exercises of recognized lodges.[3] Finally, in 1784, after nine fruitless years
of petitioning white American lodges, Grand Master Hall sought out and
obtained a Masonic warrant from the more brotherly Grand Lodge of England on September 29.[4] However unsuccessful his earliest efforts, though,
Hall's petitions for Masonic affiliation within American lodges were important because they tacitly challenged the inflated rhetoric of white American Masons as an "association of good men" allied, they claimed, "without
regard to religion, nationality, or class" (Dumenil 9). Hall's repeated appeals forced the white Masonic lie with little more than dogged persistence.

Moreover, Hall's agitation militated against the racial exclusivity of the
U.S. Continental Army as well. Less than three months after gaining fraternity in Army Lodge No. 441, and very nearly the same time he first
entreated the white Masons of Boston, Hall, in an extraordinary balancing
act of colonial progressivism, petitioned Joseph Warren and John Hancock,
leading members of the Committee of Safety (and technically Masonic
brothers), for the right of free and enslaved blacks to enlist in the revolutionary cause.[5] Fearful that Hall's activism masked a conspiratorial pretext,
the Committee of Safety of the Colonies rejected the idea of black enlistment. Later, though, in December of 1775, General George Washington,
newly in command of the Continental Armies, reconsidered Hall's peti-
tion. Threatened by the British recruitment of African Americans, yet wary
of the potential for insurrection by armed slaves, Washington issued a compromise: "As the general is informed that numbers of free Negroes are
desirous of enlisting," he declared, "he gives leave to the recruiting officers
to enlist them" (qtd. in Grimshaw 74). Although Washington would not
permit slaves to enlist, his order meant that as freemen, Hall and his Masonic brethren were eligible to fight at long last. Whether or not they did
fight for the Continental cause is not known with certainty. The evidence
remains sketchy, but most agree that the likelihood of Hall's having exer-
cised his hard-won liberty is very high. Archivist-historian Sidney Kaplan
has discovered "military records of the time [that] reveal at least six black
Prince Halls of Massachusetts in the army and navy of the revolution.
It is [therefore] probable," Kaplan concludes, "that [Prince Hall, Grand
Master of Provisional African Lodge No. 1] was one of these" (Kaplan and
Nogrady 203).

A tireless abolitionist and "leader of the colony of free colored men in
Boston" (Davis 6), Hall was intent upon gaining New England's enslaved
and free men of color a meaningful place in two of the most crucial spheres
of masculine authentication in colonial American culture, Freemasonry
and the military, where, as Mark Seltzer writes, "the social and cultural
technologies for 'the making of men' " thrived (5). His efforts point up

the single-minded earnestness with which African-American men in the colonial and Victorian periods aimed to demonstrate their manliness. Among the first black public men in America, Hall deserves primus inter pares status in the cultural history of African-American manhood. At his death in 1807, the fraters of first African Grand Lodge renamed their body Prince Hall Grand Lodge to honor the leadership of this remarkable figure in building "the only body of black men in America able to date and document their [sic] existence as an organized body from 1775 to the present" (Loretta Williams 17).

Because Hall continues to figure so centrally in the corporate identity of black Freemasons after nearly two centuries, I want to turn now to the paradox of his apotheosis within the order as a "typical [African] American," in that ironically extra-ordinary sense of the phrase advanced by Seltzer. For, as Prince Hall biographer Charles Wesley has noted, both within the fraternity and outside of it the most important treatments of Hall's life and career have been not political or literary (despite his having been recently collected in at least one major anthology of American literature) but iconic, the "impersonation of [his] life" (xvi), that is.

PRINCE HALL AS REPRESENTATIVE BROTHER(MAN)

Sparingly little about the early years of Prince Hall's life is known or documented. Accounts of Hall's birth and early life consist mostly of "lore and legend," as Kaplan has said (Kaplan 182). Without an extant autobiography or set of personal memoirs to guide the telling of his life's story, Hall's fictionalization seems to have been almost inevitable. A recent sketch of Hall's place in American literary culture avers that "[i]f Prince Hall had not actually lived, he most certainly would have been invented" (Robinson 685). Actually, the evidence suggests that Hall *was* invented in spite of having actually lived. Significantly, the earliest portrayals of Hall's life did not appear until 1903, almost a century after his death. William Grimshaw's *Official History of Freemasonry among the Colored People in North America* (1903) identified Hall as "a Mason and a preacher in the seventeenth [sic] century [who] was lifted to a lofty position by events for which there is no reasonable accounting in accordance with anything that is allied to the law of nature" (67).[6] Grimshaw offered this romantic biography:

Prince Hall was born September 12th, 1748, at Bridgetown, Barbados, British West Indies. His father, Thomas Prince Hall, was an Englishman, and his mother a free woman of French descent. . . . When twelve years old young Hall was placed as an apprentice to a leather worker. He made rapid progress in the trade. His greatest desire, however, was to visit America. When he confided this wish to his parents they gave him no encouragement, but he was determined to seize the first opportunity offered to accomplish his desire. With eager eyes he watched every sail that entered the harbor in the hope that he might hear the words "bound for America." . . . One morning in February 1765, young Prince heard the glad tidings that there was a vessel in port bound for America. . . . The vessel arrived in Boston, Mass., in March 1765. When he stepped upon the shores of New England he was seventeen years of age, small in stature, but his slight frame was surmounted with a shapely head, adorned with refined features, bright and piercing eyes, aquiline nose, mouth and chin firm and spiritual. He was in a strange land without friends or education, but [he was] determined to fight his own way. (69–70)

Grimshaw's account was accepted by Carter G. Woodson in *The Negro in Our History* in 1922 and, thenceforth, "repeated in publications and addresses across the years," so much so that "credibility has been given to [it] . . . as almost constituting a tradition" all its own (Wesley 24).

Not until Sidney Kaplan and Emma Nogrady's 1973 reprint of *Black Presence in the Era of the American Revolution* and Charles Wesley's definitive 1977 biography *Prince Hall: Life and Legacy* was Grimshaw's version of Hall's life disputed. More meticulous researchers than Grimshaw, Kaplan, and later Wesley concluded that Hall's "parents and birthplace," contrary to the specificities of Grimshaw, "are unknown." According to Kaplan's findings, "[h]is name is first seen during the 1740s as the slave of one William Hall of Boston" (Kaplan and Nogrady 203). If, indeed, our Prince Hall was the property of William Hall in 1740 and not the freeborn bootstraps hero Grimshaw imagined, then the certainty of "September 12th, 1748," Hall's birthday, is also to be questioned, particularly since his manumission papers bear no record of his birth (Wesley 15). Concerning Prince Hall's birth narrative, then, all that one can say with any certainty is put best by Wesley: "He was born somewhere and on some date" (24). Repeating Booker T. Washington on his own obscure birth ("I suspect I must have been born somewhere and at sometime" (*Up from Slavery* 9), Wesley's words, however unsuited to the trained historian, bespeak an important philosophical point not lost on the ruminations of contemporary race and cultural theorists. The "unknown" facts of Hall's birth, in other words, hint at the greater problem of racial being and nothingness wrought by the problems of slavery and white supremecy, a socioexistential dilemma of black *virtuality* according to which the well-established existentialist axiom "I think; therefore, I am" comes to be replaced by the more simply put, vexing question of black being, "I think I am." It has been precisely this dilemma of black virtuality, in fact, that has compelled so much of the effort to reconstruct black cultural history to have to rely, in greater or lesser degrees, on *invention* for its methodology. Consequently, black cultural his-

tory, to steal a phrase or more from Charles Johnson, "begins to appear
. . . as partly a product of imagination, a plastic and malleable thing
freighted with ambiguity" (79). Possibly for this reason, Wesley's opinion
of Grimshaw's earlier work was, for all its sharp criticisms, conciliatory in
its conclusion: "Grimshaw's book may have weaknesses," he grants, "but
his account became alive while clothing historical errors so that the author
is a maker of a kind of history," nevertheless (25). Grimshaw's "kind of
history," I wish to point out, is distinguished not merely by its fictional
aspect, though, but also by its pictorial imperatives.

Among a dozen or more other pictures, Grimshaw's *Official History* features a full-length portrait of Hall at the book's opening. The image of
Hall in the familiar powdered wig and knee breeches of colonial gentility
does not fail to reflect Hall's "slight frame," "shapely head," or the "refined
features" first and fastidiously detailed in an 1884 public lecture by George
Washington Williams, the eminent early black historian. Not coinciden-
tally, Williams described Hall as Grimshaw had: "We may see Prince Hall
now, a man small in stature. His slight frame is mounted by a shapely head,
adorned with refined features; his eyes are bright and piercing; his nose
aquiline; his mouth and chin, firm and spiritual. He wears a powdered wig,
a black velvet suit, an immaculate shirt with ruffles. He carries a cane in one
hand, and a roll of documents in the other" (qtd. in Wesley 12). Grimshaw's
portrait of Hall, a realistic painting duplicated in black-and-white, faithfully reproduced Williams's description. Seventy years later, however, the
painting was discovered to be "a clumsy forgery" (Kaplan 182), one of two
such visual fabrications in Grimshaw. A second portrait, one ostensibly
depicting Hall's Masonic successor Nero Prince, a free black of Boston,
was found to be "a copy of a steel engraving of Thomas Smith Webb, a
white Mason, a major in the army and an orchestra conductor," below
which Grimshaw deceptively appended Nero Prince's name. "Thus," Wesley observed, "the same likeness appears [in our historical records] for two
persons, one of Nero Prince, a black American, and the other of Thomas
Smith Webb, a white American, identically the same portrait for two men,
and again a forgery" (Wesley 21). Probably Hall's picture in *Official History*
was identically simulated. Unfortunately, as Wesley concludes, "[i]t was a
Grimshaw fabrication which most Prince Hall Masons have looked upon
with admiration and respect and carried . . . in their memories in worshipful ways. It may be that Grimshaw was well-intentioned when he is said to
have made and used this picture. He must have reasoned that having no
picture of Prince Hall, therefore, we will make one of him" (20). Well-
intentioned or not, Grimshaw's forgery should hardly surprise, given Seltzer's observations regarding the "generalized fascination with imitation
and reproduction" at the turn of the twentieth century, "part of the more
general interest in the making of persons and things" in America (55). If,

as Seltzer goes further to show, the cultural logic of the late nineteenth and early twentieth centuries supposed that individuals were productively "made" (cf. the "self-made" man) and Americanness itself was "artifactual and reproducible" (54), then Grimshaw's 1903 portraits of Prince Hall and Nero Prince may not be forgeries, strictly speaking, but worthy *copies* of masculine ideality, "models . . . [that] are valorized as heroic examples" of what the observer, as Robert Stepto says of the pictorial narrator in James Weldon Johnson's *Autobiography of an Ex-Colored Man*, "would do well to emulate" (176). Obviously setting out to portray Hall as revolutionary hero and representative man simultaneously, Grimshaw's image of Hall, in other words, might be imagined as the illustration of a generic type, a "model" black man, the copy of an at once military and Masonic masculinism, for the reproduction of black manhood in Masonic contexts.

The "system of flotation" between individual exceptionalism and the "typical" individual depends upon an abstraction whereby the human body and the collective body of the nation, race, lodge, or military unit can "stand in for each other" (Seltzer 63). Hall's portrait thus argues for this "privilege of abstraction," according to which the original (and aptly named) "framers" of Constitutional identity transformed themselves from white male subjects into republican citizens.[7] Distinguished in every physical aspect from the racist depictions of the most mundanely "typical" images of black men in eighteenth-century runaway slave advertisements, Hall, with "a roll of [presumably constitutional] documents" in hand, is "framed" in Grimshaw as constitutional and Masonic citizen, his body abstracted by an index of "bright," "spiritual," and "immaculate" features. His image resituates black masculinity, then, no longer outside of the letter of constitutional law but "squarely" within it. It implicitly opposes the image of the fugitive body—that which is inapprehensible (in its literal sense of *apprehendere*, to seize) to juridical logic.[8]

Arguably, eighteenth-century fugitive slave advertisements offered the most "typical" (i.e., standard, reproduced, imitated, copied) representations of black maleness in colonial mass culture. With the publication of *Boston News-Letter* in 1704, the birth of regular newspapers resulted in a "great boon" of runaway slave recoveries in New England. Between 1704 and 1784, historian Lorenzo Johnston Greene noted, "nearly every issue of a New England newspaper . . . carried advertisements for fugitive slaves" ("The New England Negro" 128). In the mid-Atlantic states, between 1728 and 1790 the *Pennsylvania Gazette* alone published 1,324 announcements of runaway slaves, of which 91 percent, Billy Smith and Richard Wojtowicz report, concerned male fugitives (5, 13).

Greene's study, "The New England Negro As Seen in Advertisements of Runaway Slaves," describes the problems of fugitive representation that Hall conspicuously counterposed. Because fugitive slave advertisements,

Fig. 7.1. Prince Hall. William Grimshaw, *Official History of Freemasonry among the Colored People in North America* (1903), 68.

indifferent to complex visual detail, only broadly outline the runaway's features, they are, in Greene's words, "seldom precise." The distinguishing details of height, weight, and color are mostly "vague." Of the sixty-two advertisements in Greene's sample, "only five masters attempted to portray the features of their fugitives. And even these paid little attention to the color of the eyes, the shape of the nose or the size and shape of the mouth" (132). If the proof of every rule requires an exception, as it is said, the contrast obtaining in one slave's "very thick lips" and another's "curled head of hair" proves the normative sketchiness of black male imaging in early America. But even if the specific exceptions of "thick lips" and "curled . . . hair" challenged rather than supported the rule of the nondescript, no single advertisement discussed by Greene ever approximates the visual particulars of Hall's "bright and piercing eyes" or "aquiline nose." More-over, Hall bears little trace of the "moles, scars, brands . . . impaired vision and loss of limb" (135) that betray the fugitive's status as slave instead of citizen. Whereas the fugitive body is imagined as deformed, Hall's is disciplined and dignified, armed acceptably with words, not weapons.[9] The image of the black male as an outlaw to constitutional (and, by extension, social) identity, arrested in his "typical" image even when his body re-mained at large, is substituted in Grimshaw by a radically different image: the black male as disciplinary individual and "model" citizen. His is the master('s) copy of masculine perfectibility.

In Seltzer's formulation, disciplinary individualism refers to "the re-placement of the individual and organic body by the collective body of the organization" (155). The irony of disciplinary individualism, however, of representativeness *as such*, that is, puts the very condition of subjecthood disciplinary individualism putatively confers upon Hall in jeopardy. Where the disciplinary individual submits his body, Pauline fashion, to the will and muscles of the corporate body, the "individuality of the individual" becomes "uncertain," keeping "steadily visible the tension between self-possession and self-discipline, between the particular"—Hall as black mas-culine standard—"and the generic" (Seltzer 58): Hall as standard black male. In this way, Grimshaw's treatment of Hall threatens to remand the black masculine to symbolic slave status as a self-*dis*possessed identity even as it attempts to reconstruct eighteenth-century black male representation from a position of black masculine/Masonic self-ownership.

The Masonic ideology of masculine manufacture and (re)production, articulated in the rite of the Third Degree, "the *Making* of the Master Mason" (Clawson 81; emphasis added),[10] encourages a conception of per-sons and bodies as artifacts that, like Grimshaw's biography of Hall, can be made (up) and remade. Since its reconstitution in London in the early 1700s (Carnes 22), modern Freemasonry has promoted an artifactual pro-cess, vaguely mechanical, for "producing men" (Seltzer 168). It stands to reason that Grimshaw, once "Grand Master of black Masons in the District of Columbia," thought it no offense, "having no picture of Prince Hall" (Wesley 12), to invent—indeed, to mass-produce—Hall *artifactually* as book, image, and black masculine model.

It is entirely reasonable, then, given Seltzer's characterization of the cul-tural logic of turn-of-the-century America, that Grimshaw's engagement in the man-making ritualism of Freemasonry would be so extremist; that Hall too, an adept artisan and expert tanner, was drawn so forcefully to the Masonic movement seems almost reflexive. His willingness to go to the great lengths he and his peers did to join, I advance here, was only to be expected.

THE ARTISAN HERO

In her book *Constructing Brotherhood: Class, Gender, and Paternalism*, Mary Anne Clawson argues persuasively that "in the case of Masonic fraternalism . . . the image of one particular social actor, the artisan, dominated the reality-defining drama/discourse of fraternal ritual" (13). By the time of Freemasonry's flowering in the United States, the artisan had already emerged as a national figure for republican citizenship. "Frequently held to be the model citizen of the republic" (Clawson 153), the artisan embodied the values of muscular labor, capitalist production, economic independence, and masculine self-sufficiency in response to the social and economic imperatives of early modern patriarchy and proprietorial culture. Although many of the earlier aristocratic enthusiasts of European Freemasonry promoted the architect as the proper symbol of Masonic identity, American Freemasonry championed the artisan. In becoming a Mason, in fact, a man became a figurative craftsman, whatever his actual trade or office. When he took up the standard paraphernalia of compass, square, plumb line, and leather apron for the first time, he was "express[ing] a new awareness of craft labor's contributions to . . . the success of commerce and manufacture . . . implicitly acknowledg[ing] the moral worth of economically productive activity" (Clawson 78). It is no wonder that hundreds of thousands of black men in America, Europe, and the Caribbean yearned so earnestly to belong to Masonry's symbolically authenticating ranks.[11] From an iconographic view alone, Freemasonry was well suited to the social, psychological, and political ambitions of early race men like Prince Hall, who also, importantly, tended to share a labor history a century or more old. Since before the earliest time of the black presence in the United States, in slavery and in freedom, black hands have been put to labor of craft work.

While an accurate number of black craftsmen since Jamestown 1619 may be impossible to gauge, it is indisputable that African-American men claim a long and unique artisanal history in the United States. According to Booker T. Washington's 1909 *The Story of the Negro: The Rise of the Race from Slavery*, the black crafts tradition preceded even Jamestown: "Although the slaves that were first imported from Africa were, as a rule, rude and unskilled in the industrial arts of the white man, yet the native African was not wholly without skill in the crafts, and it was not very long before some of the dark-skinned strangers had mastered the trades" (60). Quite apart from Washington's symptomatic genuflection to "the industrial arts of the white man," *The Story of the Negro* is nevertheless an extraordinary document. It stands as one of the earliest attempts to historicize African-American craftsmanship. In *The Negro American Artisan*, an even earlier effort published seven years before Washington's history, W.E.B. Du Bois averred that "[t]he Negro slave *was* the artisan of the South before the war" (68; emphasis added). As one of the then-living sources for Du Bois's study, an ex-slave named J. D. Smith recalled, "On every large plantation you could find the Negro carpenter, blacksmith, brick and stone mason" (34). Washington and Du Bois are borne out in literary representation by Frederick Douglass as a Baltimore ship caulker, Nat Turner as a carpenter and wood-carver, William Craft as a fugitive cabinetmaker, and the peerlessness of Harriet Jacobs's carpenter father.[12] For some time after the era of Douglass, Turner, Craft, and Jacobs, the African-American artisan continued to hold "undisputed sway" (Du Bois, *The Negro Artisan* 22).

Prince Hall fraternalism's appeal not only "drew upon the fact that the identity of the artisan was a gendered identity" (Clawson 14), but equally, I submit, depended on the historical relevance and respectability of the artisan in African-American masculine life. The symbolic grammar of Prince Hall Freemasonry, therefore, reveals, if only opaquely, the independent ideological and cultural formations of African-American manhood. As a uniquely black male subculture, it illustrates, in microcosm, the broader dialectics of African-American male identity construction.

MASONRY, MANHOOD, AND THE LABOR OF CONSTRUCTION

> I don't like to work—no man does—but I like what
> is in the work—the chance to find yourself, our
> own reality—for yourself—not for others—what
> no other man can ever know. They only see the
> mere show and never can tell what it really means.
> *(Joseph Conrad,* Heart of Darkness*)*
> For the descendants of slaves work . . . signifies
> servitude, misery, and subordination. Artistic
> expression, expanded beyond recognition from the
> grudging gifts offered by the masters as a token
> substitute for freedom from bondage, therefore,
> becomes the means towards both individual
> self-fashioning and communal liberation.
> *(Paul Gilroy,* The Black Atlantic: Modernity and
> Double Consciousness*)*

The "work"[13] that Prince Hall Freemasonry undertakes to transform black men into symbolic artisans, and thus citizens of the masculine body politic, reveals a dialectic of African-American male "social self-creation through labour," to borrow a phrase from Paul Gilroy (40). Although the idea of "self-creation through labour" might also signify the dialectics of white Masonic identity, I submit that black Freemasonry distinguishes itself because the artisanal consciousness Freemasonry encourages is anticipated by a historical consciousness of structure and design black men have shared as artisans in slavery and freedom. It is by this consciousness, which informs and is informed by what one might call a "work aesthetic," that black men in America have self-reflexively "built" the black masculine into their labor as men and Masons. The 1849 slave narrative of Rev. J.W.C. Pennington, "the fugitive blacksmith," for example, records Pennington's aim "to do . . . [his] work with dispatch and skill" and "a high degree of mechanical pride," in spite of the slave's toil: "I sought to distinguish myself in the finer branches of the business by invention and finish; I frequently tried my hand at making guns and pistols, putting blades in penknives, making fancy hammers, hatchets, sword-canes &c, &c. Besides I used to assist my father at night in making straw-hats and willow-baskets by which means we supplied our family with little articles of food, clothing and luxury, which slaves in the mildest forms of the system never get from the master" (8–9). Pennington's is only among the most explicit expressions of countless others that evidence the extraordinary aptitude of African-American craftsmen, slave and free, to transform resourcefully and *craftily* ("I used to assist my father *at night* . . .") the perfunctory, labor-intensive practices of everyday black life into self-affirming, self-expressive exercises of freedom and identity. In this transformation from *animal laborans* to *homo faber*, from begrudged slave laborer to self-fashioning craftsman, is something of the subterfuge that Michel de Certeau calls *la perruque*, "the worker's own work disguised as work for his employer."

In *The Practice of Everyday Life*, de Certeau explains that "the worker who indulges in *la perruque* . . . cunningly takes pleasure in finding a way to create . . . products whose sole purpose is to signify his own capabilities through his work" (25).[14] The "artisan-like inventiveness" of *la perruque* (vxiii) has enabled African-American men like Pennington to transform "labor," which, following Hannah Arendt, leaves nothing of "the subjective attitude or activity of the laborer" (93) behind, into self-reflective "work," including the mechanically resonant, ritualistic "work" of Freemasonry.[15] Prince Hall Freemasons see their symbolic self-creation as "work" and often refer to the Masonic institution as "the Craft," a name indicative of the transfigurative potential they imagined in "the labor of construction" (Wigley 27) formalized in Masonic rituals. However, Prince Hall fraternalism functions most importantly through Freemasonry's "realist tautology"—"the circular relations between interior states and material conditions (between psychology and sociology)" (Seltzer 128).

Since Freemasonry involves the symbolic "application of the rules and principles of architecture to the construction of [male subjectivity as] edifices" (Mackey, *Symbolism* 83), it is the Master Mason in the Prince Hall Craft who possesses the full knowledge of how to "construct" black masculine subjecthood. Like the mythical artisans of Jerusalem and Tyre who built Solomon's temple without "the sound of ax, hammer or any tool of iron" (Grimshaw 19),[16] the Master Mason alone knows which secrets of the Craft "unite the [male] building in one enduring and connected mass" (Mackey, *Symbolism* 97). Consequently, the singular consciousness of "one enduring and connected mass" of selfhood would appear to be the ultimate dream-wish of the conflicted born-somewhere-and-on-some-date black male subject, whom Du Bois named in *The Souls of Black Folk* a "seventh son" afforded "no true self-consciousness."[17] The interior adjustment of the fractured life of black manhood to the promise of cohesiveness represented by buildings is fundamentally, then, the surplus-producing "work" Prince Hall Freemasonry seeks to perform. In addition to the iconicity of the artisan, then, the Masonic lodge-room as artifact and edifice also expresses black masculine / black Masonic ideality. Since the seventeenth century, Freemasonry has "require[d] that certain general rules should be followed in the construction of a Lodge-room." For example, "a Lodge-room should always, if possible, be situated due East and West." Since the lodge-room's design is meant to signify doubly the ancients' quadrilateral conception of the earth, as opposed to the spherical, "any other form but that of an *oblong square* would be eminently incorrect and unMasonic"(Mackey, *Encyclopedia* 602, 102). Given that this structure reflects Masonry's cherished, if mythic, past, it is no wonder that generations of African-American men, geographically and temporally distant from their Afro-genesis, would find the Masonic lodge-room an agreeable locus for self-creation. As Muraskin has conjectured, the symbolism of the lodge-room "has presented the black man with a worldview that has aided in his creation of self-respect by supplying him with a history that is radically different from the traditional one associated with his people": it "has erased from the mind of the black Mason his actual descent from slaves" and offered an alternative ancestry in the Old World that harkens back Africentrically to "the days of the Pyramids—which according to Masonic legend is the earliest beginnings of the Order" (196–97). In the Prince Hall lodge-room, "the fact of . . . [a Mason's] former condition as [slave], or that of his [fore-]parents [has] no bearing whatever on him" (Delany, *Origin and Objects* 24); the historical nothingness of the slave identity is overcome by the lodge-room's architectural insistence on transcendent cultural memory.

Although both white and black Masons have each embraced enduring myths of Masonic origin, their myths differ markedly. While both groups "have claimed descent from the ancient Egyptians," only black Masons have maintained that "the ancient Egyptians were the original man—the black man." Muraskin discovered that not a few black Masons, therefore, have come to believe that "out of Egypt and through the black man" Masonry itself gained its special knowledge "of [the] arts, sciences and [other] forms of culture" that go into making the man. Prince Hall Masons have not wavered in their belief, in other words, that "Solomon, the builder of the Great Temple . . . upon which [the iconology of] Masonry the world over stands . . . was [also] a black man" (197). According to the Prince Hall version of Masonic beginnings, white Masonry, however thankless, owes its Masonic inheritance to the genius of the black man.

In large part, the black Masons' embrace of this gloriously gendered and racialized narrative of the Masonic genesis is attributable to the prolific writings and decided influence of Martin Robison Delany, "journalist, editor, doctor, scientist, judge, soldier, inventor, customs inspector, orator, politician and novelist," whom Gilroy describes aptly as "an early *architect* of black nationalism." Coeditor of the *North Star* from 1847 to 1849, Delany "modeled his career on standards of appropriately manly achievement . . . set in the eighteenth century by savants and philosophes whose legacy . . . was readily appropriated for his theories of racial integrity and citizenship" (Gilroy 19; 4–5, emphasis added; 21). Perhaps better known for his treatise *The Condition, Elevation, Emigration and Destiny of the Colored People of the United States Politically Considered* (1852) and for having organized the first scientific expedition from the West to the African continent in 1859, Delany was also the first Freemason in America to publish a history of the Prince Hall Craft. Elected Worshipful Grand Master of the St. Cyprian Lodge of Pittsburgh in 1852, Delany quickly published the thin but carefully researched tract *The Origin and Objects of Ancient Freemasonry; Its Introduction into the United States, and Legitimacy Among Colored Men* (1853), which "represented and documented all of his conclusions from ethnological study, that the first flowering of all [Masonic] wisdom was among the blacks of Africa" (Ullman 76). Anticipating in its conclusion his later *Principia of Ethnology* (1879), Delany's history asks, "From whence sprung Masonry, but from Ethiopia, Egypt, and Assyria—all settled and peopled by the children of Ham?" and argues passionately that to deny the black Mason this venerable history was "to deny a child the lineage of its parentage" (37). No doubt, such historical inheritance as that which Masonry offered the progeny of Africa was one of the chief appeals of Masonry to Delany. That some of the most notable of Delany's contemporaries (Frederick Douglass among them)[18] *did not* join any Masonic lodge never mitigated the order's appropriated power to comprehend the historical discontinuities of black masculine life, nor the lodge-room's capacity to evoke the ameliorative, if (re)constructed, past imagined in *The Origin and Objects of Ancient Freemasonry.*

As the lure of Freemasonry seems to have been preeminently iconological, though, and only secondarily historiographical, it is very likely that

Delany was first drawn to Masonry by its artisanal appeal. Even if his life's history does not reveal, among the vast list of vocations cited by Gilroy, that the black polyhistor ever worked as a tradesman, as an inventor, on the other hand—much more a theorist of structure and design than a practitioner—he shared in the history and consciousness of the black trade and craft tradition.[19] Early in 1852, on learning that the Pennsylvania Railroad was extending its tracks over the Allegheny Mountains toward Pittsburgh, Delany devised a means for transporting locomotives across the Alleghenies under their own steam power. His invention was a significant improvement over the usual means of employing cumbersome stationary engines to haul cars over the mountainous terrain. Delany carried the plans for his steam locomotive to a New York lawyer with hopes of acquiring a patent. Unfortunately, after several weeks of correspondence with the Patents Office in Washington, Delany's drawings were returned. Much to his despair, Delany's application had been rejected. Only U.S. citizens could hold patents, Washington explained. Although Delany had a reputation for being especially proud of his free black status, his pride could not alter the fact that, however free he was, in the eyes of the law he was not a constitutional citizen of the republic.

If it is true that something of the inventor is indeed always reflected in the invention and if, as Mark Seltzer has posited in *Bodies and Machines*, "the crisis of agency and its appeals are most evident [in the nineteenth century] in the figure of the railway locomotive" (18), then perhaps the Patent Office's rejection of Delany's application was also a more resounding rejection of the socially motile, self-determinative—even phallic—aspirations Delany's mountain-crossing locomotive might well have symbolized.

Perhaps anticipating a rejection, Delany composed the first drafts of *Condition, Elevation, and Emigration* while awaiting word on his invention from Washington. The first "full-length piece of political analysis by a black American" (Sterling 141), *Condition, Elevation, and Emigration*, grounded in "elaborate theories of nationality and citizenship it derived from a reading of European history" (Gilroy 22), bemoaned black disenfranchisement and, unexpectedly discordant with the abolitionist agenda, favored an emigrationist politics that envisioned black colonization in Central and South America. Failing miserably in its first printing, the book was beset with "misspelled names, wrong dates, [and] awkward passages" (Sterling 147), according to biographer Dorothy Sterling. Worse still for Delany, it garnered little public notice. Where Harriet Beecher Stowe's *Uncle Tom's Cabin* sold in excess of 300,000 copies in 1852, *Condition, Elevation, and Emigration* sold fewer than one thousand. Few persons of note thought *Condition, Elevation, and Emigration* worthy of remark. Only William Lloyd Garrison, the famous abolitionist, gave *Condition, Elevation, and*

Emigration substantive attention. Though he differed with Delany's emigrationist conclusions, Garrison nevertheless described the work favorably
as full of "many valuable facts and cogent appeals." His further flattery of
the author as "a vigorous writer . . . and full of energy and enterprise" (qtd.
in Sterling 149) depicted Delany in very nearly the same, vaguely machinic
("vigorous . . . full of energy"), commercial language of industrial advance
Delany's locomotive would have publicly represented (if not much more).

By 1859 Delany had traveled across Europe, explored northwestern Africa, and, with family in tow, pursued his own emigrationist course to Canada, a pilgrimage, Gilroy points out, reimagined in the epic peregrinations
of Henry Holland, the eponymous hero of Delany's serial novel *Blake; or,
the Huts of America* (21). Settling in Chatham, Ontario, where one-third of
Chatham's population of four thousand (Sterling 160) landed following the
course of the Underground Railroad, Delany chose expatriation as a sign
of his unassimilability into the American body politic.

In Chatham, Delany was a striking if "familiar sight" (Sterling 219). To
see him "at Town Hall, the Baptist Church and the colored school" clad
in the shocoto pants and dashiki (brought back from his African expedition)
was not especially unusual, according to his biographer. Although his sarto-
rial tastes were designed, in part, to counter stereotypes of African primitivism (he also frequently wore "a long dark-colored robe, with curious scrolls
upon the neck as a collar," which he claimed was "the wedding dress of
[an African] Chief" (Sterling 225), his dress was, rather, a visible material
reflection of the surplus of signification that black male bodies, mostly denied the (white, male) privilege of abstract disembodiment, inspire as outlaws to constitutional representation under racialism. For a time Delany
reveled in his "outlaw" image. With the hopefulness of the Civil War, however, his attitude toward black American enfranchisement, as well as his
dress, changed dramatically.

The political promise of a war won by antislavery forces revived in Delany a hope for "an American future for American blacks" (Gilroy 25).
"Aching to get into the struggle himself" (Sterling 233), but well beyond
the age of enlistment, he returned to the States in 1863 and volunteered
to help raise black troops for the Union cause. In a letter to then–Secretary
of War E. M. Stanton, Delany offered his energies, convinced, he wrote,
that black enlistment was "one of the measures in which the claims of the
Black Man may be officially recognized, without seemingly infringing upon
those of other citizens" (qtd. in Sterling 233). Apparently Delany knew
already what critic Michael Hatt would make clear only in the 1990s: that
by the mid–nineteenth century, "[m]asculinity defined and was defined by
the soldier's task . . . the soldier's rough and rugged lifestyle; his determina-
tion and endurance; and by his physical control . . . [demonstrated] not
least in the military requirement for discipline" (24). In Delany's letter to

Stanton, however, was an implicit avowal that black masculinity cohered in a white context. Judging "the measures" of a black man, in other words, "was a question of negotiating between sameness and difference, permitting [him] manhood without disturbing inequalities of power based on ethnicity" (29), as Hatt argues, without "seemingly infringing," that is, on the social or political "claims" of (white male) others.

With an acute sense of "the necessary relationship between nationality, citizenship and masculinity" (Gilroy 25) that I believe soldiering inevitably evokes, Delany took to recruiting ardently. For his zeal and tactical acumen in proposing to raise African-American Union troops on both sides of the Mason-Dixon, he was commissioned a U.S. Army major. Secretary Stanton issued Delany his commission on February 26, 1865. Swearing solemnly by the Constitution to fulfill the duties of his charge as the United States's first black field officer, Delany was transformed instantly from constitutional cipher and political nonconformist to disciplinary individual and "model" (black) citizen. Emblematically, the *Weekly Anglo-African* newspaper offered a dignified postcard portrait of the black major—like Prince Hall, extraordinary in one sense, "typical" in another—"taken in full uniform by the celebrated artist, Bogardus of Broadway" (Sterling 246). Once favoring the exoticism of dashiki and shocoto pants over the familiar conventions of Western dress, Delany assumed "the disciplined body of the regimented black" (Hatt 25) in his portraitured military regalia, an image of corporal asceticism prefiguring the military formalism of Marcus Garvey half a century later. No longer a menace to the representational integrity of the body politic, as soldier Delany became its willfully governed subject and defender, roles in which one could hardly have imagined so insurgent a figure as Delany were he not a Mason. For what was required by Masonry and the military alike was, above all else, a disciplined masculinism.

Given Delany's importance to the history and meaning of Prince Hall Freemasonry, and the fraternity's reciprocal influence on Delany, it is tempting to try to find evidence of Masonic arcana cached between the lines of his major writings, especially the ambitious fiction *Blake*, with all of its secret councils and masculinist politics. To mine *Blake* thoroughly for its Masonic allusions, however, is to risk erring in the direction of so much historic anti-Masonic paranoia, from that expressed by Yale College president Timothy Dwight in 1798 to the numerological auguries of Louis Farahkan in 1995, a continuum of nearly two full centuries.[20] I nevertheless want to put forward the Grand Official Council in part 2 of *Blake* not so much as a Masonic assembly—for there are women in this body—as, rather, a depiction of Masonic *seclusion*.

With its insurrectionary and nationalist objectives, the Grand Council of black liberationists appearing in chapters 60, 61, 69, 70, and 74 of the novel first serialized in the *Anglo-African Magazine* in January 1859 is por-

Fig. 7.2. Martin Robison Delany. Courtesy of Moorland-Spingarn Research Center, Howard University.

trayed as converging familiarly *in isolato* in the "southwest corner of [Madame Cordora's] mansion in an airy attic room, reserved for the purpose" (255). A pre-Garvey vanguard of Pan-Africanist politics, Delany's council of self-proclaimed "seclusionists," with all of their cabalistic pretenses of Masonic ritualism, nearly mimics the gendered politics and poetics of Masonic lodge-room design. Alhough the Council meeting-place belongs to Madame Cordora, its character is nevertheless masculinist, "the misses being admitted [only] by courtesy" (255).[21] That a guard keeps post outside the door permitting no one entry without the "closest possible inspection" is no less befitting Delany's Masonic designs. The seclusion of the Grand Council, then, imitates the topoanalytic dimensions of Masonic architecture.

Conceptually, as I showed earlier, the Masonic lodge-room aims to duplicate the universe of the ancients, a primal cosmos long since disappeared. That is its exterior objective. But the symbolism of the lodge-room moves in two directions. While the primary dimensions of the lodge-room seek to model the cartographic limits of bygone beginnings, the lodge-room's structural austerity helps the Mason to imagine the lodge-as-self. That is, the spatial concentration to which the strict boxlike framing of the lodge-room gives definition tends to simulate the unified consciousness of the Ideal-I. Furthermore, Mackey's recommendation that the "lodge-room should also be isolated where it is practicable, from all surrounding buildings" clearly appeals to the individual's consciousness of essential selfhood. From this decidedly psychoanalytic perspective, then, the design of the lodge-room is extraordinarily self-referential.

Suggestively, Mackey further specifies the formal layout of the lodge-room: "There should be two entrances to the room, which should be situated in the West. . . . The one on [the] right hand is for the introduction of visitors and . . . leading from the Tiler's room is called the Tiler's, or the *outer door*; the other, on [the] left, leading from the preparation room [where candidates await initiation], is known as the *inner door*, and sometimes called the *northwest door*" (*Encyclopedia* 602). Implicitly, this unalterable lodge-room topography posits a public (outer) and private (inner) conveyance into the lodge-as-self homologous with Raymond Williams's formulations of the *material sign*, i.e., the "outer door" of public representation, and the *inner sign*, or the "inner door" entering into the private negotiations of Masonry and manhood. (Appropriately, the two auxiliary rooms into which the "inner door" and "outer door" enter and exit are also known among insiders as "secret . . . closets" [Mackey, *Encyclopedia* 432].) Although both entry and egress of the "southwest corner" of Madame Cordora's mansion, the material sign and the inner sign respectively, are resolutely *Western* semiologies, the problem of the (black) masculine ideal is inextricable from its Western contexts of race, sex, and representation.

The public/private dichotomy of representation suggested by lodge-room design, however, is not unique to the gendered identity of Masonry. Significantly, it is as crucial to the familiar Du Boisian notion of racial "double consciousness" as it is to Masonic identity. Perhaps no less important than the black/white, African/European binarisms that typically characterize "the twoness" of black American identity, the public/private dialectic is no strange division of consciousness to Prince Hall Freemasons. They are among those whom Lawrence Levine described as a "people who have walked through American history with their cultural lanterns obscured from the unknowing and unseeing eye of outside observers" (442). Levine's depiction of black cultural life imaginatively highlights the concord of strategic dissimulations in public culture that African Americans have privately engineered for their protection. As a mimetic reproduction of a familiar structure of consciousness, then, the lodge-room is especially signifying for the Prince Hall Mason.

Relatedly, the recent work of Eric Lott on the "seeming counterfeit"[22] theatrics of black minstrelsy offers the "darky" performance as one of the paradigmatic forms of cultural practice revealing the particularistic efforts of African-American *men* to insure the dividing line between private and public self-representation. Lott argues that when black actors took the minstrel stage after the Civil War, their burnt-cork and "lamp black" performances, far from redeeming their bodies from the appropriating gaze of the white public, merely reappropriated them, further disguising the "authentic" character of black male subjectivity. "It was possible for a black man in blackface, without a great deal of effort, to offer *credible imitations of white men imitating him*," Lott maintains (113). I find this performed will to keep apart the public and private selves of African-American male subjecthood deeply invested in the symbolic architecture of the Prince Hall lodge-room. Not unagreeably, its discrete influence on several generations of African-American men has doubtless helped to ease many of the private anxieties of historic black masculine identity.

INTERIOR DESIGNS

Given the number of legal prohibitions restricting African-American sociability in the eighteenth and nineteenth centuries, it is remarkable that Prince Hall Freemasonry survived its first one hundred years. In 1770s Massachusetts, for example, a 9:00 P.M. curfew for free blacks probably curtailed the amount of "work" fledgling African Lodge No. 1 could carry out (Greene, *The Negro* 299). States like South Carolina went so far as to forbid the assembly of slaves or free blacks "in a confined or secret place" altogether.[23] An entire range of repressive measures between those of Massachusetts, at one extreme, and South Carolina, at the other, were also enacted in most other states from Connecticut in the North to Tennessee and Georgia in the South. Nevertheless, by 1865, the end of the Civil War, Prince Hall lodges had been securely established in fourteen states, including Maryland, Kentucky, Louisiana, and South Carolina (Loretta Williams 44). That black Masonry thrived in spite of these black codes is testament to the covertness and cunning by which black masculine identity has kept itself hidden from the arrestive encroachments of public specularity. Architecturally, I hope finally to make clear, this will to secrecy and silence is reflected in the uncompromising insularity of the lodge-as-self.

In form and function, the Prince Hall lodge-room has been an enduring sanctuary for black masculine subjectivization for over two centuries. Its integrity as a refuge from specular objecthood is guaranteed by the architectural imperative of "lofty walls" to "preclude the possibility of being overlooked by cowans or eavesdroppers" (Mackey, *Encyclopedia* 432). Whatever else Masonic authorities intended "lofty walls" to signify, in the context of black male specularity and the madness engendered by racist *oversight*, they cannot escape casting the Masonic lodge-room as an asylum, structural as much as social, for the black Mason's most essential self-interests.

As to the interior layout and furnishings of the lodge-room, Mackey's *Encyclopedia* gives the following blueprint: "In a Lodge-room the dais should be elevated on three steps, and provided with a pedestal for the Master. . . . The pedestal for the Senior Warden in the West should be elevated on two steps, and that of the Junior Warden in the South on one. . . . The tabernacle also forms an essential part of the Chapter room. This is sometimes erected in the center of the room. . . . There are some other arrangements required in the construction of a [lodge-]room, of which is unnecessary to speak" (433). By limning only the most essential features of this blueprint, forsaking "unnecessary" details, Mackey implicitly underscores the symbolic importance of the three named offices: the Master, the Senior Warden, and the Junior Warden. Significantly, in the symbolism of these three posts lies the gender and sexual subtexts of Freemasonry that I believe are faithfully recapitulated in Delany's *Blake*.

From yet another cosmological view, "the Master and Wardens are symbols of the sun, the lodge-room of the universe, or world," themselves further symbols in the secret language of Masonry of the fecundating power of the Phallus or *membrum virile*, and the Cteis or female "receptacle." The Phallus and Cteis, sun and universe, represent "the two different forms of the generative principle," male and female, which "perfect the circle of generation" in nature (Mackey, *Symbolism* 115, 112–13). Reflecting the notion "that the procreative and productive powers of nature might be conceived to exist in the same individual" (114)[24] the union of Phallus and

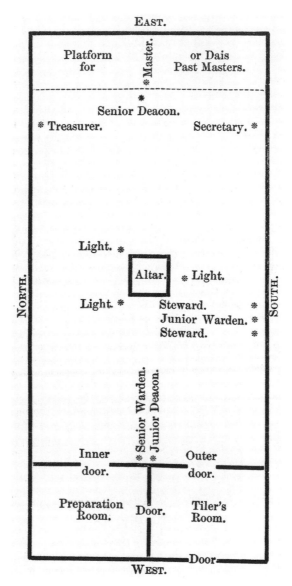

Fig. 7.3. An arrangement of the lodge-room in the United States. Albert Mackey, *Encyclopedia of Freemasonry and Its Kindred Sciences* (1892), 601.

Cteis, which the special layout of the lodge-room represents, signifies among Masons an androgynous subjectivity intent upon displacing women from the generative process of masculine self-creation "with an alternative practice, at once [artifactual] and male" (Seltzer 28). While the lodge-room as Cteis bears a conspicuously uterine character (it is here, one recalls, that men are "born again"),[25] the androgenetic/androgynistic principle in Masonry upsets female-uterine relation. In an act of what Seltzer calls the "confiscation of the generative function," an act that might be thought of as *homo-obstetric*, the Master Mason actualizes "a compensatory male response to [an ostensibly] threatening female productivity . . . underwriting . . . what appears as an absolute differentiation of gender powers and 'principles' " (28). Maternity, that is, is not required for the initiate to be "born into the Masonic light" (Mackey, *Symbolism* 218). Paternity alone is sufficient.

This gynecological hermeneutic for understanding the form and functions of the lodge-room, however, does not settle everything. Pushing the tropological imagination, Paul Smith's idea of *vas*, a schematic trope for thinking about the male imaginary in rather dynamic terms, helps to explain further the metaphysical designs of the lodge-as-self. As Smith explains in his essay by the same name, *vas* is literally a vessel or a container in the Latin—another "receptacle,"that is, but a fundamentally different one from the Cteis. Smith understands *vas* as a metaphor for the dialectics of the "male body and the male imaginary" (1011) in synchrony. Related to "the 'vas deferens' of the male sexual gear, and the . . . castratory idea of 'vasectomy' " (1016), *vas* also signifies those "unsymbolizable" (1020) drives of masculine identity "which are left aside by the [overused] metaphor of the phallus" (1011). That is, as a "flexible and movable container where accumulations of imaginary 'substance' are built up and from which they can be lost" (1019), *vas* "carries" with it significations that the phallus alone cannot easily achieve. As a mimetic reflection of Smith's principle, the "contained" space of the lodge-room as masculine self conceals certain unsymbolizable conditions of intimate male selfhood that most Masons would probably rather not own publicly. The ideas implicit in Masonry's symbolic androgyny and homo-obstetrics are simply unrepresentable in public language and not nearly phallic enough. Since Lacan has argued that the unsymbolizable is tantamount to the death of the subject, it is perfectly logical why the Phallus, the symbolizable of masculine identity, is held up by black Masons for public representation. Such a self-protective impulse would seem to have made Freemasonry an appealing recourse to the risk of racial oversight and public overexposure.

To enlist in the ranks of Prince Hall Freemasonry, then, is inevitably to take on a structure of consciousness that, reconstituting the black masculine, conceives of the lodge-as-self. In accord with the Bourdieuvian *dialec-*

tic of the internalization of externality and the externalization of internality, the architectonics of the lodge-room replicate externally and reinforce internally the organization of the Prince Hall Masonic mind, establishing the preconditions for a historical "edifice complex" among black Masons and non-Masons who, nevertheless, share the same problems of history, identity, and public specularity. Few institutions, then, besides Prince Hall Freemasonry illustrate so lucidly how the black masculine is "made in America."

NOTES

1. An incomplete list of other prominent black Freemasons before 1912 would also include Paul Cuffee, James Forten, Alexander Crummell, Edward Bouchet, W.E.B. Du Bois, and Jack Johnson

2. One of fifty foreign military lodges stationed in the American colonies. See Morse 16.

3. Among other restrictions, Hall and his fellow Masons could not legitimately initiate other free men of color, so that from 1775 to 1784 only fifteen black men in the country were Masons.

4. Prince Hall to William Moody of London (March 2, 1784):

Dear Brother I would inform you that this Lodge hath been founded almost eight [*sic*] years and we have had only a Permit to Walk on St. John's Day and to Bury our Dead in manner and form. We have had no opportunity to apply for a Warrant before now, though, we have been importuned to send to France for one, yet we thought it best to send to the Fountain from whence we received the Light, for a Warrant; and now Dear Br. we must make you our advocate at the Grand Lodge, hoping you will be so good (in our name and Stead) to Lay this Before the Royal Grand Master and the Grand Wardens and the rest of the Grand Lodge, who we hope will not deny us nor treat us Beneath the rest of our fellow men, although Poor yet Sincere Brethren of the Craft. (Qtd. in Wesley 210)

Owing to a number of communication failures and broken trusts, the official document did not arrive in the colonies until April 29, 1787. Hall's extant letters and correspondences with the Mother Grand Lodge of England reveal that the charter "was personally delivered to Prince Hall by James Scott, a sea captain and brother-in-law of the eminent John Hancock." The charter numerically redesignated Provisional African Lodge No. 1 as African Lodge No. 459, following a peculiarly Masonic logic. See Loretta Williams 17.

5. According to William Grimshaw, fifty-one of the fifty-five signers of the Declaration of Independence, including Warren and Hancock, were Masons. It is very unlikely, however, that any of them recognized a fraternal connection with Hall. See Grimshaw chap. 51.

6. Subsequent histories dispute Grimshaw's assertion that Hall was a preacher.

7. "Privilege of abstraction" is Seltzer's phrase. See Berlant on abstract disembodiment and constitutional citizenship.

8. Robert Reid-Pharr has posited the fugitive or "runaway" in dialectical relation to the "domestic" black body: where the runaway body is "profligate," the domestic is "respectable." My conception of the fugitive differs, I think, only insofar as I posit it in opposition to the disciplined black body, which connotes a specifically male dialectic. Reid-Pharr, *Conjugal Union*.

9. Hall also counters the runaway slave advertisements' "typical" image of the illiterate slave. Greene writes, "From the advertisements, the runaways would appear to have been overwhelmingly illiterate, for all but one of the owners said nothing concerning the ability of their slaves to read and write. Whether these slaves were generally illiterate or whether the masters apparently believed that literacy or lack of it in their slaves would have little to do with their recovery cannot be ascertained" ("The New England Negro" 139). In the context of this study, the actual literacy rate among the runaways is not as important as the perception of "overwhelming" illiteracy among them.

10. Significantly, the rite of the Third Degree is "usually considered the dramatic centerpiece of [all] Masonic ritual[s]."

11. For a historical overview of Prince Hall Masonic membership's numerical and regional trends, see Muraskin. For prominent Prince Hall Masons since 1723, including notable clergymen, artists, athletes, and activists, see Cox.

12. "I was born a slave; but I never knew it till six years of happy childhood had passed away. My father was a carpenter, and considered so intelligent and skillful in his trade, that, when buildings out of the common line were to be erected, he was sent for from long distances, to be head workman. On condition of paying his mistress two hundred dollars a year, and supporting himself, he was allowed to work at his trade, and manage his own affairs. His strongest wish was to purchase his children" (Jacobs 341).

13. "Work" is Freemasonry's own term for "the initiation of a candidate into its mysteries" (Mackey, *Symbolism* 266).

14. In some ways, *la perruque* accords with the notion in African-American cultural studies of *masking* as a survival strategy. In this case, however, the masking is not performed but produced, worked by hand into an object.

15. Drawing on ancient Greek categories, Arendt distinguishes labor, the activity of the body that slavishly "minister[s] to the necessities of life" (80), from work, the activity of productive hands that are "capable of producing a 'surplus'" (88). According to the Greeks, "to labor meant to be enslaved by necessity, and this enslavement was inherent in the condition of human life. Because men were dominated by the necessities of life, they could win their freedom only through the domination of those whom they subjected to necessity by force. The slave's degradation was a blow of fate and a fate worse than death, because it carried with it a metamorphosis of man into something akin to a tame animal. A change in a slave's status, therefore, such as manumission by his master or a change in general political circumstance . . . automatically entailed a change in the slave's 'nature'" (84). If there is any ideological continuity between ancient Greek and modern American forms of slavery, then it is clear why Hall's efforts on behalf of enslaved and free blacks to serve in the Continental Army and to perform the "work" of Freemasonry were so earnest: manumission makes the slave human; "work" makes him a man.

16. For a Masonic commentary on this idea as it relates biblically to Solomon, see Mackey, *Symbolism* 85–99.

17. "[T]he Negro is a sort of seventh son, born with a veil, and gifted with second-sight in this American world,—a world which yields him no true self-consciousness. . . . One ever feels his two-ness,—an American, a Negro; . . . two warring ideals in one dark body, whose dogged strength alone keeps it from being torn asunder" (Du Bois, *Souls of Black Folk* 45).

18. "Frederick Douglass chided blacks in fraternities for time spent in rituals of secrecy rather than actions for [social] change" (Loretta Williams 84).

19. This possibility is made all the more likely when one considers that, besides Delany, black inventors Henry Blair, the first black inventor to receive a U.S. patent; Lewis Latimer, an associate of Thomas Edison and Alexander Graham Bell, and creator of the carbon filament now used in the lightbulb; and Granville T. Woods, whose better known inventions include the steam boiler, the incubator, and automobile air brakes, were also Prince Hall Masons. See Cox.

20. On Timothy Dwight and anti-Masonic sentiment, see George Johnson; on Louis Farakhan, refer to Freund.

21. I am indebted to Reid-Pharr's essay "Violent Ambiguity" for concisely articulating the gender politics at work in the Grand Official Council.

22. "As a figure for early blackface acts, 'the seeming counterfeit' is perfectly apt. To the extent that such acts merely seemed [like the counterfeit productions of blacked-up white men], they kept white involvement in black culture under control, indeed facilitated that involvement; but the power disguised by the counterfeit was also often invoked by it, suggesting the occasional ineffectiveness, the mere seeming, of the counterfeit itself" (Lott 113).

23. Linda Warfel Slaughter, *Freedmen of the South*. Quoted in Loretta J. Williams 30.

24. This cosmology is, to a significant degree, harmonious with the religious worldview that many historians and scholars of Afro-Christian history, including Mechal Sobel, C. Eric Lincoln, John Mbiti, Albert Raboteau, and Cheryl Townsend Gilkes, believe accompanied Africans to the New World. As Gilkes writes, "Indeed African religious systems, regardless of how patriarchal they were, exalted both the male and female in the various collective expressions of the holy (the cult)" (80).

25. For a lucid discussion of the maternal qualities of the lodge-room, see Carnes 119–21.

WORKS CITED

Arendt, Hannah. *The Human Condition*. Chicago: U of Chicago P, 1958.

Berlant, Lauren. *The Anatomy of National Fantasy: Hawthorne, Utopia, and Everyday Life*. Chicago: U of Chicago P, 1991.

Bullock, Steven C. *Revolutionary Brotherhood: Freemasonry and the Transformation of the American Social Order, 1730–1840*. Chapel Hill. U of North Carolina P, 1996.

Carnes, Mark C. *Secret Ritual and Manhood in Victorian America*. New Haven: Yale UP, 1989.

Clawson, Mary Ann. *Constructing Brotherhood: Class, Gender, and Fraternalism.* Princeton: Princeton UP, 1989.

Conrad, Joseph. *Heart of Darkness: An Authoritative Text, Backgrounds, Sources and Criticisms.* Ed. Robert Kimbrough. New York: Norton, 1988.

Cox, Joseph Mason Andrew. *Great Black Men of Masonry, 1723–1982.* Bronx: Blue Diamond, 1982.

Crawford, George. *Prince Hall and His Followers.* New York: Crisis, 1914.

Davis, Harry E. *A History of Freemasonry among Negroes in America.* [Cleveland?]: The United Supreme Council, Ancient & Accepted Scottish Rite of Freemasonry, Northern Jurisdiction, USA (Prince Hall Affiliation), 1946.

de Certeau, Michel. *The Practice of Everyday Life.* Trans. Steven Rendall. Berkeley: U of California P, 1984.

Delany, Martin. *Blake; or, the Huts of America.* Boston: Beacon P, 1970.

———. *The Condition, Elevation, Emigration, and Destiny of the Colored People of the United States Politically Considered.* 1852. New York: Arno, 1968.

———. *The Origin and Objects of Ancient Freemasonry; Its Introduction into the United States, and Legitimacy Among Colored Men.* Pittsburgh: Haven, 1853.

Du Bois, W.E.B. *The Souls of Black Folk.* 1903. New York: Singet-NAL, 1969.

———, ed. *The Negro Artisan.* . . . Rpt. in *Atlanta University Publications* 2 (1902). New York: Arno, 1969. No. 7.

Du Bois, W.E.B., and Augustus Dill, eds. *The Negro American Artist.* . . . Rpt. in *Atlanta University Publications* 1 (1912). New York: Arno, 1969. No. 17.

Dumenil, Lynn. *Freemasonry and American Culture, 1880–1930.* Princeton: Princeton UP, 1984.

Freund, Charles Paul. "From Satan to Sphinx: The Masonic Mysteries of DC's Map." *Washington Post* November 5, 1995: CO3.

Gilkes, Cheryl Townsend. "The Politics of Silence: Dual-Sex Political Systems and Women's Traditions of Conflict in African-American Religion." *African American Christianity.* Ed. Paul E. Johnson. Berkeley: U of California P, 1994. 80–110.

Gilroy, Paul. *The Black Atlantic: Modernity and Double Consciousness.* Cambridge: Harvard UP, 1993.

Greene, Lorenzo Johnston. *The Negro in Colonial New England 1942.* New York: Atheneum, 1968.

———. "The New England Negro As Seen in Advertisements for Runaway Slaves." *Journal of Negro History* 29 (1944): 125–46.

Grimshaw, William. *Official History of Freemasonry among the Colored People in North America.* . . . 1903. New York: Negro Universities P, 1969.

Hatt, Michael. " 'Making a Man of Him': Masculinity and the Black Body in Mid-Nineteenth-Century American Sculpture.' " *Oxford Art Journal* 15, no. 1 (1992): 21–35.

Jacobs, Harriet. *Incidents in the Life of a Slave Girl. The Classic Slave Narratives.* Ed. Henry Louis Gates, Jr. New York: Mentor-Penguin, 1987. 333–513.

Johnson, Charles. *Being and Race: Black Writing since 1970.* Bloomington: Indiana UP, 1988.

Johnson, George. "Pierre, Is That a Masonic Flag on the Moon?" *New York Times* November 24, 1996: 4E.

Johnson, James Weldon. *The Autobiography of an Ex-Colored Man*. 1912. New York: Penguin Books, 1990.

Kaplan, Sidney. *The Black Presence in the Era of the American Revolution, 1770–1800*. Washington, D.C.: New York Graphic Society/Smithsonian Institution, 1973.

Kaplan, Sidney, and Emma Nogrady. *The Black Presence in the Era of the American Revolution*. Rev. ed. Amherst: U of Massachusetts P, 1989.

Levine, Lawrence W. *Black Culture and Black Consciousness: Afro-American Folk Thought from Slavery to Freedom*. New York: Oxford UP, 1978.

Lott, Eric. *Love and Theft: Blackface Minstrelsy and the American Working Class*. New York: Oxford UP, 1993.

Mackey, Albert G. *Encyclopedia of Freemasonry and Its Kindred Sciences. . . .* Rev. ed. Philadelphia: Everts, 1892.

———. *The Symbolism of Freemasonry: Illustrating and Explaining Its Science and Philosophy, Its Legends, Myths, and Symbols*. Chicago: Cooke, 1947.

Morse, Sidney. *Freemasonry in the American Revolution*. Washington, D.C.: Masonic Service Association of the United States, 1924.

Muraskin, William A. *Middle-Class Blacks in a White Society: Prince Hall Freemasonry in America*. Berkeley: U of California P, 1975.

Pennington, J.W.C. *The Fugitive Blacksmith: Or, Events in the History of James W. C. Pennington, Pastor of a Presbyterian Church, New York, Formerly a Slave in the State of Maryland, United States*. 3d ed. Westport: Negro Universities P, 1971.

Reid-Pharr, Robert. *Conjugal Union*. New York: Oxford UP, 1999.

———. "Violent Ambiguity: Martin Delany, Bourgeois Sadomasochism and the Production of Black National Masculinity." *Representing Black Men*. Ed. Marcellus Blount and George P. Cunningham. New York: Routledge, 1996. 73–94.

Robinson, William H. "Prince Hall." *The Heath Anthology of American Literature*. Vol. 1. Ed. Paul Lauter et al. Lexington: Heath, 1990. 685–86.

Seltzer, Mark. *Bodies and Machines*. New York: Routledge, 1992.

Smith, Billy G., and Richard Wojtowicz, comps. *Blacks Who Stole Themselves: Advertisements for Runaways in the Pennsylvania Gazette, 1728–1790*. Philadelphia: U of Pennsylvania P, 1989.

Smith, Paul. "Vas." *Feminisms: An Anthology of Literary Theory and Criticism*. Ed. Robyn Warhol and Diane Price Herndl. New Brunswick: Rutgers UP, 1991. 1011–29.

Stepto, Robert B. *From Behind the Veil: A Study of Afro-American Narrative*. 2d ed. Urbana: U of Illinois P, 1991.

Sterling, Dorothy. *The Making of an Afro-American: Martin Robison Delany, 1812–1885*. New York: Doubleday, 1971.

Ullman, Victor. *Martin P. Delany: The Beginnings of Black Nationalism*. Boston: Beacon, 1971.

Walker, David. *Walker's Appeal in Four Articles. . . .* 2d ed. 1830. New York: Arno, 1969.

Washington, Booker T. *The Story of the Negro: The Rise of the Race from Slavery*. Vol. 2. New York: Doubleday, 1909.

———. *Up From Slavery*. 1901. New York: Mangum, 1968.

Wesley, Charles. *Prince Hall: Life and Legacy*. Washington, D.C.: United Supreme Council Southern Jurisdiction-Prince Hall Affiliation, 1977.

Wigley, Mark. *The Architecture of Deconstruction: Derrida's Haunt*. Cambridge: MIT P, 1993.

Williams, Loretta J. *Black Freemasonry and Middle-Class Realities*. University of Missouri Studies 69. Columbia: U of Missouri P, 1980.

Williams, Raymond. *Marxism and Literature*. Oxford: Oxford UP, 1977.

Woodson, Carter G. *The Negro in Our History*. Washington, D.C.: Associated Publishers, 1922.

CHAPTER 8

Unseemly Commemoration: Religion, Fragments, and the Icon

JENNY FRANCHOT

The sacred is invested in the trace that is at
the same time its negation.
(Pierre Nora, "Between Memory and History:
Les Lieux de Memoir")

1

What is the status of religious experience as an object of interpretation in intellectual culture today? I would like to approach this question by examining two scenes from nineteenth-century American fiction, one in Harriet Beecher Stowe's *The Minister's Wooing* (1859) and the other in George Washington Cable's *The Grandissimes: A Story of Creole Life* (1880). In these and similar nineteenth-century novels, I believe, we can trace a larger cultural experience of the loss of religious belief and its re-creation as visual memory, or more precisely as souvenir and entertainment, one fit for visual scrutiny and memorial appropriation as the "seen."

In the wake of the Enlightenment, the status of religion in intellectual culture is that of a loss, a collection of images and texts that are now irrevocably a recollection, a memorial of past faith, or, depending on one's perspective, of past illusion. This condition of belief, the attachment to invisible realities, is ours through not being ours. We know of others' belief or attachment to the invisible only through the visible traces left behind, through the images and texts that attest to an encounter with the unseen. In a sense, the situation of intellectual culture vis-à-vis religious experience reenacts the classic problem of distance from the divine familiar to theological and mystical traditions: those who approach divinity and then report on it dwell always in the trope of inexpressibility. A doubled exasperation haunts Western culture's encounter with its deity—an exasperation not only with "his" overbearing yet neglectful, raging yet rueful character, but also with our ability to represent that character. We are made in his image, according to biblical tradition, but cannot discern his image. Records of encounters with the deity are always pointing to an insufficiency, even a failure of witnessing. He is fragment, a backside vanishing from Moses. But in becoming subject of our recollection, in becoming a memento of a lost faith, this exasperation has often been minimized, sometimes even replaced, by the colonizing conviction that our past Western selves—the Other in this case—constitute a whole, an object of our condescension or nostalgia, surveillance, and repressed desire. Contradiction, alienation, and loss belong to the conqueror; neither the native nor the past self is granted depth.

If we consider the Anglo-American past in terms of postcolonial conceptions of othering and strategies of the "gaze," religion emerges as a "stereotype" of the kind that, according to Homi Bhabha, figures the colonized as a mode of representation dependent on contradictory urges toward "fixity" and "ambivalence" (139–70). Stereotypes of lost belief appear most typically in museums, on public television, or in history movies: in all three places visuality is critical. We gaze on accoutrements and art of past centuries—saintly faces, biblical scenes, church interiors, crucifixes. Or we encounter their representations in books where print, born in the era of Protestant iconoclasm, set itself in conscious competition with the image: the visibility of text—shorn of color, shape, and the libidinal, idolatrous lure of graphic representation—potentially offers unmediated contact with an invisible deity.[1] Such images and texts filling museums and libraries are, for secular culture, the Other, the loss by which, ironically, we have come to know ourselves: we are *not* belief. We are that which we have lost.

Belief's transformation into pastness is, in fundamental respects, the narrative of Western culture's birth into the modern. The Other to modernism, religion has become a repository of the visual and has itself become a "mental" image (Mitchell 14–19). Just as the past is "religious," religion itself is a sign of the quaint, scaled down into a memory like our conception of childhood, which, Susan Stewart argues, is seen "as if it were at the other end of a tunnel—distanced, diminutive, and clearly framed" (44). As memorabilia or as pathology, religion is imagined as an "other" state of being that is stranger and smaller—the "doll-like Middle Ages" that so fascinated Henry Adams in *Mont-Saint-Michel and Chartres* (1913), a perspective that now characterizes our bemused scrutiny of contemporary cults. Religion has become its own relic, its pastness an insignia of the inaccessible but also, as with our childhoods, of the authentic. Religion's scaled-down dimensions register our possession of it instead of its possession of us. As memento of our Western childhood, religion is thus miniaturized into objects available for visual appropriation as commodity, souvenir, or ornament.

The effort of early Protestant reformers to arrive at a purified form of Christianity is central to this othering and miniaturization—this construction of faith as something to be remembered through being scaled down to the "seen." Augustine's argument that knowing God ultimately entails an act of remembering that which he had always known is important to later Protestant efforts to construct a purified Western memory of Christ that knows itself by the superiority of its internal sight of Christ to the visual artifacts of a repudiated Catholic culture. The elder William Bradford, setting out to learn Hebrew in his last years so that he could acquire the language God spoke (see Rosenmeier), is a classic instance of this Protestant memorial project to circumvent the contaminations of Roman Catholic materiality, to get back to a pure time not through the image but through the greater purity of words. Such procedures of memorial purification, at once iconoclastic and nostalgic, ironically enough contributed to the othering of religion: Catholic culture was denigrated into the seen in order to establish the purified precincts of Protestant spirituality. Critical thought today moves within the wake of this iconoclasm, still positing itself against the claims of adequate representation, melancholically content with the fragments produced by its iconoclastic energies. Current appreciation for the fragmentation and hybridity of diasporic consciousness and voice is one among many instances in contemporary cultural studies where we encounter these pleasures of iconoclastic skepticism.[2]

In becoming subject to critical reflection, religion now dwells in front of us as a visual and textual fragment to be remembered precisely as that which is not us: a subject not only *for* memory, but deeply constitutive of Western memory. We possess religion through encounters with text and image, a "seeing" that understands itself as a not believing. Central to this process of secularization, this experience of liberation and loss, is the descent of belief into private and material domains as personalized object. The sacred falls into the mundane region of the seen, the knowable, the fragment.

A disassemblage of a prior unity, the Judeo-Christian tradition has, since the eighteenth century, fallen into iconic fragments—the detritus of a once powerful, overarching, and "invisible" ideology. Was the Protestant "part" a unity by virtue of its claims to having restored Christianity to its apostolic purity? If so, how did it both emerge from Catholic corruption and yet claim purity? Or was the Protestant "part" a fragment, shamefully broken off as Catholic polemicists accused and condemned to a derivative, impure status until returned to its proper place in the encompassing unity of Rome? Voicing such anxieties over the fragmentary status of Protestantism, nineteenth-century Anglo-American writing is preoccupied with alternative religions, especially Catholicism and to a lesser but significant extent, in the postbellum era, with voudou. Both Rome and Africa emerge as metaphoric sites of fetishized consciousness, a depository of material items forced into illicit, even grotesque assemblage that bespeak libidinal power.

Centuries of iconoclastic rhetoric have produced not only literal and meta-phoric fragments but also a continuing preoccupation with the dangers of the idol, the fetish, the miniature object hidden within.[3] Subject to the iconoclastic energies of reform, the space between deity and believer has been swept clean of the visual, and yet, paradoxically, religion now rests before us as a collection of the visible, wrested from ideology into the humbled dimension of the artifact. In this case the visible does not refute skepticism, but rather, as talisman of undecidability and inescapable mate-riality, it signifies the absence of proof.

2

Walking along the Newport beaches in the late eighteenth century, the Protestant heroine of Stowe's *The Minister's Wooing* improbably stumbles across one such religious fragment: an engraving of the Madonna lying tangled in seaweed. Washed ashore (presumably from the Old World), the Catholic image is immediately adopted as a "waif" by our rigorous Calvinist heroine whose purity exceeds that of the Virgin Mary (a comparison hinted at throughout the story). Stowe's account of her Protestant heroine's even-tual marriage, not to the Edwardsean Calvinist minister but instead to a more attractive suitor, sets as its fundamental narrative problem the project of female asceticism within the obligations of the marriage plot. How is the Protestant heroine to be at once saint and wife, an ascetic and a procreative homemaker? *The Minister's Wooing*, both sentimental novel and manual of personality development, details the construction of interior spirituality in a Calvinist culture that disdains external aids to or representations of spiri-tual work. The portrait our Protestant Mary stumbles upon is central to this characterological project of passionless procreation, for it functions as Other and fragment to her invisible and whole interiority. Her encounter anticipates the reproduction of Christianity entire as fragment, as memo-rial accessory to secular culture.

In an act of delicate ethnic cleansing, the Protestant Mary nails her Cath-olic Mary on the wall of the secret garret where she retires to meditate and spin yarn, producing bundles of literal whiteness. Hung directly opposite a portrait of a woman who suffered martyrdom during the Salem witchcraft crisis, Mary's Madonna serves as marginalized image and raw material for the production of her invisible sentimental piety. Eighteenth- and nine-teenth-century gothic, sentimental, and eventually realist narratives are re-plete with similar visual encounters with Catholic religious fragments that bespeak loss and ruin in a context of possessive appropriation: the religious past, humbled into the fragmentary, iconic dimension, functions as visual accessory in the development of novelistic character and of the novel's "inner language" as it is produced in the experience of reading.[4] Religious warfare gives way in the eighteenth and nineteenth centuries to acts of stylistic religious appropriation. Stowe's heroine can pick up Catholicism entire in an act of ecumenical housewifery, reincorporating Protestant New England's hated Other as accessory to sentimental female identity.[5]

This pious Protestant rhetoric of iconoclasm is characterized, then, by disavowal of its own violence. The assault upon an abandoned competitor faith's political and ethnic cultures involves the fragmentation and appropriation of the image as commodity or souvenir. The Madonna's transit from her status as mother of God to ornament in the Protestant Mary's garret emblematizes this iconoclastic process whereby preservation of the image masks its loss of significance. One can excoriate the seen as the "Whore of Babylon," the "Antichrist," the scheming "Jesuit"—demonizations that gain force from the reduction of ideology into figure, into bodies that can then be disassembled. Such reduction of a rival faith to the scale of the body is reenacted in Mary's treatment of the Madonna: as a portrait walling Mary's private interior, the mother of God is reduced to a bodily Other whose boundaries mark the limitless reach of the disembodied.

Hung on the garret wall, the portrait of the Madonna becomes a memorial site for the reformulation of the sacred from a collective tradition to an improvisational style of spiritual being. The Madonna can appear opposite the Salem witchcraft victim because, from the novel's devotional perspective, they go together nicely as versions of alternative feminine spirituality. Secularization records coincident processes of iconoclasm: fragmentation of the image and privatization of religious meaning out of corporate consensus. The nineteenth-century cult of domesticity, which has drawn so much critical attention in the past three decades, provides us with an archive of these aftereffects of iconoclasm. In Victorian novels like Charlotte Brontë's *Villette* (1853), George Eliot's *Middlemarch* (1871–72), Nathaniel Hawthorne's *Scarlet Letter* (1850), and Henry James's *Portrait of a Lady* (1881), visual fragments of an abandoned "Romanism" function as vestigial traces for what must remain, ideologically speaking, the invisible processes of an improvisational, Protestant perfectionism. Such broken sacramental signs are critical to these novels' postsacramental semiotics, for, as material markers at once numinous and fallen, these Catholic fragments deploy the ambiguity of the fragment to testify to the superior immateriality and wholeness of fictional character.

The uneven descent of sacred objects from holiness to inauthenticity typically elicited nostalgia for a prior, more communally sanctioned sacramentalism and disquiet toward the materiality newly perceived by the iconoclastic eye in viewing religious objects as separated items or fragments, ineluctably divorced from the wholeness of spirit. In particular, the nostalgic perception of Catholic fragments recorded in Protestant novels' encounters with monastic ruins, sacred iconography, or Rome itself was laced with the libidinal anxiety of othering. This linked yearning and distaste ambiguously positioned the religious fragment both within the bourgeois subject (as erotic or subversive enticement) and without (as supernatural force). Gothic fictions like M. G. Lewis's *The Monk* (1796) configure this dual position by dramatizing the monastery as a memorial site of commemoration and incarceration. The implicitly Protestant (or even post-Protestant) reader's progress through such founding gothic fictions is at once a touristic movement "out there" into a newly colonized space of religious otherness—a spatialized terrain of corridors and cells inhabited by the religious Other (the raging, libidinal monk)—and an intrapsychic movement "down into" the Western past.

The trope of incarceration is of course crucial to gothic discourse in the Enlightenment as it seeks to liberate Western thought from the "confinements" of superstition. The washed-up portrait of the Madonna reveals sentimental fiction's eventual inversion of this trope of incarceration: the frightening religious past is now diminished and framed, the monastic corridor has opened onto the beach, the cell onto the decorated garret. The portraits that haunt gothic fictions no longer haunt but decorate, serving as stylistic models for sentimental piety's perfection of personality. Furnished with the Madonna, Mary's garret is an early figuration of the space of advertising, where the commodified representations of spiritual perfection depend upon acquisitions, ones that will wall the interior space of personality in contemporary culture.

Historical novels like Stowe's *The Minister's Wooing* and Cable's *The Grandissimes* construct history as the material site for locating this purified national character. History in such novels serves not only as place and time but also as "body," a space of the carnal that gives form to what Hawthorne anxiously referred to as the ghostliness of literary character. As image, or that which is seen, history is the place of the fragmented, repudiated body that anchors the iconoclastic energies of the fictional imagination as it seeks to create character and plot out of emptiness. The past holds the body, as Hawthorne's narrator observes of the Elizabethan females who crowd in to watch Hester on the scaffold: "Morally, as well as materially, there was coarser fibre in those wives and maidens of old English birth and breeding, than in their fair descendants" (37). The theological ruminations of *The Scarlet Letter*'s narrator suggest America's past as an abandoned eroticism associated with the iconic domain of the Catholic image. To tell the story of America in the historical novel is to recount progressive forgettings of this bodily past, purifications from old- and new-world religious, class, and racial contaminants, emptyings of the image. The narrative of American national identity is a story of refinement, disembodiment, and forgetting.

Paradoxically, what enables this process of forgetting is the image, the visible shred of the past—whether it be a portrait of the Madonna or the rag of scarlet cloth Hawthorne picks up in "The Custom-House." Such relics initiate a process of remembering crucial to the organization of these nineteenth-century historical fictions—"mixed, hybrid, mutant, bound intimately with life and death" (Nora 19), these memorial sites provide the carnality of history that empowers fiction's iconoclastic critique.[6] Intoxicated with the pleasures of religious othering—the displacement of traditional asceticism by improvisational processes of "refinement"—the nineteenth-century Protestant novel silences the flesh in its new preoccupation with sentimental sentience, the breathless "now" of American purity. Central to this memorial national project, iconic fragments such as the rag of scarlet cloth, the portrait of the Madonna, and, as we shall see in Cable's *The Grandissimes*, the voudou amulet construct the past as visual fragment promising a criminal materiality at the heart of national origin. The image serves at once as speech and discretion, voice and shroud. Not text, the image at once remains subordinate to the imperial powers of discourse to emplot and interpret, while, as we know from reading *The Scarlet Letter*, it disdains the global reach of discursive interpretation, eluding its grasp. Generated by the iconic fragment, the project of American historical romance is to "remember" a past otherwise censored by language, to provide a visible form for otherwise repressed truths. The logic of historical romance, then, is deeply paradoxical: correctly, deeply, fully to remember by fabricating memories, to know their fictionality through bodily memorial sites.

3

In 1803 a New Orleans slave woman is sent by her quadroon mistress to kill a white man. Although the quadroon is universally feared in both the white and black Creole communities for her skills as a voudou priestess, her talents backfire when her accomplice is captured. The slave woman, Clemence, is caught in a steel trap laid by a member of the white Grandissime clan, a man who is intent on catching whoever has been "fixing" his uncle with voudou charms. This describes in brief the setting for one of the most troubling scenes in nineteenth-century American fiction: the death by torture of a woman at the hands of a white supremacist, a character as irritated by the slave religion of voudou as by race, a man "beset with the idea that the way to catch a voudou was—to catch him; and as he had caught numbers of them on both sides of the tropical and semitropical Atlantic, he decided to try his skill privately" (Cable, *Grandissimes* 311).

Filling the penultimate pages of Cable's *Grandissimes*, Clemence's lynching at the hands of Captain Jean-Baptiste Grandissime is a double murder: Clemence's protracted death marks not just an intimately physical destruction of an individual but the killing of an entire religion, or more precisely, of that of Clemence and of a religious stereotype—"voodoo"—as constructed by the Euro-American colonial imagination from its centuries-long encounter with African and new-world African religious practice.

Students of the black Atlantic and the American South have studied voudou both as remnant of West African cultures after the trauma of enslavement and diaspora and as evidence of African spiritual and political resilience in the New World.[7] Perhaps the best-known literary treatment of voudou's creative potential, Zora Neale Hurston's *Of Mules and Men*, presents the rites of "hoodoo" as providing access to an ultimate authenticity, the richest site of hidden folk culture and of incipient female authorial power. Karen Brown's recent anthropological classic, *Mama Lola: A Voudou Priestess in Brooklyn*, presents immigrant Haitian voudou as a regenerative polytheism and feminism that can heal our impoverished, secular sensibility. In its depiction of voudou ceremonies and ritual behaviors in French colonial New Orleans, Cable's novel anticipates these recent appreciations of voudou as a beguiling instance of racial and religious heterogeneity, a multicultural practice that therapeutically mixes not only the races but, theologically speaking, the flesh and the spirit. Mulattoes, Creoles, full Africans—virtually all the characters in *The Grandissimes* except for the Anglo- and German-Americans—practice voudou and often together.

Cable's representation of this colonial religious culture provoked deep anger among local readers. An anonymous pamphlet published shortly after the novel accused Cable of being a jackal whose ironical but probing portrait of Creole culture's involvement with voudou disinterred a "cherished corpse"; Cable's exposé was equivalent to miscegenation, charged the author, with no less a personage than the famed New Orleans voudou priestess herself, Marie Laveau (qtd. in Turner 102). While Cable's various local-color sketches of voudou practice constitute a good deal of the novel's touristic charm, the scene of Clemence's death reveals voudou's paranoid position in the Euro-American imagination. In the chapter title sarcastically denoting Clemence's death as "Voudou Cured," we see the interplay between the intimacies of bodily suffering and the abstractions of racial and religious othering, as quaintness balloons into horror. Clemence is the "Voudou" and, crucially, Clemence is "voodoo"; she is stereotype and scapegoat, the point of fixity for an abstraction's materialization and contraction.

Critically, Clemence's capture moves from interrogation into murder with the abrupt disclosure of an iconic fragment: the sculpted arm of a murdered slave, itself enclosed in a tiny coffin that is shaken loose from her clothing. The moment, rich with the violence of illicit seeing, marks the ultimate revelation of the religious Other in a novel that otherwise provides merely enticing glimpses into New Orleans voudou practice. "He removed the lid and saw within, resting on the cushioned bottom, the image, in myrtle-wax, moulded and painted with some rude skill, of a ne-gro's bloody arm cut off near the shoulder—a *bras-coupé*—with a dirk grasped in its hand" (314). This miniaturized object has been designed by Palmyre, the voudou priestess, as a signature for Clemence to leave at the murder site. The cutoff arm memorializes the death by torture some de-cades earlier of a slave who, on being sold into slavery, had named himself "Bras-Coupé" to signal his now useless status to his tribe, and whose ensu-ing resistance to slavery cost him his life. A relic of slave insurgency, Palmyre's sculptured arm radically condenses the narrative complexities of Bras-Coupé's story that otherwise filter through the novel's master narra-tive as the fragmentary legend that everyone is seeking to hear and to tell. The coffin finally arrests Bras-Coupé for our readerly curiosity and domin-ion. The miniature limb is also the visual evidence that spurs Grandissime on in the torture of Clemence. As icon of the religious Other, it is instantly deciphered as evidence of her criminality, while its moment of disclosure subtly repositions that criminality as curio of Anglo-American postbellum regionalism. With the visual emergence of the waxen arm, voudou emerges as the site of ultimate violence, which is duplicated in a considerably milder register by the narrative's stance of genial Protestant condescension to vou-dou practice as infantile superstition likely to attract the colonial Catholic imagination but rightly giving way to the novel's master narrative of bour-geois progress.[8]

Clemence's lynching ruptures the genteel conventions of historical ro-mance otherwise deployed with local charm in the story's parallel marriage plot that happily pairs two white couples in the end. While local papers largely defended the novel, Cable's portrayal of Southern religious practice and brutality outraged some local readers. For instance, Grace King charged that Cable had "stabbed the city in the back in a dastardly way to please the Northern press" (qtd. in Rubin 263).[9] Mark Twain praised Cable on the same grounds, however: "When a Southerner of genius writes mod-ern English, his book goes . . . upon wings; and they carry it swiftly all about America and England, and . . . Germany—as witness the experience of Mr. Cable and Uncle Remus, two of the very few Southern authors who do not write in the southern style" (qtd. in Goldman 151). But the novel turns from its brilliant "winged" writing of Clemence's lynching and from Cable's self-described insistence that he "meant to make *The Grandissimes* as truly a political work as it ever has been called" ("My Politics" 14) into the marriage plot at its conclusion, a collapse that reproduces the very silence about race relations otherwise so powerfully attacked in the novel.[10]

As in *The Scarlet Letter* the national past of *The Grandissimes* is reconstructed as a site of potential subversion only to be buried again. It is opened to our view so that we might see the interior of the national body as criminal, lust-ridden, and layered with religious secrets. But as suggested by Dimmesdale's notorious "hush" bidding Hester be quiet, these narratives of national identity lead us from detection, revelation, and contrition back into suppression.

Reception of Cable's novel has always been embroiled in the very questions of regional, ethnic, and racial identity at the heart of the novel's focus on Louisiana's humiliating subordination to a hated American government. The novel portrays the white Creoles as outraged natives for whom any participation in the new colonial authority is, as the leading Creole of the community explains to the new American governor, "odious—disreputable—infamous" (101). Clemence's death, within this context of imperial transfer, is a colonial drama of scapegoating, of power infamously executed by the soon-to-be powerless against the most abject.

After Grandissime captures his "Voodoo," the sympathetic narrative voice fully accedes to Clemence's oscillating patois (colonial French, Afro-English, and standard English), the torture unleashing the celebrated polyglossic culture of colonial New Orleans into its horrific double, the heteroglossic near-gibberish of suffering: " 'Qui ci ça?' asked the Captain, sternly, stooping and grasping her burden, which she had been trying to conceal under herself. 'Oh, Miché, don' trouble dat! Please jes tek dis-yeh trap offen me—da's all!' " (313). Clemence's escalating desperation is marked in the text by her alternations between French and English and typographically by the alternation between roman and italicized print: "*[O]h! fo' de love o' God, Miché Jean-Baptiste, don' open dat ah box! Yen a erin du tout la-dans, Miché Jean-Baptiste; du tout, du tout!* . . . Oh! you git kill' if you open dat ah box, Mawse Jean-Baptiste! *Mo' parole d'honneur le plus sacré*—I'll kiss de cross!" (313). Jean-Baptiste's discovery of the waxen arm jettisons Clemence into a dizzying linguistic performance that splinters into a near chaos of dialects as she is strung up to be hanged only to be let down and ordered to run so that she can be shot in the back. Illicit seeing triggers verbal virtuosity as the pages of sadistic interrogation and lamentation that describe the death of "the Voodoo" and of voudou break religious and racial otherness apart into a vastness of competing languages. Clemence's oscillations between dialects not only commemorate this death but visualize language itself: the standard typography is invaded by italicizations and phoneticisms. Clemence's verbal struggle to arrest her death pits the mute religious icon against speech's mobility, transformative capacities, and multiple national identifications. Clemence's language soaks in the power of the unseen dimension, while its very materiality and visibility paradoxically register its impotence. Thus while the scene's various rhetorical devices of amplification, repetition, and dialect alternation measure the absence of language's communicative power, those same devices, in rendering language more visible, preserve (if only partially) the memorial power of the iconic.

For the novel's implicitly Northern, Anglo-American readership, Cable's multilingual representation of New Orleans and the lynching in particular constructs a South at once bewildering in its racial, religious, and linguistic complexities—a mysterious regional Other for the national eye—and scaled down to the simplicity of the regional, translated into the comprehensibility of the quaint. Representative of the ascendant Anglo-American culture, the novel's protagonist, the German-American immigrant Joseph Frowenfeld, must struggle to clarify these doubled realities of Southern life. Frowenfeld is alternately mystified and horrified by the various colonial Others who people New Orleans, and whose evident racial miscegenation figures in the mixture of languages that beset him in the pharmacy he establishes: colonial French, "negro French" (321), metropolitan French, patois, African English, and Creolized English. Frowenfeld's own Protestant German heritage rapidly becomes synonymous with the novel's Americanness, an identity characterized by semicomprehension, a cognitive emptiness whose political and religious equivalents advertise themselves as forms of purity. Stranded in English, Frowenfeld is both student and incipient master in all spheres domestic, political, and religious. To decipher the languages of New Orleans is implicitly to purify Southern miscegenation, to replace the regional with the national, Catholicism with Protestantism, voudou with Frowenfeld's apothecary. And finally, the novel replaces torture with the sentimental domesticity of Frowenfeld's eventual marriage to a Creole woman. Frowenfeld, who cannot understand the coded speech Clemence speaks to him as she travels through the town square selling cakes, ultimately deciphers Clemence precisely by not understanding her. Although at the center of the novel, he does not witness her persecution or death and is never shown assimilating its implications.

Clemence's outraged speech at her death is already familiar as the intercultural speech of the black, white, and mulatto communities—all of whom know how to speak the speech of the other and how to corrupt their own and others' languages depending upon the communicative urgencies of context. For instance, Cable's rendition of Clemence's pleading pronunciation of "*accident*" (313) fuses Afro-English and Afro-French pronunciations. The term's slippage into italics makes this fusion visible. We are continually confronted with the estranging effect of "seeing" the novel's language as we both read it and read the narrative voice's efforts to interpret it for us. Italics signal the transition from one language to another as a "descent" from the standard into the variant, from the naturalized imperial viewpoint into the marginalized speech of the Other. In this way italics function as typographical equivalents of the stereotype, of Palmyre viewed as a "woman of the quadroon caste, of superb stature and poise, severely handsome features, clear, tawny skin and large, passionate black eyes" (57).

The narrator's standard English—that "hated tongue prescribed by the new courts" (65)—sets up a doubled relation of conquest to its characters. Their French must be represented as "peculiar" (66) both aesthetically and politically—an exoticism whose other side is mastery of the racial Other. Frowenfeld, bewildered immigrant and suitor, stands in for Cable's postbellum, implicitly Northern reader: New Orleans as the South appears before him "in a strange tongue . . . a volume whose displaced leaves would have to be lifted tenderly . . . re-arranged, some torn fragments laid together again" (103). Both 1803 New Orleans and the postbellum South are "romantic" fragments whose decipherment depends upon our patient submission to a linguistic instruction that Frowenfeld avoids.

With the disclosure of the tiny coffin Cable produces race and religion in miniaturized form, jointly and horrifically compacted in the term "Voudou"—the essence to be caught, rendered visible, and ultimately "cured." The discovery of the coffin, then, instances the materialization of the colonized Other as both individual and alternative religious tradition. This materialization transgresses the propriety of the hidden or twilight region of the half-seen that harbors various figurations of the mulatto as uncanny by emerging into a flagrant visibility that must be rendered invisible again, murdered through an extended verbal representation. Voudou thus operates on dual levels of iconic representation, a fit subject for the nostalgic, miniaturizing perspective of "local-color romance" and at the same time so blasphemous that it must be subjected to a ritualized death by torture. Miniaturization aggrandizes the very contexts that it excludes.[11] The horror of this double capture is summarized in the coffin's capture of the reader's gaze. As Bachelard observes of miniature houses, "false objects that possess a true psychological objectivity," Palmyre's miniaturized image of Bras-Coupé uses the hapless inadequacy of image fashioning—the necessarily fragmentary representation of divinity—to voice a new-world history of racial violence and mystification. The "inversion of perspective" (Bachelard 149) achieved through miniaturization echoes that involved in slavery's radical diminution of personhood.[12] Similarly, in the scaled-down representation characteristic of regional fiction, the region is the "small" to the nation's greatness, materiality to the Union's immateriality.

The coming into-sight of the coffin's contents figures the ultimate penetration of the recesses of the subordinated Other, the achieved access into the confines of superstition. Looking in on the coffin's contents recapitulates the fascinated investigation of monastic interiors so popular in anti-Catholic fiction, while the discovery of a body part therein echoes Protestant horror at the various disassembled body parts at the heart of othered religious traditions, such as new-world cannibalist practices or old-world Roman Catholic dismemberments in the Inquisition or destruction of illegitimate offspring in convents.[13] And, as the revelation of Palmyre's vengeance, the sighting of the coffin's contents forges a link between the novel's fragmentary narrative (the whispered renditions of Bras-Coupé's story) and the culminating disclosure. It invites us to consider the imagistic renditions of the religious Other: as the duplicitous phantom and as the material object. Bras-Coupé's waxen arm is the "it" that locates, homogenizes, and finally arrests the linguistic heterogeneity of the text, grounds an otherwise anarchic word, and clarifies the speech of the Other.

But Palmyre's sculpture raises further questions about the reassemblage of the body of the religious Other, for, in providing a radical form that entraps the fragmentary retellings of Bras-Coupé's story, it reincorporates him into the national body. Cable's historical romance is a doubled detective narrative: we struggle to find out both the story of Bras-Coupé and the story of America's relationship to France, Spain, Germany, England, Africa, and the West Indies. We resist the knowledge that America has indeed a past whose regional truths are not cut off from the national one but intrinsic to it. Imperial formation and bodily dismemberment or disfigurement are linked narratives. Not only are the wages of imperialism violence, but also the imperial nation is formed through the severing of parts of the national body or history. The story of America, like *The Grandissimes* and *The Scarlet Letter*, is at base a crime story: Who is guilty of the murder of Bras-Coupé and Clemence? How did the nation become "white" in the face of all this nonwhiteness, innocent in the face of all this terror, and empty in the face of all these material traces? While Hester's cloth letter evokes a suppressed Catholic embodiment, Palmyre's arm, in its very rude fleshiness, doubly simulates the body, a repetitiveness that reveals a religious sensibility wholly other to Christianity. The religious Other is dependent upon a literal synecdoche for its voicing. Both the legend and its method of resurrection spill out when the coffin's contents are disclosed. If the scarlet *A* reveals the subversive art of needlework, Bras-Coupé's arm, clutching a knife, reveals another (but far more troubling) womanly art of revenge—voudou.

Bras-Coupé's fragmented body and story supply the enticement of the untold, the true history of the South's racial violence that will be reiterated in Clemence's death. As history it is the inner, contestatory truth of the romance, a truth of region that does battle with the nationalist ideology of plantation romance, which encloses it. Eventually restored to completed sequence, it is, ironically, suppressed when Bras-Coupé's body, reduced to a miniature arm, becomes a relic. Preserved in the form of the carefully molded waxen arm, Bras-Coupé's existence is resurrected from the apolitical, fragmented status of legend into the urgencies of political narrative, only to precipitate a release of vengeful violence against voudou. This captive/resistant body and its metaphoric name are literalized and commemorated by Palmyre's religious art, which forces it into sight as "voodoo." This viewing, like the Protestant Mary's viewing of the Madonna on her wall, moves ineluctably toward eclipse of the religious Other.

And yet this image suggests a curious semiotic relation, for it visualizes something that, literally speaking, never existed: the cutoff arm. The molded waxen arm does not portray the face of a man (the man who called himself "Bras-Coupé") but a part of him that claimed only metaphoric existence, that is, a self likened to a cutoff arm. Palmyre's relic materializes an abstraction of slavery—its theft of personhood. But this political truth is a fiction, an imaginative illustration that she supplies to Bras-Coupé's conversion of himself into text. Even more paradoxically, Cable resupplied his heroic slave with the arm traditionally cut off or missing in local legends. Writing to his daughter after the novel's publication, Cable noted that some local opposition to *The Grandissimes* was provoked by his revision of the Bras-Coupé legend. Cable made his hero whole-bodied. "They considered . . . that my version of it was faulty, because I had taken the liberty of saving Bras-Coupé's arm whole. The fact that he certainly did chop it off seemed to them to be a precious verity of history not to be trifled with, and I believe the insistence upon this point was a conscious tribute to the African's magnificent courage" (Stephens 388).[14] Cable's restoration of Bras-Coupé's arm is a bid for realism, an effort to demythologize the legend's critique of slavery in order to sharpen it. Yet Bras-Coupé's essentially allegorical status remained prominent in Cable's characterization of him, for after Bras-Coupé names himself, the narrative voice reports that he thus made himself into "a type of all Slavery, turning into flesh and blood the truth that all Slavery is maiming" (171). Cable's metaphorical representation of the missing arm narrows the character into near allegory. Ironically, Cable's view of Bras-Coupé as voluntarily rendering into bodily terms the abstractions of slavery is contradicted by the name's significance, which marks the loss of the capacity to be useful, to make meaning, and to signify. The two authors, Bras-Coupé and Cable, are joined in rivalry. If, as one critic notes, Cable grafted "the 'fact' of self-mutilation from his readings on Santo Domingo" (Stephens 405) onto local legends of insurgent slaves who had been injured or punitively maimed, his metaphorization of the bras-coupé lends a carefully proscribed Haitian militancy to the figure of the American slave. Fully "armed," Cable's Bras-Coupé suppresses the specter of African violence; the boundaries of the American slave body remain intact, as do the boundaries of the nation. The plot of *The Grandissimes* implies that Haitian revolutionary violence will be contained within a more powerful white violence: the disclosure of the waxen limb now

armed with a knife—synecdoche of revolution—precipitates the cata-
strophic assault upon Clemence and, ultimately, the banishment of
Palmyre and her revolutionary iconography.

Cable's novel bids us reflect on how the religious Other is commemorated as figure of both the criminal and the quaint—a process of miniaturization essential to the construction of an expansionist national identity
out of theological ruin and racial violence. If Stowe's historical romance
anticipates the transformation of religion entire into souvenir and decorative accessory, Cable's exploration of the deviant religious icon suggests
another, more disturbing implication to Western iconoclasm. The destruction of the icon liberates thought, or, in the terms of *The Grandissimes*, the
cutoff arm generates and is nobly commemorated by the novel's masterful
realism. But the destruction of the icon at the novel's conclusion also
forecloses further interpretation. Clemence drops to the earth and no one
knows who has fired the bullet. Nor does anyone pick up the coffin, even
as a souvenir. It is closed to view but not in the way Clemence had
prayed for.

NOTES

1. Accounts of Protestant iconoclasm that have shaped my understanding of
print culture's competition with the image include Phillips and Ong.

2. Examples of this diasporic consciousness can be found in Bhabha, Smith, and
Gilroy. For a penetrating meditation on the pleasures of minimalism at the heart
of Reform sensibility, see Kristeva.

3. Bhabha's account of the construction of the colonial subject can be profitably
applied to thinking about the construction of the religious subject and object. While
Bhabha uses primarily racial and sexual terms in his account of the colonial Other
as "fetish," I do not mean to fold religion in as one more category of difference
within "the binding of a range of differences and discriminations that inform the
discursive and political practices of racial and cultural hierarchization" (67), but
rather to suggest how the entire field of religion qua religion has been constructed
as a colonial domain within postmodern studies as indigenous, lost, and primitive.
Indeed, colonialism and secularization are reciprocal processes of reification and
reduction to the status of the "trinket." See also Mitchell's account of the fetish as
the "antithesis of the scientific image, epitomizing irrationality in both its crudity
of representational means and its use in superstitious rituals. It is a 'producer' of
images, not by means of mechanical reproduction, but by organic 'breeding' of its
own likeness" (162).

4. I borrow the phrase "inner language" from Stewart 17.

5. For an account of Stowe's logic of affective ownership in *The Minister's Wooing*, see Merish.

6. Nora situates contemporary practices of commemoration within larger cultural experiences of the loss of tradition: "No society has ever produced archives as

deliberately as our own, not only by volume, not only by new technological means of reproduction and preservation, but also by its superstitious esteem, by its veneration of the trace. Even as traditional memory disappears, we feel obliged assiduously to collect remains, testimonies, documents, images, speeches, any visible sign of what has been, as if this burgeoning dossier were to be called upon to furnish some proof to who knows what tribunal of history. The sacred is invested in the trace that is at the same time its negation" (14–15).

7. For classic accounts, see Raboteau, Thompson, and Brown. Also see Mulira.

8. Swann argues that the novel's politics are in the service of the "bourgeois revolution" against the "stagnations of caste" (260), among which, although Swann does not discuss them, are the practices of voudou.

9. Alice Hall Petry makes the nice point that it was ironically only the outraged white Southern reaction that correctly surmised the dark side of Cable's vision, precisely what we today appreciate as his greatness; it was Northern readers who were strangely blind to the terror in his writing, seeing more charm than scandal in his portrayals of religion.

10. Swann argues that, to the contrary, Cable's return to the relative trivialities of the white marriage plot invites us to "place that sentimentality" (273).

11. Stewart argues that the "miniature has the capacity to make its context remarkable; its fantastic qualities are related to what lies outside it in such a way as to transform the total context" (46).

12. Bachelard notes the "inversion of perspective" involved in fantasy tales of miniaturization as well as the freedom from imprisonment and implicit mastery of reality it provides.

13. For accounts of European and Euro-American fears of cannibal dismemberment, see Dening, de Certeau, and Greenblatt. For accounts of Protestant legends about Catholic dismemberment, see Franchot. Bhabha's discussion of "gathering" as the best available way to conceive of existence in the wake of diaspora attempts to find in fragmentation a source of political and intellectual strength, to convert the sign of a fragmented otherness into that of a redemptive postmodern consciousness. My awareness of these issues has been heightened by Caroline Walker Bynum's fine studies.

14. Stephens supplies a useful account of the various source legends that fed into Cable's initial treatment of the Bras-Coupé legend in his short story "Bibi," a short story then modified into the story of Bras-Coupé that forms the crux of *The Grandissimes*. (As Stephens argues, Cable's reading of Mérimée exposed him to the "linkage of the African slave trade with Creole culture, the confrontation of African, Creole, and Anglo-American values, gothic action, and searching irony" [398].) The internationally renowned pianist Louis Moreau Gottschalk includes in his memoirs his childhood memories of a Bras-Coupé as a bogeyman haunting the woods around New Orleans—a figure whose legendary abilities at the "bamboula" dance Gottschalk later transcribed into his famous concert piece "Bamboula: Danse des Nègres," a piece whose revolutionary implications made it a favorite among audiences in the revolutionary year 1848.

WORKS CITED

Bachelard, Gaston. *The Poetics of Space*. Trans. Maria Jolas. New York: Orion, 1964.

Bhabha, Homi K. *The Location of Culture*. London: Routledge, 1994.

Brown, Karen McCarthy. *Mama Lola: A Voudou Priestess in Brooklyn*. Berkeley: U of California P, 1991.

Bynum, Caroline Walker. *Fragmentation and Redemption: Essays on Gender and the Human Body in Medieval Religion*. New York: Zone Books, 1992.

——. *The Resurrection of the Body in Western Christianity, 200–1336*. New York: Columbia UP, 1995.

Cable, George Washington. *The Grandissimes: A Story of Creole Life*. Harmondsworth, Eng.: Penguin, 1988

——. "My Politics." *The Negro Question: A Selection of Writings on Civil Rights in the South*. Ed. Arlin Turner. New York: Anchor-Doubleday, 1958. 1–25.

de Certeau, Michel. "Montaigne's 'Of Cannibals.' " *Heterologies: Discourse on the Other*. Trans. Brian Massumi. Minneapolis: U of Minnesota P, 1986. 67–79.

Dening, Greg. *Mr. Bligh's Bad Language: Passion, Power, and Theatre on the Bounty*. Cambridge: Cambridge UP, 1992.

Franchot, Jenny. *Roads to Rome: The Antebellum Protestant Encounter with Catholicism*. Berkeley: U of California P, 1994.

Gilroy, Paul. *The Black Atlantic: Modernity and Double Consciousness*. Cambridge: Harvard UP, 1993.

Goldman, Arnold. "Life and Death in New Orleans." *The American City: Literary and Cultural Perspectives*. Ed. Graham Clarke. New York: St. Martin's, 1988. 146–78.

Greenblatt, Stephen Jay. *Marvelous Possessions: The Wonder of the New World*. Chicago: U of Chicago P, 1991.

Hawthorne, Nathaniel. *The Scarlet Letter: An Authoritative Text, Essays in Criticism, and Scholarship*. Ed. Seymour Gross et al. 3d ed. New York: Norton, 1988.

Hurston, Zora Neale. *Mules and Men*. New York: Perennial Library, 1990.

Kristeva, Julia. "Holbein's Dead Christ." *Black Sun: Depression and Melancholia*. Trans. Leon S. Roudiez. New York: Columbia UP, 1989. 105–38.

Merish, Lori. "Sentimental Consumption: Harriet Beecher Stowe and the Aesthetics of Middle-Class Ownership." *American Literary History* 8 (1996): 1–33.

Mitchell, W.J.T. *Iconology: Images, Text, Ideology*. Chicago: U of Chicago P, 1986.

Mulira, Jessie Gaston. "The Case of Voodoo in New Orleans." *Africanisms in American Culture*. Bloomington: Indiana UP, 1990. 34–68.

Nora, Pierre. "Between Memory and History: *Les Lieux de Memoir*." *Representations* 26 (1989): 7–25.

Ong, Walter J. *The Presence of the Word: Some Prolegomena for Cultural and Religious History*. New Haven: Yale UP, 1967.

Petry, Alice Hall. "Native Outsider: George Washington Cable." *Literary New Orleans: Essays and Meditations*. Ed. Richard S. Kennedy. Baton Rouge: Louisiana State UP, 1992. 1–7.

Phillips, John. *The Reformation of Images: Destruction of Art in England.* Berkeley: U of California P, 1973.

Raboteau, Albert J. *Slave Religion: The "Invisible Institution" in the Antebellum South.* New York: Oxford UP, 1978.

Rosenmeier, Jesper. " 'With My Own Eyes': William Bradford's *Of Plymouth Plantation.*" *Typology and Early American Literature.* Ed. Sacvan Bercovitch. Amherst: U of Mass P, 1972. 69–106.

Rubin, Louis D., Jr. *George W. Cable: The Life and Times of a Southern Heretic.* New York: Pegasus, 1969.

Smith, Theophus Harold. *Conjuring Culture: Biblical Formations of Black America.* New York: Oxford UP, 1994.

Stephens, Robert O. "Cable's Bras-Coupé and Mérimée's 'Tamango': The Case of the Missing Arm." *Mississippi Quarterly* 35 (1982): 387–405.

Stewart, Susan. *On Longing: Narratives of the Miniature, the Gigantic, the Souvenir, the Collection.* Baltimore: Johns Hopkins UP, 1984.

Stowe, Harriet Beecher. *The Minister's Wooing.* New York: Derby and Jackson, 1989.

Swann, Charles. "*The Grandissimes*: A Story-Shaped World." *Literature and History* 13 (1978): 257–77.

Thompson, Robert Farris. *Flash of the Spirit: African and Afro-American Art and Philosophy.* New York: Random House, 1983.

Turner, Arlin. *George W. Cable: A Biography.* Durham: Duke UP, 1956.

CHAPTER 9

Tex-Sex-Mex: American Identities, Lone Stars, and the Politics of Racialized Sexuality

JOSÉ E. LIMÓN

JOHN Sayles's 1996 film *Lone Star* will provide closure to an argument I wish to make concerning certain American identities. I will also have occasion to revisit another classic treatment of such identities in the film *High Noon*. Before film became their primary discourse, these identities were first fully articulated in nineteenth-century dime novels of the West, many of which were, like *Lone Star*, set in Texas. A now very distant discursive cousin of the Sayles film called, in fact, *Little Lone Star* (1886) and written by one Sam Hall features Anita, "a physically precocious" young Mexican woman living on a Texas hacienda, "whose passions and complexion are compared to the red-hot volcanoes of her native Mexico" (Pettit 39). She is being threatened with rape by Caldelas the Coyote, a vicious, degenerate Mexican bandit, until she is rescued by a strong, clean-cut, fair-haired Anglo-Texan cowboy named William Waldron. Anita reciprocates the sexual interest of the "fair-haired hero" (Pettit 39). Such identities were to be on display again and again in fiction, film, song, and even television advertising. Who can forget the Frito Bandito, cartoon cousin of Caldelas the Coyote? We thus have inherited a potent and perduring American cultural iconography of Anglo-American/Mexican relations that has a special intensity in Texas.

In this essay, I take up the intertwined theoretical spheres of postcolonialism, race, and sexuality to reexamine this iconography in the conflicted social history of these two peoples. I suggest that this iconographic relationship goes beyond simple mutual stereotyping; it has politically critical ambivalence. Sayles's *Lone Star* offers a radical revision of this iconography and its inherent ambivalence, a revision consistent with a major shift in the social relations between Anglos and Mexicans, at least in Texas, at the present moment.

ICONOGRAPHY, SEXUALITY, AND THE COLONIAL ORDER

The male Anglo icon is a tough, swaggering, boastful—sometimes taciturn—hard-drinking, hard-riding, straight-shooting cowboy. We also usu-

ally visualize a tall, strong, lean, handsome, and of course white figure—
John Wayne in any of his Westerns. These bodily attributes contrast with
a fat, slovenly, dark, mustachioed, and often drunken, deceitful, and treach-
erous Mexican male with whom our Anglo cowboy is usually at personal
and political odds—for example, the Mexicans in *Little Lone Star* and in
Sam Peckinpah's *The Wild Bunch* (1969). The figure of a Mexican woman
brought into close sexual conjunction with the cowboy mediates these two.
She is usually an upper-class, very attractive, light-complected, often
"Spanish" senorita, such as Alejandra in Cormac McCarthy's otherwise
subtle, "modernist" *All the Pretty Horses* (1992). Those of us who came of
age in the late 1950s may recall Marty Robbins's popular song "El Paso"
(1959), beginning, "Out in the west Texas town of El Paso, I fell in love
with a Mexican girl." While attractive like the Spanish senorita, this "girl,"
Selena, has a distinctively "darker" sexual semiosis. She is, characteristically, a "bar-girl," or prostitute, and sometime lover to the song's cowboy
hero, like *Little Lone Star*'s Anita. This figure of "darker" and lower-class,
illicit sexuality—usually positioned on the real and figurative border—is
more common in the popular imagery than the senorita. Robbins's cow-
boy-narrator, Gary Cooper's Will Kane, and McCarthy's John Grady Cole
may be attracted to, have sex with, and even fall in love with such a figure,
but usually these relationships are not culturally meant to last, as we see in
a nineteenth-century cowboy song:

> Me and Juana talkin' low
> So the "madre" couldn't hear—
> How those hours would go a-flyin',
> And too soon I'd hear her sighin',
> In her little sorry tone—
> "*Adios, mi corazon*"
>
> . . . .
>
> Never seen her since that night;
> I kain't cross the Line, you know.
> She was Mex and I was white;
> Like as not it's better so.

(Lomax 67–68)

More often than not, our cowboy must take up romantic permanency with
his own racial-cultural kind:

> I'm free to think of Susie—
> Fairer than the stars above,—
> She's the waitress at the station
> And she is my turtle dove.
>
> . . . .

I take my saddle, Sundays,—
The one with inlaid flaps,—
And on my new sombrero
And my white angora chaps;
Then I take a bronc for Susie
And she leaves her pots and pans
And we figure out our future
And talk o'er our homestead plans.

(Lomax 65–66)

Yet another song fills out the spiritual dimensions of this female figure:

You wonders why I slicks up so
On Sundays, when I gits to go
To see her—well, I'm free to say
She's like religion that-a-way.
Jes sort o' like some holy thing,
As clean as young grass in the spring;

(Lomax 72)

Anglo women are represented, on the one hand, as religious, virtuous, faithful, hardworking housewives or potential housewives—pretty, if sometimes a bit homey. According to Pettit, in *High Noon* the "prim and proper" Amy, just such an Anglo woman, does not forsake Will Kane on his wedding day, for example (205). On the other hand, we have the image of the tough-talking, somewhat sexually available, take-charge, Anglo woman who can drink—Miss Kitty of the old television series *Gunsmoke* (1955–75). A related version is the older-woman-in-charge, such as Jordan Benedict's feisty unmarried sister, Luz, in Edna Ferber's *Giant*, as both novel (1952) and film (1956; produced by George Stevens and Henry Ginsburg). Susie in the cowboy song has a bit of this type, and more recently we have the ex-prostitute Anglo character Lorena, in Larry McMurtry's *Streets of Laredo*, as both novel and television miniseries.

This cultural complex attracted significant analytical attention in the 1960s, even as early as 1958, with Américo Paredes's *"With His Pistol in His Hand": A Border Ballad and Its Hero*. In the 1960s Chicano and Chicana cultural critics offered a critical reading of its iconography, although Anglo scholars generally share the view as well.[1] They unequivocally implicated these recurrent images in the history of Anglo conquest and the quasi-colonialism of Mexican communities, not only in what later became the Southwest, but in Mexico as well. Casting Mexican women, in particular, as sexually promiscuous made them morally available within a code of racism ratifying and extending the right of Anglo conquest to the realm of the sexual. By taking "his" woman, the Anglo colonizer further diminished the already desexualized Mexican male even as the Anglo male body was sexually affirmed. Anglo males thus extracted not only economic surplus value from Mexicans but also what Chicano Marxist critic Guillermo Flores calls "racial-cultural surplus value" (194). In their extensive review of American literature treating this subject, Alfredo Mirandé and Evangelina Enríquez conclude: "The progressively bleak picture we have presented . . . reveals a pathetic series of depictions of the Chicana in American literature. From the coquettish senorita to the lusty whore . . . a series of portrayals unfolds that pays little tribute to Mexican femininity. Underscoring this series, which recedes into negativity, is the theme of an encounter between two very different cultures which produces a pattern of initial attraction that quickly gives way to rejection, seduction, and finally, relegation to inferior status of one by the other" (158). Otherwise highly critical of such representations, Mirandé and Enríquez offer one ambivalent passage that, as early as 1979, began to lead me away from my own former view that this iconography simply reproduces colonialist dominance: "Although their [Mexican women's] deficiencies are cited as frequently as their attractions, it is noteworthy that their exotic qualities often triumph when they are compared with their American sisters" (143).

The very persistence and predictability of the iconography, together with the advent of certain strains of postcolonial theory and the passage of time and change of circumstance, now lead me in a direction that lends full valence to the exotic and erotic character of these figurations, even as it restores a part of the iconography often left out of such analyses: hardworking, faithful, religious, sort-of-pretty Anglo Susie and the somewhat later "Latin Lover." An intriguing passage focused on Texas in Arnoldo De Leon's 1983 *They Called Them Greasers: Anglo Attitudes toward Mexicans in Texas, 1821–1900* further encouraged this new direction: "The image of Mexicans as irresponsible and promiscuous laid the foundation for another important theme in nineteenth-century Texas—the sexual desire of white men for Mexican women. White men took Mexican senoritas to bed, perhaps more often than can ever be known. But the sexual relations were not just something that naturally came to be: on the contrary, they occurred only after the physical drive of white men wrestled with the discriminating psyche that resisted such relations" (39). Charles Ramirez-Berg has also taken something of this anticipatory perspective to my own work but in Lacanian theoretical terms; in such images, he says, "the Other is (temporarily) idealized as the path back to wholeness, until what always happens—does happen—the subject realizes that the Other is lacking. In terms of Hispanic stereotypes, it might be speculated that the stereotypes have persisted in cinema—since the earliest years of this century—because they fulfilled a need of the Anglos" (291).

The alternative reading I would offer of this iconography conceptually departs from De Leon's perhaps unintended double entendre on the Anglo "*discriminating* psyche."[2] The Anglo male's struggle is not so much between his psyche and something distinct called the physical; rather, it is deeply intrapsychic even as it is social. The problem of "discrimination" is not confined to external social relationships; it is a struggle to discriminate between deeply internalized political relationships and allegiances. Needed also relative to Ramirez-Berg's Lacanian thesis is a historicization of an otherwise quite persuasive psychoanalytic insight that informs my own account as well. One must account for these complexities of desire with greater historical specificity as to social change and conditions that might be loosely termed colonialist.[3]

POLITICAL ECONOMY, SEXUALITY, AND AMBIVALENCE

I am swayed in this direction by Homi Bhabha's recent theoretical work on race, sexuality, and colonialism. Robert Young explains how Bhabha exploits a somewhat repressed distinction that Edward Said made in his now famous formulation of Orientalism as the discursive project through which the West came to fashion its inherently denigrating view of the colonized cultural Other. Employing a psychoanalytic perspective, Bhabha pursues Said's brief notice of a latent as well as a manifest Orientalism, or what Young terms "an unconscious positivity of fantasmatic desire" (161). By emphasizing the extent to which the two levels fused, Young explains, Bhabha shows us "how colonial discourse of whatever kind operated not only as an instrumental construction of knowledge but also according to the ambivalent protocols of fantasy and desire" (161). Bhabha would move us away from a rigid, univocal understanding of such cultural constructions toward *ambivalence*: "To recognize the stereotype as an ambivalent mode of knowledge and power demands a theoretical and political response that challenges deterministic or functionalist modes of conceiving of the relationship between discourse and politics. The analytic of ambivalence questions dogmatic and moralistic positions on the meaning of oppression and discrimination" (66–67). He would have us shift from "the ready recognition of images as positive or negative, to an understanding of the *processes of subjectification* made possible (and plausible) through stereotypical discourse" (67). Rather than simply judge such a construction as the sexy senorita "bad" image, he would have us "displace" it, by engaging with its "*effectivity*; with the repertoire of positions of power and resistance, domination and dependence that constructs colonial identification subject (both colonizer and colonized)" in forms of difference that are racial and sexual. "[S]uch a reading reveals . . . the boundaries of colonial discourse," Bhabha believes, "and it enables a transgression of these limits from the space of that otherness" (67). "In making ambivalence the constitutive heart of his analyses," Young explains, "Bhabha has in effect performed a political reversal at a conceptual level in which the periphery—the borderline, the marginal, the unclassifiable, the doubtful—has become the equivocal, indefinite, indeterminate ambivalence that characterizes the centre" (161).

How can ambivalence help us understand the cultural iconography in which, against a degenerate Mexican male, the Anglo cowboy seeks a Mexican woman, even as Susie waits ready to homestead with her pots, pans, and religion? How can we now rethink the relationship of this expressive complex to quasi-colonialism in the Southwest, especially Texas—a quasi-colonialism that included land usurpation and physical violence, but, more significantly, the daily extraction of labor power and racial-cultural gratification and status within a code of racial segregation often enforced through the power of the state, which prevailed well into my own lifetime? In the summer of 1962, I drove back to south Texas with other angry, disappointed, working-class Mexican guys, on a senior trip to Anglo-dominated central Texas, after we were refused admission to the wonderful swimming areas in a town named San Marcos, fed by three rivers—named in the seventeenth century as the San Antonio, the Guadalupe, and the Medina. We listened to Robbins's "El Paso" on the car radio. What did it mean not only to listen to such a song with some pleasure but also actually to sing along in chorus about a heroic but lonesome Anglo cowboy longing for an attractive Mexican bar-girl? What pleasure could segregated Mexican boys, or those who segregated them, take in a musical performance seemingly reproducing their social relationship, a relationship still more viciously dominant in the nineteenth-century Texas setting of this song? Is this not a case of what Renato Rosaldo calls "imperialist nostalgia," which "uses a pose of 'innocent yearning' both to capture people's imagination and to conceal its complicity with often brutal domination" (70)? For such instances from the Mexican border, I want to suggest a more complicated signification.

Frederick Pike reminds us of the way nineteenth-century middle-class Anglo-America conflated sexual repression and control with capitalist expansion. "For the businessmen intent upon building America's economic foundations," he tells us, "thrift seemed a cardinal virtue; and thrift meant establishing strict control over spending—both dollars and sperm. . . . Nineteenth-century defenders of American middle-class respectability assumed that excess spending of male sperm was bad both for the nation's economy and its morality" (53). The lack of this capitalist virtue was then projected onto what later came to be called the Third World, which, for such Americans, meant Latin America and, according to Pike, the American South. Challenges to such a capitalism—the 1960s, for example—have always carried with them a sexual practice critiquing repression, along with more instrumentalist political-economic analyses and actions.

I want to suggest that the American cowboy, the Mexican female figure of illicit sexuality, and the "prim and proper" Anglo female figure represent a scenario of ambivalence played out in partial and unconscious challenge to the ruling cultural order. Significantly, this scenario's central figure of ambivalence is a cowboy, a figure on the lower rungs of American capitalism at its most expansive moment, working in the West and in Texas, a periphery of the American capitalist culture centered in the East and Midwest well into the twentieth century (Montejano 309–20). A complicated ambivalent resistance to this expansive culture has always been sited on the cowboy. While many such figures represent societal law and order—Matt Dillon in *Gunsmoke*, for instance—loner figures like Clint Eastwood are already at the critical margins of society. When either enters the realm of the sexual Other, however, the critical possibilities are enhanced if we give full valence to the rhetorically sexualized Mexican woman for what this figure might say about the subject who so persistently desires her. In the figure of the desiring cowboy we can, indeed, see the colonizing agent—white, tall, strong gunfighter—but we can also detect a fissure in the colonial enterprise, a break with the sexual repression concomitant with the ruling order that desire for the racial Other accentuates. At its most extreme, the agent of colonialism may actually die in his quest for the Other. In the song "El Paso," the Anglo cowboy finally dies in Selena's arms. We also need to recall her desire for him. Critics often read such a woman's active pursuit as yet another example of colonial dominance—she longs for his domination. However, as bell hooks notes of such racialized Otherness, "within this fantasy . . . the longing for pleasure is projected as a force that can disrupt and subvert the will to dominate. It acts to both mediate and challenge" (27)—although, I would add, never wholly undo. We may imagine such mutual longing as always ambivalent guerrilla-like activity destabilizing the unitary, repressed colonialist capitalist culture at its most primal site of value.

Such a sexualized destabilization without clear victory is, I think, the critical value of *High Noon*'s appearance in the early 1950s, when the segregation and labor exploitation of Mexican-Americans was everywhere evident in Texas and the rest of the nation. As a Mexican boy growing up in the aforementioned San Marcos, Texas, in the mid-'50s, Tino Villanueva, now a well-known poet, drew deep racial instruction from *Giant* (see his *Scene from the Movie* Giant [1993]), while I, in southern Texas, watched Stanley Kramer's *High Noon* in utter fascination. Perhaps more *boy* than Mexican, I, like many other Americans, was wholly taken by Gary Cooper as town marshal Will Kane awaiting, in his small nineteenth-century Western town of Hadleyville, gunfighters from Texas sworn to kill him at high noon. But one now sees the significance of Helen Ramirez, the town madam and Will Kane's former lover, played by Katy Jurado. At first, wholly within the tradition of the eroticized Mexican woman, she is inevitably contrasted with Amy, Kane's new bride. A Quaker, Amy will not abide her husband's impending violence and decides to leave him, though later she abruptly changes her mind. Out of her very sexual marginality, however, Helen has forged a distinctive subversive identity within the town's repressive moral and political economy. Her professional sexual practice has led to a "primitive" accumulation of capital, which she has used to convert herself into a "legitimate" and competent businesswoman, owner of a saloon and a store. Her combined sexual and economic power allows her to hold sway over the town's white male community as they make ritual, obsequious visits to her queenly apartment above the bar to curry favor while their repressed white wives wait at home.

In a long and telling middle scene, she and Kane confront each other at the height of Kane's crisis, and it is abundantly clear that Kane has fully experienced her evident passion and still cares deeply for her as does she for him. Imbedded in their dialogue is a brief but fulsome exchange of deeply romantic words uttered in Spanish, probably lost on the predominantly Anglo audience since they are inserted without any translation and are therefore already subversive. These words speak massive cultural volumes to any native member of the Spanish-speaking world: "Un año sin verte" (A year without seeing you), she says to him as she gazes deeply into his eyes; "lo se" (I know), he answers. He answers in such an informed Spanish that it is clear that he has been interpellated by the language just as he has by her entire sexual-cultural being. Indeed, he knows a great deal, more than he will be willing to admit, but she knows that in *their mano a mano* he has capitulated to the other side. She decides to leave town with their love never permanently fulfilled.

They see each other only once more. Helen is riding to the train station in a buggy with Amy, who is also leaving town; they pass Kane standing in the street awaiting his assailants. Amy looks away from him, but Helen's eyes lock onto Kane's, and through her eyes the camera holds him for a full five seconds as he returns her steady parting gaze. So how could this passionate romance have failed? Why does Kane leave Helen for Amy and the life of a small shopkeeper? The implication is quite clear: he has been unable to escape the racism and the sexual/economic repression of the town's capitalist moral economy. Helen comments on this economy as she gets ready to leave: "I hate this town. I've always hated it, to be a Mexican woman in a town like this." Kane leaves Helen for Amy even though Helen is the superior figure; she even rhetorically forces Amy to assist in his final moment of crisis as the gunfight begins. At the end of the film, he and Amy emerge victorious over some part of this economy, but it is also clear that they have both derived great strength from the racial-sexual Other—Helen

Ramirez—even as Kane denies her claim on his sexual and moral sensibility. She will, of course, lose Kane to Amy and leave town. In her final scene, however, Helen is on the train, and as the camera focuses on her strong, beautiful, Mexican face, we clearly sense that she has achieved some large measure of victory in this contest even as the film at the end too quickly erases her strong, sexualized, Mexican female presence to make narrative way for the white reunited couple, triumphant heroes of the rising yet repressed bourgeois social order in the later nineteenth century.

One conventional, circumscribed reading of *High Noon* is that the town has morally failed the heroic Will Kane, and that this serves as a critical commentary on the McCarthyite 1950s, when society failed to act against the "bad men" until it was almost too late. But as a perhaps unintended critical commentary on the Anglo-Mexican racial politics of this period, the film is a local intervention often ignored in efforts to nationalize and universalize the film. While heroic in one way, Kane fails in another. I submit that after their climactic meeting Kane labors with his own racially motivated moral failure to fully respond to Helen's plenitude and thereby to transcend the racialized political-economic moral order. Even as he survives the gunfight and restores his marriage with Amy, it is clear that his petit bourgeois world has been forever destabilized by his prior knowledge of the Mexican sexual Other. Helen's parting gaze is on him forever and "un año sin verte" plus many more may never be enough to undo her ambivalent yet powerful incursion into Will Kane's life.

THE UNFORGIVEN, PRIM AND PROPER CULTURE,
AND LATIN LOVERS

If the Mexican woman in her full sexuality has critical possibilities, what of the clearly despised Mexican male? With none of the exoticism, the eroticism, or freer play given that of the Mexican woman, he is a rhetorical construction for which the term *stereotype* is in unforgivingly full force. In this discursive encounter men read other men in a discursive *mano a mano*. Denigration of the Mexican male is conventionally understood as the articulation of colonialism directed specifically at the male body that traditionally offered the greatest opposition, namely, the heroic male figures of the Texas-Mexican border ballads, or *corridos*. In the context of the Anglo male's politically and psychologically necessary desire for Mexican women, however, we begin to see here a psychoanalytic relationship of identity and difference, narcissism and aggressivity. The Mexican and Anglo males narcissistically identify with each other as equally available sexual partners for Mexican women. Indeed, Américo Paredes suggests that the ideal Mexican cowboy or *vaquero*, quite contrary to the stereotypic image, was more likely to be tall, lean, and dark with green or tawny eyes, more like his

Anglo counterpart than not (*"With His Pistol in His Hand"* 111). However, such a Mexican man would still have a cultural advantage over his Anglo mirror image relative to Mexican women, if only by his Spanfluency. In response, the Anglo, who controls this discursive site, produces a maximum form of difference and aggressivity so as to deny wholly the identity of the Mexican man, which, if it were acknowledged, puts him at a disadvantage in his quest. When it comes to the construction of Mexican males by Anglo males, there can be no rhetorical quarter given, no ambivalence.

Ambivalent toward Mexican women as he is, the Anglo male neverthe-less recognizes the limits of his transgression and returns to Susie. And what else is Susie—pots, pans, hard work, religion, and all (likely including a timid sexuality)—but the figure of the dominant culture that compels this resolution. In the white "settlement" of the West, such women represented the most effective form of colonialism, bringing with them the daily habitus of households, social etiquette, religion, and schools for the reproduction of fundamental colonial values (Deutsch 63). The schoolmarm emerges as the ultimate pairing for our cowboy once he is done with his transgressive experimentation at the border. As mothers, such women were also obli-gated to reproduce Anglo culture, literally, in its numbers, but also through socialization. J. Frank Dobie, an archetypal cowboy, grew up on a Texas ranch in the late nineteenth century and told of his very religious mother, who was a schoolteacher in south Texas before marrying his rancher father, bore six children, and eventually persuaded her husband to move the family into town (71–82). Giving up his range life for the sake of such civilizing women is another vector of cowboy ambivalence, as "A Cowboy's Son" also suggests:

> Whar y'u from, little stranger, little boy?
> Yu was ridin! a cloud on that star-strewn plain,
> But y'u fell from the skies like a drop of rain
> To this world of sorrow and long, long pain.
> Will y'u care fo' yo' mothah, little boy?
>
> When y'u grows, little varmint, little boy,
> Y'u'll be ridin' a hoss by yo' fathah's side
> With yo' gun and yo' spurs and yo' howstrong pride.
> Will y'u think of yo' home when the world rolls wide?
> Will y'u wish for yo' mothah, little boy?
>
> When y'u love in yo' manhood, little boy,—
> When y'u dream of a girl who is angel fair,—
> When the stars are her eyes and the wind is her hair,—
> When the sun is her smile and yo' heaven's there,—
> Will y'u care for yo' mothah, little boy?

(Lomax 88)

In this cowboy world, the mother, conflated with the "angel fair" girl, exerts civilizing power along with domesticity. Though "fathah" appears as cowboy mentor with horse, gun, and pride, the song never asks the question "Will y'u care for yo' fathah?"

The Anglo male's ambivalent transgression with the Other as sexualized Mexican woman is usually resolved in the direction of this hegemonic Anglo woman-centered culture, from where such a woman might also recognize her greatest enemy. For we learn again from J. Frank Dobie's autobiography that his mother had specifically instructed her sons never to "debase themselves by living with Mexican women" (89). As I have suggested about Will Kane in *High Noon*, this resolution of ambivalence often occurred with nostalgia:

> Her eyes were brown—a deep, deep brown:
> Her hair was darker than her eyes;
> And something in her smile and frown,
> Curled crimson lip and instep high,
> Showed that there ran in each blue vein,
> Mixed with the milder Aztec strain,
> The vigorous vintage of Old Spain.
>
> .   .   .   .
>
> The air was heavy, the night was hot,
> I sat by her side and forgot, forgot;
> Forgot the herd that were taking rest,
> Forgot that the air was close oppressed.
>
> .   .   .   .
>
> And I wonder why I do not care
> For the things that are, like the things that were.
> Does half my heart lie buried there
> In Texas, down by the Rio Grande?
>
> (Lomax 24–26)

Thus far I have been dealing with a cultural iconography born out of the nineteenth century with a specific siting in the West and, to some considerable degree, in Texas. The twentieth century brings another image, broadly Latin American; it might be said to begin in the early 1920s with the film career of the Italian Rudolph Valentino and his portrayal of the "Latin Lover" and to have developed up through our own time in a lineage that includes, most prominently, Gilbert Roland, Desi Arnaz (before he loved Lucy), Fernando Lamas, Ricardo Montalban, Zorro, Julio Iglesias, and—in contemporary, funkier versions—Jimmy Smits and Antonio Banderas. How does this strong, slender, suave, sophisticated, slightly accented, slightly dark, simmering, sultry—is it necessary to say sexy?—figure work into this iconography? It seems not unreasonable to view this image in relation to two factors emerging out of the period between the two world wars and gaining potency after the second: first, the greater cultural tolerance at the national level for Latin America, especially Mexico, as a result, in significant part, of the latter's enlistment on the Allied side in World War II—what Helen Delpar has called "the enormous vogue of things Mexican"; and second, the increasing structural and cultural freedom of Anglo-American women—the presumed desiring audience for this icon. Recall how often in films and TV shows she meets the "Latin Lover" while she is on vacation somewhere in Latin America either by herself or with a girlfriend. Ricky came to love Lucy while she was vacationing in Havana with Ethel sometime before 1959, for example.[4] In the relationship of these latter-day Anglo women—now at some considerable distance from Susie and J. Frank Dobie's mother—to this figure of Latin male sexuality, do we not have a relationship similar to the traditional Anglo male–Mexican woman conjunction? Does this relationship not also make a momentary ambivalent claim to greater though transgressive fulfillment, although the Anglo woman also usually finds permanence elsewhere?[5]

In the preceding, I have tried to shift us from a directly correlated relationship between such iconography and quasi-colonialism to one of ambivalence. The colonized thus become a site for witnessing a fissure or decentering within the colonizer, remaining unequal. A larger realm of freedom for colonized and colonizer would require termination of even this ambivalence and a revision of the social relations that have sustained it. John Sayles's recent film *Lone Star* suggests such a termination by radically revising the history of this iconography.

BLOOD ONLY MEANS WHAT YOU LET IT

A murder mystery, *Lone Star* is set in contemporary small-town southern Texas along the U.S.-Mexico border.[6] Through flashbacks it spans the years from the 1930s to the present. In the 1990s Sam Deeds—the young, tough, lean, soft-spoken Anglo county sheriff—is trying to solve the murder of Charlie Wade, the former corrupt, tyrannical, and racist sheriff, whose remains were accidently found in the desert after his mysterious disappearance some forty years previously. Between these two sheriffs' tenure, the office was filled by Sam's father, Buddy Deeds, said to have been the living definition of the epic Texas male. Although Buddy too is now dead, he becomes a prime suspect in Wade's murder. Buddy served as Wade's deputy before becoming sheriff, and they clashed over Wade's corruption. Led by Hollis, the mayor and a former deputy to both Wade and Buddy, the town—Anglo, Mexican, and African-American—remains loyal to both Buddy's epic quality and his patronage politics. Revered almost as much as

Buddy, his now dead Anglo wife, Muriel, is said to have been "an angel of a woman." In the course of his investigation, Sam comes upon repressed information that revisits the traditional iconography.

Sam eventually discovers the identity of Wade's killer, but this other knowledge of past and present racialized sexualities gives the story greater significance. It sketches the evolution of Anglo-Mexican relations in Texas and radically revises the traditional iconography. Buddy presided as sheriff in the period roughly from the late 1950s to the early 1970s. Though not Charlie Wade, he still participated in maintaining a colonialist social order in which the local Mexicans knew their place; he did not, for example, permit his teenage son, Sam, to date Pilar, a Mexican-American, and was livid when he caught them necking at a local drive-in theater. The reason for these strictures turns out to be more complex than simple racism: Pilar is the attractive daughter of Mercedes Cruz, the owner of a successful local Mexican restaurant and herself a beautiful woman in her youth. Mercedes's husband, Eladio Cruz, had died some years earlier. While Sam has become sheriff, Pilar has become an activist high school history teacher. As the murder investigation proceeds, Sam and Pilar rekindle their romantic relationship, an involvement culminating in a slow romantic dance to jukebox music after hours in her mother's restaurant. As befits the social forces they come to represent, they dance to the 1960s tune by Ivory Joe Hunter with the refrain "Since I met you baby, my whole life has changed," sung, however, in Spanish by Freddy Fender.

As late as the mid-1960s, colonial order still prevailed in many parts of Texas, of which the administrations of both Charlie Wade and Buddy Deeds are very accurate representations. Buddy changes the style of administration, however, from one of violent coercion to one in which, in Gramscian terms, the state justifies and maintains its dominance by winning the active consent of the dominated (see Adamson 165). Buddy, our archetypal Texas male, played out the sexualized cultural politics of ambivalence. While married to an Anglo woman with an appropriately angelic name, Muriel, he completed the traditional constellation of images through a love affair with the beautiful Mercedes. As with Kane and Ramirez, this is an affair that questions the cultural totality of the ruling order, especially since the erstwhile "Mexican" Pilar is his daughter and therefore Sam's half-sister. It remains for his son Sam and *his* daughter Pilar to move beyond this dialectic of rule and ambivalence into a greater realm of freedom.

As the film ends, Sam and Pilar are sitting on the hood of a car parked at the now abandoned drive-in theater as Sam tells her all that he has discovered about their mixed parentage. Sam and Pilar, like Will Kane and Helen Ramirez, must make a critical decision. They can go their separate ways, or they can continue and make permanent through marriage their relationship despite, or perhaps through, this knowledge. The film ends without an absolutely clear resolution. For me, there is nothing now in the social order to prevent the legal and moral consummation of their love. They are free to do what Kane, in his shallow heroism, could not. I am not persuaded that Pilar and Sam will forsake each other on *their* wedding day about-to-be. It is entirely appropriate that this final scene and decision take place in the now decaying drive-in theater where they once made illicit teenage love: the theater and the lovemaking symbolize another era when the colonial order was still in full force (when Mexicans were not allowed to swim in the swimming areas of San Marcos fed by the San Antonio, Medina, and Guadalupe rivers).

"Forget the Alamo," says Pilar, as she and Sam appear to decide to forge a relationship based not on sexually transgressive ambivalence but rather on a clear recognition of their relative equality and the public continuation of their love. A college-educated intellectual, she has social status equaling whatever cultural capital still accrues to him as an Anglo in the 1990s. As a public school teacher—indeed a teacher of history, the "queen" of the sciences—she revises the image of the Mexican woman at the sexual and social margins of society, often as a prostitute. In effect, Pilar appropriates the traditional image of the civilizing Anglo schoolmarm with a critical difference: she is a civilized and civilizing individual while maintaining a full and healthy display of her sexuality. Her initiation in a Mexican restaurant of the sex she will enjoy with Sam revises the iconographic sexual encounter between Anglo cowboy and Mexican woman in a cantina. Not a cantina, this is a socially sanctioned space; the fact that it is not only a Mexican but also a Mexican-owned restaurant testifies to the full emergence of a Mexican-American social class that would now effectively demand an equal place in society. Other well-educated Mexican-American figures appear who are on the verge of taking over civil and state society, replacing the Hollises and Sams, or at least sharing power with them. Represented by clean-cut, earnest young Mexican-American males—a journalist and a mayoral candidate who will replace Hollis and Sam—they are garbed in the coats and ties of civil society. These Mexican-American male figures have no discernible sexual valence in the film, negative or positive; they are at a considerable distance from both the rapacious Mexican bandit and the "Latin Lover."

This implied ending of the colonial order has much to do with the sexualized kinship twist that Sayles has given his story. The fact that Pilar and Sam are simultaneously lovers and blood brother and sister reinforces their sexually constituted love with the enduring bonds of consanguineous affiliation. Their half blood relations suggest that these two social sectors are now also united in brother-sisterhood, though still with some, perhaps minimal, social distance. Public equals and in unambivalent love, in semi–

brother-sisterhood, still aware of their ethnicities, Pilar and Sam are willing, in her words (and it is critical that she say them), to "forget the Alamo."[7] She is a teacher of history, and one senses that she means to negate history in the present by moving beyond the colonial, if ambivalent, sexual and social worlds of her parents. Is this a utopian vision? Perhaps, but the foremost social historian of these matters in Texas, with great sociological supporting data, wrote in 1986: "From the long view of a century and a half, Mexican-Anglo relations have traversed a difficult path, from the hatred and suspicion engendered by war to a form of reconciliation" (Montejano 297); "[T]his does not mean that ethnic solidarity has become a matter of the past; it means rather that it has become subordinated to the voices of moderation from both communities. The politics of negotiation and compromise have replaced the politics of conflict and control" (Montejano 306). Negotiation and compromise characterize a good marriage, one beyond domination, inequality, stereotypic iconographies, and ambivalence.[8] Seen in the context of a correlation of social forces now underway in Texas, New Mexico, and perhaps other parts of Mexican America, *Lone Star* is a film that seems to end the legacy of *Little Lone Star*; it invites us to review this iconographic and social history even as it seems to propose productive forgetfulness in the name of a larger vision long overdue. Relative to this conflicted history, is Sayles an obscurantist or, in Alan Stone's words, "a prophet of hope"?

NOTES

1. See my review of this Chicano critique. The principal Anglo-American scholarship is that of Pettit, preceded by Cecil Robinson's *With the Ears of Strangers: The Mexican in American Literature* (1963).

2. I was also motivated in this direction by Américo Paredes' brief and general yet intriguing assessment of this iconography in his 1978 essay "The Problem of Identity in a Changing Culture" (43).

3. I do not wish to adhere to any rigid definition of colonialism, internal or otherwise, relative to this Mexican-American community that represents a mixture of landed conquered people dating back to the sixteenth century and third- and fourth-generation children of immigrants, as well as more recent ones. My loose sense of such a colonial order between Anglos and Mexicans in the United States would suggest that in some respects, especially in the realm of culture, the Anglos and Mexicans have interacted in a manner that bears some similarities to classic examples of world colonialism. This seems to me to be especially the case in the realm of sexuality. For a fine discussion of the history of the concept of "colonialism" relative to Anglos and Mexicans in the Southwest, see Almaguer.

4. My discussion here is indebted to Gustavo Pérez Firmat on Desi Arnaz and Lucille Ball (chaps. 1 and 2).

5. There is also the more complicated case where an Anglo male such as D. H. Lawrence imagines Anglo women desiring Mexican men, combining the "Latin Lover" with something of the degenerate Mexican bandit. As Marianna Torgovnick tells us, for Kate in Lawrence's *Plumed Serpent*, "Mexico can also offer Mexican men, especially 'silent, semi-barbarous men' in whom she finds 'humility, and the pathos of grace . . . something very beautiful and truly male, and very hard to find in a civilised white man. It was not of the spirit. It was of the dark, strong, unbroken blood, the flowering of the soul' " (163).

6. My heading is a phrase uttered by Otis Payne, the central African-American character in *Lone Star*. Except for a rather forced implication of Otis in the murder plot at the very end, the Mexican and African-American stories rarely come together. I think Sayles was imagining the film's appeal to a larger national audience too likely to see *Lone Star* as just another border "Western."

7. Sayles has to foreclose the possibility of biosocial reproduction, however; so Pilar, for past medical reasons, can no longer get pregnant. Yet Sam and Pilar have nothing to prove on this score; already products of such racialized sexuality, they foretell the shape of the new social order. Admittedly, this is an ambiguous ending, although it is clear that Sayles expected his audience to understand that Pilar and Sam would stay together. See Stone.

8. We must note that this "marriage" does not seem to include recent undocumented Mexican immigrants such as those working in the kitchen of Mercedes's restaurant. In her movement from hostility to some sympathy for this population, Mercedes represents Mexican-American ambivalence toward Mexican immigrants. See de la Garza et al. 10–102; and Gutiérrez 207–16.

WORKS CITED

Adamson, Walter L. *Hegemony and Revolution: A Study of Antonio Gramsci's Political and Cultural Theory*. Berkeley: U of California P, 1980.

Almaguer, Tomas. "Ideological Distortions and Recent Chicano Historiography: The Internal Colonial Model and Chicano Historical Interpretation." *Aztlán: A Journal of Chicano Research* 18 (1987): 7–28.

Bhabha, Homi K. *The Location of Culture*. London: Routledge, 1994.

de la Garza, Rodolfo O., et al. *Latino Voices: Mexican, Puerto Rican, and Cuban Perspectives on American Politics*. Boulder: Westview, 1992.

De Leon, Arnoldo. *They Called Them Greasers: Anglo Attitudes toward Mexicans in Texas, 1821–1900*. Austin: U of Texas P, 1983.

Deutsch, Sarah. *No Separate Refuge: Culture, Class, and Gender on an Anglo-Hispanic Frontier in the American Southwest, 1880–1940*. New York: Oxford UP, 1987.

Dobie, J. Frank. *Some Part of Myself*. 1967. Austin: U of Texas P, 1980.

Firmat, Gustavo Pérez. *Life on the Hyphen: The Cuban-American Way*. Austin: U of Texas P, 1994.

Flores, Guillermo. "Race and Culture in the Internal Colony: Keeping the Chicano in His Place." *Structures of Dependency*. Ed. Frank Bonilla and Robert Girling. Oakland: Sembradora, 1973. 189–223.

Gunsmoke. CBS. 1955–75.

Gutiérrez, David G. *Walls and Mirrors: Mexican Americans, Mexican Immigrants, and the Politics of Ethnicity*. Berkeley: U of California P, 1995.

Hall, Sam. *Little Lone Star, or, the Belle of the Cibolo*.1886.

High Noon. Dir. Fred Zinneman. Prod. Stanley Kramer. With Gary Cooper and Katy Jurado. United Artists, 1952.

hooks, bell. *Black Looks: Race and Representation*. Boston: South End, 1992.

Limón, José E. "Stereotyping and Chicano Resistance: An Historical Dimension." *Aztlán: Chicano Journal of the Social Sciences and the Arts* 4 (1973): 257–70. Rptd. in *Chicanos and Film: Representation and Resistance*. Ed. Chon A. Noriega. Minneapolis: U of Minnesota P, 1992. 3–17.

Lomax, John A., comp. *Songs of the Cattle Trail and Cow Camp*. New York: Macmillan, 1919.

Lone Star. Dir. John Sayles. Prod. R. Paul Miller and Maggie Renzi. With Kris Kristofferson, Matthew McConaughey, Chris Cooper, and Elizabeth Peña. Columbia, 1996.

McCarthy, Cormac. *All the Pretty Horses*. New York: Vintage, 1992.

McMurtry, Larry. *Streets of Laredo*. New York: Simon, 1993.

Mirandé, Alfredo, and Evangelina Enríquez. *La Chicana: The Mexican-American Woman*. Chicago: U of Chicago P, 1979.

Montejano, David. *Anglos and Mexicans in the Making of Texas, 1836–1986*. Austin: U of Texas P, 1987.

Paredes, Américo. "The Problem of Identity in a Changing Culture: Popular Expressions of Culture Conflict along the Lower Rio Grande Border." *Views across the Border: The United States and Mexico*. Ed. Stanley Ross. Albuquerque: U of New Mexico P, 1978. 68–94. Rptd. in *Folklore and Culture on the Texas-Mexican Border*. Ed. Richard Bauman. Austin: Center for Mexican-American Studies, University of Texas, 1993. 19–47.

———. *"With His Pistol in His Hand": A Border Ballad and Its Hero*. Austin: U of Texas P, 1958.

Pettit, Arthur G. *Images of the Mexican American in Fiction and Film*. Ed. Dennis E. Showalter. College Station: Texas A&M UP, 1980.

Pike, Frederick B. *The United States and Latin America: Myths and Stereotypes of Civilization and Nature*. Austin: U of Texas P, 1992.

Ramirez-Berg, Charles. "Stereotyping in Films in General and of the Hispanic in Particular." *Howard Journal of Communications* 2 (1990). 286–314.

Robinson, Cecil. *With the Ears of Strangers: The Mexican in American Literature*. Tucson: U of Arizona P, 1963.

Rosaldo, Renato. *Culture and the Truth: The Remaking of Social Analysis*. Boston: Beacon, 1989.

Stone, Alan A. "The Prophet of Hope." *Boston Review* October–November 1996: 20–22.

Torgovnick, Marianna. *Gone Primitive: Savage Intellects, Modern Lives*. Chicago: U of Chicago P, 1990.

Young, Robert J. C. *Colonial Desire: Hybridity in Theory, Culture and Race*. London: Routledge, 1995.